mâci-nêhiyawêwin
Beginning Cree

SOLOMON RATT | ILLUSTRATIONS BY **HOLLY MARTIN**

University of Regina Press

A version of the story on pages 273-276 appeared previously as "Shaking-Spear
papāmohtīw/Shaking-Spear Wanders About," in *Woods Cree Stories*, published
by University of Regina Press, 2014.

Printed and bound in Canada at Friesens.

COVER AND TEXT DESIGN: Duncan Campbell, University of Regina Press
COVER ART: "From Back Home Cree Guy," 2014, mixed media on paper,
22½″ × 22½″, by George Littlechild
INTERIOR ILLUSTRATIONS: Holly Martin

Library and Archives Canada Cataloguing in Publication

Ratt, Solomon, author
     mâci-nêhiyawêwin = Beginning Cree / Solomon Ratt ; illustrations by
Holly Martin.

Includes bibliographical references.
Issued in print and electronic formats.
Text in English and Cree.
ISBN 978-0-88977-435-3 (paperback).—ISBN 978-0-88977-436-0 (pdf)

     1. Cree language—Textbooks for second language learners—English
speakers. I. Martin, Holly, illustrator II. Title. III. Title: Beginning Cree.

PM986.R38 2016   497'.323   C2016-903545-X
                                  C2016-903546-8

We acknowledge the support of the Canada Council for the Arts for our pub-
lishing program. We acknowledge the financial support of the Government of
Canada. / Nous reconnaissons l'appui financier du gouvernement du Canada.
This publication was made possible through Creative Saskatchewan's Creative
Industries Production Grant Program.

This book is dedicated to future generations.

TABLE OF CONTENTS

Acknowledgements

This book is a result of teaching introductory Cree via satellite, online course offerings, and in the classroom. It is an introductory course on the Cree language with basic grammar using topics that occur in everyday situations. It is primarily designed for those who have no easy access to fluent speakers, so the exercises and grammar explanations are geared for self-study. It has been my experience that those who successfully learn another language have been those who have devoted a lot of time in self-study.

I give thanks to the many students who have been in my classes using a form of this book throughout the years. Many thanks to my teacher and mentor, Jean Okimâsis, for her guidance throughout my teaching career. Without her encouragement I may have pursued another career. Thanks also to Arok Wolvengrey and Jean Okimâsis for proofreading this volume. Any mistakes can be attributed to myself. I often find my original dialect of Cree (TH-Cree) gets in the way of my working in the Y-Cree dialect. And, finally, I must give special thanks to my student Holly Lydia Martin who was more than enthusiastic to tackle the graphics in this book. And lastly, a great thank you to Donna Grant and Duncan Campbell for the excellent layout!

kinanâskomitinâwâw
I thank you all!

Solomon Ratt
November 2015

CHAPTER ONE
INTRODUCTION

1. THE CREE

The Cree are the most widespread of Canada's First Nations peoples. According to Statistics Canada figures of 1996 there are approximately 87,555 speakers of the Cree language in Canada. There are five main dialects of Cree spoken in Canada:

- The R dialect speakers, commonly known as "Atikamekw (Cree)," live in the southwestern regions of Quebec;
- The L dialect speakers, known as "Moose Cree," live on the western shores of James Bay, especially in Moose Factory, Ontario, hence the name;
- The N dialect speakers, known as the "Swampy Cree," range from northern Ontario throughout the interior of Manitoba and mid-eastern part of Saskatchewan;
- The TH dialect speakers, known alternately as "Woods Cree" or "Rock Cree," can be found in northern Manitoba and north-eastern Saskatchewan;
- The Y dialect speakers, known as the "Plains Cree," range along the Great Plains regions of southern Saskatchewan as well as north-western Saskatchewan and northern Alberta.

Not all of these dialects of Cree are mutually intelligible although their grammar systems are basically the same. The R dialect is the one that is most radically different from the other four dialects; thus, it is the most difficult to understand by the other speakers of Cree. In Saskatchewan, speakers of the three dialects found here, the N, Y and TH, can communicate in Cree, but there are certain differences in word usages that sometimes need explanation. No dialect is better than any other. This introductory book will be done in the Y dialect.

Of the 74 First Nations in Saskatchewan there are 10 Saulteaux Nations, 7 Dene Nations, 8 Nakota/Dakota/Lakota Sioux Nations and 49 Cree Nations. Of the Cree Nations, 3 are TH-dialect, 3 are N-dialect, and the remaining 43 are Y-dialect. Although there appears to be a healthy number of Cree speakers in the parental age generations in some communities, most Cree communities fear the threat of language loss because the children are not learning the language.

Efforts are underway in many communities to revive the Cree language, with some communities establishing Cree immersion programs while others have core language programs. The programs use a number of methods including aural-oral language teaching and grammar-based programs, and most have introduced writing in what has been an oral language prior to the coming of the missionaries into Cree country. There are two basic writing systems: the syllabics system introduced to the Cree in the mid-nineteenth century and the Standard Roman Orthography (SRO). In this text we will work only with the SRO.

1.1 THE STANDARD ROMAN ORTHOGRAPHY

For this introductory text on Cree we will write Cree using the Standard Roman Orthography (SRO). What follows is a brief introduction on the SRO (for further information see: *How to Spell It in Cree: The Standard Roman Orthography* by Jean Okimâsis and Arok Wolvengrey: miywâsin ink, 2008). One advantage of using the SRO for writing Cree is its consistency: one letter represents one sound. In contrast to Cree SRO, English may have one sound represented by different letters or combination of letters as is evident in the following examples of the sound [ij]: Caesar (ae), each (ea), amoeba (oe), people (eo), meet (ee), me (e), machine (i), seize (ei), piece (ie), psychology (y). The same sound, [ij], is represented in Cree SRO as **î**.

1.1.A CONSONANTS

The Cree SRO has 10 consonants: **c h k m n p s t w y**. The consonants are pronounced similar to their English counterparts, for the most part, but the **c, k, p**, and **t** need special attention.

The "**c**" in Cree is pronounced like the "**ch**" in "**ch**arge", or, depending on dialect, like the "**ts**" in "ca**ts**". The following are some of the more common words in Cree with a "c":

cêskwa – *wait*	cî – *a polarity question indicator*
mîciso – *eat* (VAI)[1]	mîcisowinâhtik – *a table* (NI)

In English, the "**k**" can be silent, as in "know," or it can be pronounced with a puff of air following it, as the "k" in "kipper", or without the puff of air, as in "skipper". The Cree "**k**" is pronounced like the "k" in "skipper" without the puff of air – except when following an "h"; then the "k" does have a softer sound. Some of the more common words in Cree with a "k" include the following:

kiya – *you*	kiyawâw – *you* (plural)
kîsta – *you too*	kîstawâw – *you* (plural) *too*

In English, the "**p**" can be silent, as in "pneumonia", or have an "f" sound when followed by an "h", as in "phone", or can have a puff of air as in "pot", or have no puff of air as in "spot". In Cree the "**p**" has no puff of air and is pronounced like the "p" in "spot" – except when following an "h"; then it has a softer sound. Some of the more common words in Cree with a "p" include the following:

pêyak – *one*	pîsim – *sun/month* (NA)
pêyakwâw – *once*	pîsimwasinahikan – *calendar* (NI)

---

1 The following abbreviations are for the grammatical items here:
   VAI – animate intransitive verb
   VII – inanimate intransitive verb
   NA – animate noun
   NI – inanimate noun

In English, the **"t"** can have a puff of air, as the "t" in "tan", or have no puff of air, as the "t" in "Stan". The Cree **"t"** is pronounced with no puff of air, much like the "t" in "Stan". Some of the more common words in Cree with a "t" include the following:

tânisi – *how/how are you*   tâniwê – *where* (use for NI)
takwâkin – *It is fall.* (VII)   tâniwâ – *where* (use for NA)

1.1.B VOWELS

In Cree we use seven vowel sounds to write in the SRO. We have three short vowel sounds: **a, i, o;** and four long vowels marked by either a circumflex or macron (bar) over the vowel: **â, î, ô, and ê.**

SHORT VOWELS
The short vowels include: **a, i, and o:**

The short **a:** - pronounced like the first "a" in "appeal":
  apisîs – *a little bit*   awas – *go away*
  api – *sit* (VAI)   awîna – *who*

The short **i:** - pronounced like the "i" in "it":
  itôta – *do it* (VTI-1)[1]   itwaha – *point to it* (VTI-1)
  itwê – *say* (VAI)   isiyihkâsow – *she/he is named* (VAI)

The short **o:** - pronounced like the "oo" in "shook":
  otin – *take someone* (VTA)   otina – *take it* (VTI-1)
  omisi – *this way*   pipon – *It is winter.* (VII)

LONG VOWELS
The long vowels are marked with either a circumflex or a macron (bar) over the vowel: **â, î, ô, and ê:**

The long **â:** - pronounced like the "a" in "fa" as in "do, ray, me, fa, so, la, ti, do":
  âstam – *come here*   âstamitê – *over this way*
  âskaw – *sometimes*   âha – *yes*

The long **î:** - pronounced like the "e" in "me":
  mîna – *also*   nîpin – *It is summer.* (VII)
  sîkwan – *It is spring.* (VII)   wîpac – *soon/early*

---

1   VTI-1 – transitive inanimate verb-class 1
     VTA – transitive animate verb

The long **ô:** - pronounced like the "o" in "or":

    ôta – *here*   ôtê – *over here*

    ahpô êtikwê – *maybe*   namôya – *no/not*

The long **ê:** - pronounced like the "ay" in "day":

    êkota – *there*   êkotê – *over there*

    nêhiyaw – *a Cree* (NA)   nêhiyawê – *speak Cree* (VAI)

1.1.C SRO: CHANTS

CONSONANTS

c-c-c-c:	cêskwa, cêskwa, cêskwa pitamâ. *Wait, wait, wait a bit.*
h-h-h-h:	hâw, hâw, hâw mâka. *Okay, okay, okay then.*
k-k-k-k:	kâya, kâya, kâya itôta. *Don't, don't, don't do it!*
m-m-m-m:	mahti, mahti, mahti nêhiyawêtân. *Please, please, please, let's speak Cree.*
n-n-n-n:	namôya, namôya, namôya cêskwa. *No, no, not yet!*
p-p-p-p:	pêtâ, pêtâ, pêtâ kimasinahikan. *Bring it, bring it, bring your book.*
s-s-s-s:	sôhki, sôhki, sôhki-sêsâwî. *Hard, hard, exercise hard!*
t-t-t-t:	tâpwê, tâpwê, tâpwê takahki. *Truly, truly, it is truly great!*
w-w-w-w:	wîcih, wîcih, wîcih kiwîcêwâkan. *Help him, help her, help your companion.*
y-y-y-y:	yîkatê-, yîkatê-, yîkatê-kwâskohti. *Aside, aside, jump aside!*

VOWELS

a-a-a-a: apisîs, apisîs, apisîs nêhiyawêk.
A little, a little, speak (you – plural) *a little Cree!*

â-â-â-â: âskaw, âskaw, âskaw âkayâsîmo.
Sometimes, sometimes, sometimes speak English.

ê-ê-ê-ê: êkosi, êkosi, êkosi itôta.
That's it, that's it, do it like that.

i-i-i-i: itwaha, itwaha, itwaha iskwâhtêm.
Point to it, point to it, point at the door.

î-î-î-î: îkatêna, îkatêna, îkatêna êwako.
Set it aside, set it aside, set that one aside.

o-o-o-o: omisi, omisi, omisi itwê.
This way, this way, say it this way.

ô-ô-ô-ô: ôtê, ôtê, ôtê pê-itohtê.
This way, this way, come this way.

1.1.D DICTATION

Write out the words the instructor says in the spaces below:

_____   _____

_____   _____

_____   _____

_____   _____

_____   _____

_____   _____

1.1.E MIMIMAL PAIRS

Minimal pairs are two words with only one sound difference. Examples from English would include:

> pat – bat
> fit – sit
> fat – fit
> pot – pit

The difference in sounds can be in consonants or in vowels. Cree also has minimal pairs. Here are a few more common ones:

nahapi – *Sit down!* (VAI)
nahâpi – *See clearly!* (VAI)

api – *Sit!* (VAI)
ati – *begin* (IPV)

atim – *a dog* (NA)
akim – *Count him/her!* (VTA)

maskisin – *a shoe* (NI)
mâskisin – *S/he is crippled from a fall.* (VAI)

ôma – *this* (PR-in)
ôta – *here* (PR)

awa – *this* (PR-an)
ana – *that* (PR-an)

asam – *Feed him/her!* (VTA)
asâm – *a snowshoe* (NA)

maskosis – *a bear cub* (NA)
maskosîs – *a small piece of grass* (NI)

pisiw – *a lynx* (NA)
pêsiw – *Bring him/her!* (VTA)

ôta – *here* (PR)
ôtê – *over here* (PR)

niya – *me/I* (PR)
niyâ – *Lead/go ahead* (IPC)

nitomisin – *I have an older sister/s.* (VAI)
nitômisin – *I am greasy/oily.* (VAI)

nîsta – *me too* (PR)
nîstâ – *my brother-in-law* (vocative)

pôsiw – *S/he gets on board.* (VAI-3rd person)
pisiw – *a lynx* (NA)

pasow – *S/he smells it.* (VAI)
pâsow – *S/he dries up.* (VAI)

Cree has many minimal pairs that appear in pronouns (PR) and in verb (V) pairs as the following illustrate:

niya – *me/I* (PR)
kiya – *you* (PR)

niya – *me/I* (PR)
wiya – *s/he/him/her* (PR)

kiya – *you* (PR)
wiya – *s/he/him/her* (PR)

nîsta – *me too* (PR)
kîsta – *you too* (PR)

nîsta – *me too* (PR)
wîsta – *her/him too* (PR)

kîsta – *you too* (PR)
wîsta – *her/him too* (PR)

nitisiyihkâson – *I am named/called (my name is)* (VAI-1st person singular)
kitisiyihkâson – *You are named/called (your name is)* (VAI-2nd person singular)

nitohcîn – *I am from* (VAI-1st person singular)
kitohcîn – *You are from* (VAI-2nd person singular)

nititahtopiponân – *I am of that age* (VAI-1st person singular)
kititahtopiponân – *You are of that age* (VAI-2nd person singular)

In addition to minimal pairs, there are also minimal sets and near minimal pairs. The near minimal pairs can create some problems in spelling and understanding as shown in the following:

acâhk – *star* (NA)
ahcahk – *spirit* (NA)

akik – *mucous* (NA)
âhkik – *seal* (NA)

niyânan – *five*
niyanân – *us*

ohcîw – *s/he is from* (VAI-3rd person)
ôcêw – *a housefly*

As is evident from the foregoing, we must be vigilant in writing the Cree words, if we want to write them correctly. Here are other minimal pairs which can cause problems:

kisik – *and also* (IPC)
kîsik – *the sky* (NI)

itapi – *Sit that way!* (VAI)
itâpi – *Look that way!* (VAI)

tahkon – *Carry him/her!* (VTA)
takon – *Add it to it!* (VTA)

pêhêw – *S/he waits for s.o.* (VTA)
pihêw – *a grouse/partridge* (NA)

êkâwiya – *Don't!*
okâwiya – *her/his mother*

pâskisam – *S/he shoots at it.* (VTI-1)
paskisam – *S/he cuts it.* (VTI-1)

sêkihêw – *S/he scares s.o.* (VTA)
sâkihêw – *S/he loves s.o.* (VTA)

itôta – *Do it!* (VTI-1)
itohtah – *Take s.o. somewhere!* (VTA)

paskinam – *S/he breaks s.t. off.* (VTI)
pâskinam – *S/he uncovers s.t.* (VTI)

sâkinêw – *S/he holds it out.* (VTA)
sakinêw – *S/he holds onto it.* (VTA)

iskwêwasâkay – *a woman's dress/coat* (NI)
iskwêwasakay – *a woman's skin* (NA)

atotêw – *S/he makes a request of someone.* (VTA)
âtotêw – *S/he tells a story about someone.* (VTA)

kinosêw – *a fish* (NA)
kinosiw – *S/he is long.* (VAI)

miskon – *liver* (NI)
mîskon – *Feel him/her!* (VTA)

pimisin – *S/he lies down.* (VAI)
pîmisin – *S/he lays sideways.* (VAI)

pimotêw – *S/he shoots arrows at s.o.* (VTA)
pimohtêw – *S/he walks.* (VAI)

pimiciwan – *There is a current.* (VII)
pîmiciwan – *There is a cross-current.* (VII)

otah – *Defeat him/her!* (VTA)
ôta – *here* (PR)

DO:

A.   DICTATION: 10 WORDS IN CREE CHOSEN FROM THE PRECEDING VOCABULARY.

B.   MARK THE LONG VOWELS IN THE FOLLOWING WORDS:

nahapi – *See clearly!*　　maskisin – *She/he is crippled.*　　oma – *this*
nahapi – *Sit down!*　　　maskisin – *a shoe*　　　　　ota – *here*
asam – *Feed him/her.*　　maskosis – *bear cub*　　　　pasow – *She/he smells it.*
asam – *a snowshoe*　　　maskosis – *small grass*　　　pasow – *She/he is dry.*

C.   GETTING TO KNOW EACH OTHER: FIRST AND SECOND PERSONS

Go from student to student saying the following information to them, a section at a time. First do the name section with all the students, then move on to the next section. Once you have completed all the sections, then you can do all four sections with each of the students. Students do not get to see these until after the class.

1. NAME:

SPEAKER A: _____ nit**isiyihkâso**n. *My name is* _____.

kiya mâka, tânisi kit**isiyihkâso**n? *How about you, what is your name?*

SPEAKER B: _____ nit**isiyihkâso**n. *My name is* _____.

2. PLACE OF ORIGIN:

SPEAKER A: _____ kayahtê nit**ohcî**n. *I am originally from* _____.

kiya mâka, tânitê kayahtê kit**ohcî**n. *How about you, where are you originally from?*

SPEAKER B: _____ kayahtê nit**ohcî**n. *I am originally from* _____.

3. PLACE OF PRESENT RESIDENCE:

SPEAKER A: _____ mêkwâc ni**wîki**n. *I now live in* _____.

kiya mâka, tânitê mêkwâc ki**wîki**n? *How about you, where do you live now?*

SPEAKER B: _____ mêkwâc ni**wîki**n. *I now live in* _____.

4. AGE:

SPEAKER A: _____ nit**itahtopiponâ**n. *I am* _____ *years old.*

kiya mâka, tân**itahtopiponê**yan? *How about you, how old are you?*

SPEAKER B: _____ nit**itahtopiponâ**n. *I am* _____ *years old.*

D. GETTING TO KNOW EACH OTHER: FIRST, SECOND AND THIRD PERSONS

Go from student to student saying the following information to them, a section at a time:

1. NAME: go to the first student in the circle with your information and your question:

SPEAKER A:_____ nit**isiyihkâso**n. *My name is*_____.

kiya mâka, tânisi kit**isiyihkâso**n? *How about you, what is your name?*

SPEAKER B: _____ nit**isiyihkâso**n. *My name is* _____.

Go to the next student in the circle with your information and the information provided by the previous student then ask the question:

SPEAKER A: _____ nit**isiyihkâso**n. *My name is* _____.

_____ **isiyihkâso**w awa. (point to the previous student)

This one's name is _____.

kiya mâka, tânisi kit**isiyihkâso**n? *How about you, what is your name?*

SPEAKER C: _____ nit**isiyihkâso**n. *My name is*_____.

SPEAKER A: Point to the previous student then ask: tânisi **isiyihkâso**w awa? *What is this one's name?*

SPEAKER C: _____ **isiyihkâso**w awa. *This one's name is* _____.

2. PLACE OF ORIGIN:

SPEAKER A: _____ kayahtê nit**ohcî**n. *I am originally from* _____.

kiya mâka, tânitê kayahtê kit**ohcî**n? *How about you, where are you originally from?*

SPEAKER B:_____kayahtê nit**ohcî**n. *I am originally from* _____.

Go to the next student in the circle with your information and the information provided by the previous student then ask the question:

SPEAKER A: _____ kayahtê nit**ohcî**n. *I am originally from* _____.

_____ kayahtê **ohcî**w awa. (point to the previous student)

This one is originally from _____.

kiya mâka, tânitê kayahtê kit**ohcî**n? *How about you, where are you from originally?*

SPEAKER C: _____ kayahtê nit**ohcî**n. *I am originally from* _____.

SPEAKER A: Point to the previous student then ask:
tânitê kayahtê **ohcî**w awa? *Where is this one originally from?*

SPEAKER C:_____ kayahtê **ohcî**w awa. *This one is originally from* _____

3. PLACE OF PRESENT RESIDENCE:

SPEAKER A: _____ mêkwâc ni**wîki**n. *I now live in* _____.

kiya mâka, tânitê mêkwâc ki**wîki**n? *How about you, where do you live now?*

SPEAKER B: _____ mêkwâc ni**wîki**n. *I live in* _____.

Go to the next student in the circle with your information and the information provided by the previous student then ask the question

SPEAKER A: _____ mêkwâc ni**wîki**n. *I now live in* _____.

_____ mêkwâc **wîki**w awa. (point to the previous student)

This one now lives in _____.

kiya mâka, tânitê mêkwâc ki**wîki**n? *How about you, where do you live now?*

SPEAKER C: _____ mêkwâc ni**wîki**n. *I now live in* _____.

SPEAKER A: Point to the previous student then ask:
tânitê mêkwâc **wîki**w awa? *Where does this one live now?*

SPEAKER C: _____ mêkwâc **wîki**w awa. *This one now lives in* _____.

4. AGE:

SPEAKER A: _____ nit**itahtopiponâ**n. *I am* _____ *years old.*

kiya mâka, tân**itahtopiponê**yan? *How about you, how old are you?*

SPEAKER B: _____ nit**itahtopiponâ**n. *I am* _____ *years old.*

Go to the next student in the circle with your information and the information provided by the previous student then ask the question

SPEAKER A: _____ nit**itahtopiponâ**n. *I am* _____ *years old.*

_____ **itahtopiponê**w awa. (point to the previous student)

This one is _____ *years old.*
kiya mâka, tân**itahtopiponê**yan? *How about you, how old are you?*

SPEAKER C: _____ nit**itahtopiponâ**n. *I am* _____ *years old.*

SPEAKER A: Point to the previous student then ask: tân**itahtopiponê**w awa? *What is this one's age?*

SPEAKER C: _____ **itahtopiponê**w awa. *This one is* _____ *years old.*

	STEM			
subject	**isiyihkâso**–be named	**ohcî**–be from	**wîki**–reside/live	**itahtopiponê**–age
I/me	nit**isiyihkâso**n	nit**ohcî**n	ni**wîki**n	nit**itahtopiponâ**n
You	kit**isiyihkâso**n	kit**ohcî**n	ki**wîki**n	kit**itahtopiponâ**n
S/he	**isiyihkâso**w	**ohcî**w	**wîki**w	**itahtopiponê**w

1.2 DIALOGUE ONE

A: tânisi.

B: namôya nânitaw. kiya mâka?

A: pêyakwan. _____ NAME _____ nitisiyihkâson.
kiya mâka, tânisi kitisiyihkâson?

B: _____ NAME _____ nitisiyihkâson.

A: kayahtê _____ PLACE _____ ohci niya.
kiya mâka, tânitê ohci kiya kayahtê?

B: _____ PLACE _____ ohci niya kayahtê,
mâka *Regina* mêkwâc niwîkin. **OR**
Regina ohci niya, êkota mîna mêkwâc niwîkin.

kiya mâka, tânitê mêkwâc kiwîkin?

A: *Regina* mêkwâc nîsta niwîkin.
okiskinwahamâkan niya.
kiya mâka, okiskinwahamâkan cî kîsta?

B: âha, okiskinwahamâkan nîsta.

A: *Hello, how are you?*

B: *Fine. How about you?*

A: *The same. My name is _____ .*
How about you, what's your name?

B: *My name is _____ .*

A: *I am from _____ originally.*
How about you, where are you from originally?

B: *I am originally from _____ ,*
but I live in Regina now. **OR**
I am from Regina, I also live there now.

How about you, where do you live now?

A: *I live in Regina now too.*
I am a student.
How about you, are you a student too?

B: *Yes, I am a student too.*

VOCABULARY

tânisi – *Hello, how are you.*
namôya nânitaw – *fine*
kiya mâka? – *How about you?*
kitisiyihkâson – *your name is*
tânitê – *where*
êkota – *there*
nîsta – *me too*
okiskinwahamâkan – *a student*

namôya – *no*
kiya – *you*
pêyakwan – *the same*
ohci – *from*
mêkwâc – *now*
mîna – *also/too*
kîsta – *you too*
kayahtê – *originally*

nânitaw – *about*
mâka – *but*
nitisiyihkâson – *my name is*
niya – *I/me*
niwîkin – *I live/reside*
kiwîkin – *you live*
okiskinwahamâkêw – *a teacher*

1.3 INTRODUCTORY INFORMATION ABOUT FAMILY

The following Animate Intransitive Verbs (VAI) appear in the first person (I) and second person (you) in the foregoing dialogue: **isiyihkâso** – *be called/named*; and **wîki** – *live/reside*. Note, the paradigm below includes the third person (he/she) form:

<table>
<tr><td colspan="2" align="center">isiyihkâso</td><td colspan="2" align="center">wîki</td></tr>
<tr><td colspan="2" align="center">nitisiyihkâson – I am called/named</td><td colspan="2" align="center">niwîkin – I live</td></tr>
<tr><td colspan="2" align="center">kitisiyihkâson – You are called/named</td><td colspan="2" align="center">kiwîkin – You live</td></tr>
<tr><td colspan="2" align="center">isiyihkâsow – She/he is called/named</td><td colspan="2" align="center">wîkiw – She/he lives</td></tr>
</table>

DO: Take a photograph of a person and provide that person's name, age, place of origin, and place of residence to your classmates. Information provided should be in the same form as in **dialogue two** following this chart of kinship terms:

BASE NOUN	1st person possessive	2nd person possessive	3rd person possessive
omosômimâw *a grandfather*	nimosôm *my grandfather*	kimosôm *your grandfather*	omosôma *his/her grandfather*
ohkomimâw *a grandmother*	nohkom *my grandmother*	kohkom *your grandmother*	ohkoma *his/her grandmother*
okâwîmâw *a mother*	nikâwiy *my mother*	kikâwiy *your mother*	okâwiya *his/her mother*
ohtâwîmâw *a father*	nohtâwiy *my father*	kohtâwiy *your father*	ohtâwiya *her/his father*
okosisimâw *a son*	nikosis my son	kikosis your son	okosisa her/his son
otânisimâw *a daughter*	nitânis *my daughter*	kitânis *your daughter*	otânisa *her/his daughter*
omisimâw *an older sister*	nimis *my older sister*	kimis *your older sister*	omisa *her/his older sister*
ostêsimâw *an older brother*	nistês *my older brother*	kistês *your older brother*	ostêsa *his/her older brother*
osîmimâw *a younger sibling*	nisîmis *my younger sibling*	kisîmis *your younger sibling*	osîmisa *his/her younger sibling*
awâsis *a child*	nitawâsimis *my child*	kitawâsimis *your child*	otawâsimisa *her/his child*

1.3.A DIALOGUE TWO

Two people talking about a relative.

A: awîna awa? (*Who is this?*)
B: nitânis awa. (*This is my daughter.*)
A: tânisi isiyihkâsow kitânis? (*What is your daughter's name?*)
B: *Megan* isiyihkâsow nitânis. (*My daughter's name is Megan.*)
A: tânitê ohcîw kitânis? (*Where is your daughter from?*)
B: *Regina* ohcîw nitânis. (*My daughter is from Regina.*)
A: tânitê mêkwâc wîkiw kitânis? (*Where does your daughter live now?*)
B: *Regina* mêkwâc wîkiw nitânis. (*My daughter lives in Regina now.*)
A: tânitahtopiponêw kitânis? (*How old is your daughter?*)
B: nîsitanaw itahtopiponêw nitânis. (*My daughter is twenty years old.*)

1.3.B DIALOGUE THREE

Two people talking about someone else's relative: note the use of **yiwa** at the end of the verbs which ended in **w** in dialogue two.

C: awîna ôhi otânisa? (*Whose daughter is this?*)
D: _____ anihi otânisa. (*That is_____'s daughter.*)
C: tânisi isiyihkâsoyiwa otânisa? (*What is his/her daughter's name?*)
D: *Megan* isiyihkâsoyiwa otânisa. (*His/her daughter's name is Megan.*)
C: tânitê ohcîyiwa otânisa? (*Where is his/her daughter from?*)
D: *Regina* ohcîyiwa otânisa. (*His/her daughter is from Regina.*)
C: tânitê mêkwâc wîkiyiwa otânisa? (*Where does his/her daughter live now?*)
D: *Regina* mêkwâc wîkiyiwa otânisa. (*His/her daughter lives in Regina now.*)
C: tânitahtopiponêyiwa otânisa? (*How old is his/her daughter?*)
D: nîsitanaw itahtopiponêyiwa otânisa. (*His/her daughter is twenty years old.*)

NOTE: the **yiwa** form of the verb above is the form the verb takes when talking about someone else's relative's information. It is known as the obviative form of the verb. The subject of the obviative form of the verb is *his/her* (_____) and in the above case it is **otânisa** – *his/her daughter.*

NEW VAIS FROM ABOVE:

itahtopiponê – *be of a certain age*   ohcî – *be from*

DO: Following the format in **dialogue three** above, have students talk about another classmate's information.

1.4 NUMBERS, MONTHS, DATES

A. NUMBERS

BASE NUMBERS:	-add "-osâp" or "-sâp" to the base numbers for units 11 - 19	-add "-omitanaw" to the base numbers for units of ten from 20 to 100
pêyak–1	pêyakosâp–11	mitâtaht–10
nîso–2	nîsosâp–12	nîs(om)itanaw–20**
nisto–3	nistosâp–13	nistomitanaw–30
nêwo–4	nêwosâp –14	nê(wo)mitanaw–40
niyânan–5	niyânanosâp–15	niyân(an)omitanaw–50
nikotwâsik–6	nikotwâsosâp–16	nikotwâsomitanaw–60
têpakohp–7	têpakohposâp –17	têpakohpomitanaw–70
ayênânêw–8	ayênânêwosâp–18	ayênânê(wo)mitanaw- 80
kêkâ-mitâtaht* - 9	kêkâ-mitâtahtosâp -19 Or kêkâ-nîsitanaw	kêkâ-mitâtahtomitanaw–90
mitâtaht–10	The units above can also be used with the units from 20 to 90 to say 21-29 etc.	mitâtahtomitanaw–100

*kêkâ-mitâtaht literally means *almost ten*. The **kêkâ** comes from **kêkâc** – *almost* and can be used for other numbers like 19 – **kêkâ-nîsitanaw** (*almost 20*); **kêkâ-nistomitanaw** then is 29 (*almost 30*) and so on down the line.

**The letters in brackets here and elsewhere on this chart are often left out when speaking. That process will be evident in further writings of the above numerical units.

B. MONTHS

The list of months provided below is from *Cree: Language of the Plains* (Okimâsis, 2004, pp. 57–58).

Month in Cree	Common event during Moon phase	Month in English
kisê-pîsim	The Great Moon	January
mikisiwi-pîsim	The Eagle Moon	February
niski-pîsim	The Goose Moon	March
ayîki-pîsim	The Frog Moon	April
sâkipakâwi-pîsim	The Budding Moon	May
pâskâwihowi-pîsim	The Hatching Moon	June
paskowi-pîsim	The Moulting Moon	July
ohpahowi-pîsim	The Flying Up Moon	August
nôcihitowi-pîsim takwâki-pîsim	The Mating Moon The Autumn Moon	September
pimihâwi-pîsim pinâskowi-pîsim	The Migrating Moon The Leaf Falling Moon	October
ihkopîwi-pîsim	The Frost Moon	November
pawâcakinasîsi-pîsim	The Frost Exploding Moon	December

C. DATES

Saying the date in Cree has several forms depending on the context.

1. If the information provided deals with the current date, use the following:

_____DATE_____ akimâw mêkwâc awa pîsim.

It is the _____DATE_____ of the month now.

QUESTION AND ANSWER:
Q. tâniyikohk akimâw mêkwâc awa pîsim? *What is the date right now?*
A. <u>nisto</u> akimâw mêkwâc pîsim. *It is the 3rd of the month now.*

2. If the information is a recurrent event like a birthday use the following:

In talking about yourself use the following:

_____DATE_____ ê-akim**iht** _____MONTH_____ mâna nitipisk**ên**.

I have a birthday on the_____DATE_____ of _____MONTH_____.

QUESTION AND ANSWER:
Q. tânispîhk mâna kâ-tipiska**man**? *When do you have a birthday?*
A. <u>nêwo</u> ê-akimiht <u>sâkipakâwi-pîsim</u> mâna nitipiskên. *I have a birthday on the 4th of May.*

3. In talking about someone else the "ê-akimiht" becomes "ê-akim**im**iht" and the month ends in "wa" and the verb "tipiska" becomes "tipisk**am**".

_____DATE_____ ê-akim**im**iht _____MONTH_____ mâna tipisk**am**.

She has a birthday on the_____DATE_____ of _____MONTH_____.

QUESTION AND ANSWER:
Q. tânispîhk mâna kâ-tipisk**ahk**? *When does she/he have a birthday?*
A. <u>nêwo</u> ê-akim**iht** <u>sâkipakâwi-pîsim**wa**</u> mâna tipisk**am**.
   She/he has a birthday on the 4th of May.

4. If the information provided is upcoming then the **future conditional** form of "ê-akimiht" "akim**ihci**" is used:

_____DATE_____ akim**ihci** _____MONTH_____ ni**wî**-tipiskên.

I am going to have a birthday on the_____DATE_____ of _____MONTH_____.

Regardless of which of the two "*it is counted*" one uses, "akimâw" or "ê-akimiht," the date always comes before the month.

1.5 CHAPTER ONE EXERCISES

EXERCISE 1. Use the chart below to talk about yourself and members of your family:

PERSON	NAME?	ORIGIN?	RESIDENCE?	STUDENT?
1st: Speaker speaks of him/herself	nitisiyihkâson	ohci niya kayahtê	mêkwâc niwîkin	okiskinwahamâkan niya
2nd: The one spoken to	kitisiyihkâson	ohci kiya kayahtê	mêkwâc kiwîkin	okiskinwahamâkan kiya
3rd: The one spoken about	isiyihkâsow	ohci wiya kayahtê	mêkwâc wîkiw	okiskinwahamâkan wiya
3rd person obviative: someone else's kin	isiyihkâsoyiwa	ohcîyiwa kayahtê	mêkwâc wîkiyiwa	okiskinwahamâkaniyiwa wiya

QUESTIONS:

A. ABOUT THE ONE SPOKEN TO:

   1. tânisi kitisiyihkâson?
   2. tânitê ohci kiya?
   3. tânitê mêkwâc kiwîkin?
   4. okiskinwahamâkan cî kiya?

B. ABOUT THE KIN OF THE ONE SPOKEN TO:

   1. tânisi isiyihkâsow k_____?
   2. tânitê ohci wiya k_____?
   3. tânitê mêkwâc wîkiw k_____?
   4. okiskinwahamâkan cî wiya?

C. ABOUT THE KIN OF THE ONE SPOKEN ABOUT:

   1. tânisi isiyihkâsoyiwa o_____a?
   2. tânitê ohci wiya o_____a?
   3. tânitê mêkwâc wîkiyiwa o_____a?
   4. okiskinwahamâkaniyiwa cî wiya

      o_____a?

ANSWERS:

   1. _____ nitisiyihkâson.
   2. _____ ohci niya.
   3. _____ mêkwâc niwîkin.
   4. âha, okiskinwahamâkan niya.

   1. _____ isiyihkâsow n_____.
   2. _____ ohci wiya n_____.
   3. _____ mêkwâc wîkiw n_____.
   4. âha, okiskinwahamâkan wiya.

   1. _____ isiyihkâsoyiwa o_____a.
   2. _____ ohci wiya o_____a.
   3. _____ mêkwâc wîkiyiwa o_____a.
   4. âha, okiskinwahamâkaniyiwa wiya

      o_____a.

EXERCISE 2. Have students prepare a project for in-class presentation similar to the exercise above. The students will bring a photograph of a relative to class and talk about them including the following information:

1. How the person is related:

   (*Relative from Exercise 4 – page 21*) awa. – *This is my* _____ .

2. Name of person:

   (*Name*) isiyihkâsow. – *Her/his name is* _____ .

3. Age:

   (*Age: take from 1.4 – page 14*) itahtopiponêw. – *She/he is* _____ *years old.*

4. Place of Birth:

   (*Place of birth*) kî-nihtâwikiw. – *She/he was born at* _____ .

5. Birth-date:

   (*Date*) ê-akimimiht (*Month*) mâna tipiskam. – *She/he has a birthday on* _____ .

6. Where the person was raised:

   (*Place*) kî-pê-ohpikiw. – *She/he was raised in* _____ .

7. Where the person went to school:

   (*Place*) kî-pê-kiskinwahamâkosiw. – *She/he went to school in* _____ .

8. Present residence of the person:

   (*Place*) mêkwâc wîkiw (*Kinship term*). – *She/he lives in* _____ *right now.*

9. Present occupation of the person (see list in next section):

   okiskinwahamâkaniwiw mêkwâc (*Kinship term*) – *She/he is presently a student.*

NOTE: okiskinwahamâkan – *a student* is a noun but this can be made into a verb by the inclusion of "**iwi**" to the noun to make it into a VAI: okiskinwahamâkan**iwi**- *be a student*, so: okiskinwahamâkan**iwiw** – *she/he is a student.*

LIST OF OCCUPATIONS AND OTHER ITEMS OF IDENTIFICATION:

ENGLISH	NOUNS	VERBS: VAI stem forms
Student	okiskinwahamâkan	okiskinwahamâkaniwi
Teacher	okiskinwahamâkêw	okiskinwahamâkêwi
Child	awâsis	awâsisiwi
Mother	okâwîmâw	okâwîmâwi
Father	ohtâwîmâw	ohtâwîmâwi
Chief	okimâhkân	okimâhkâniwi
Councillor	wiyasiwêwiyiniw	wiyasiwêwiyinîwi
Carpenter	mistikonâpêw	mistikonâpêwi
Fisherman	opakitahwâw	opakitahwâwi
Trapper	owanihikêw	owanihikêwi
Farmer	okistikêwiyiniw	okistikêwiyinîwi
Doctor	maskihkîwiyiniw	maskihkîwiyinîwi
Nurse	maskihkîwiskwêw	maskihkîwiskwêwi
Lawyer	opîkiskwêstamâkêw	opîkiskwêstamâkêwi
Dentist	mîpit-maskihkîwiyiniw	mîpit-maskihkîwiyinîwi
Bus Driver	opimohtahiwêw	opimohtahiwêwi
Janitor	okisîpêkihtakinikêw	okisîpêkihtakinikêwi
Firefighter	otâstawêhikêw	otâstawêhikêwi
Police	simâkanis	simâkanisiwi
Soldier	simâkanisihkân	simâkanisihkâniwi
Secretary	masinahikêsîs	masinahikêsîsiwi
Babysitter	okanawêyimâwasow	kanawêyimâwasôwi
Mechanic	pîwâpisko-iyiniw	pîwâpisko-iyinîwi
Maintenance person	osîhcikêwiyiniw	osîhcikêwiyinîwi
Optometrist	miskîsiko-maskihkîwiyiniw	miskîsiko-maskihkîwiyinîwi
Priest	ayamihêwiyiniw	ayamihêwiyinîwi
Probation officer	okitêyihcikêw	okitêyihcikêwi
Conservation Officer	okanawêyihcikêw	okanawêyihcikêwi
Teacher	okiskinwahamâkêw	okiskinwahamâkêwi

NOTE: The above forms can be used in the following way:
1. okiskinwahamâkan awa. – *He/she is a student.*
2. okiskinwahamâkaniwiw awa. – *He/she is being a student. (He/she is a student.)*
3. okiskinwahamâkêw ôma niya. – *I am a teacher.*
4. nitokiskinwahamâkêwin. – *I am being a teacher. (I am a teacher.)*

EXERCISE 3. One student will present the above information to the class and another will ask questions after the presentation. Here is a sample exercise, with the presenter's information in one column and the questions a classmate would ask in the other column.

PRESENTER: showing photo	QUESTIONS TO ASK CLASSMATES
nisîmis awa. *This is my younger sibling.*	awîna ôhi wîtisâna?* *Whose sibling is this?*
Patrick isiyihkâsow nisîmis. *My younger sibling is named Patrick.*	tânisi isiyihkâsoyiwa** osîmisa awa? *What is the name of his/her younger sibling?*
kêkâ-mitâtahtosâp itahtopiponêw nisîmis. *My younger sibling is 19 years old.*	tânitahtopiponêyit osîmisa awa? *How old is his/her younger sibling?*
wanihikêskanâhk kî-nihtâwikiw nisîmis. *My younger sibling was born on the trapline.*	tânitê kâ-kî-nihtâwikiyit osîmisa awa? *Where was his/her younger sibling born?*
nistosâp ê-akimimiht*** ihkopîwi-pîsimwa mâna tipiskam nisîmis. *My younger sibling's birthday is on November 13th.*	tânispîhk mâna kâ-tipiskamiyit osîmisa awa? *When does his/her younger sibling have a birthday?*
iskonikanihk kî-ohpikiw nisîmis. *My younger sibling was raised on the reserve.*	tânitê kâ-kî-pê-ohpikiyit osîmisa awa? *Where was his/her younger raised?*
iskonikanihk kî-pê-kiskinwahamâkosiw nisîmis. *My younger sibling went to school on the reserve.*	tânitê kâ-kî-pê-kiskinwahamâkosiyit osîmisa awa? *Where did his/her younger sibling go to school?*
ôtênâhk mêkwâc wîkiw nisîmis. *My younger sibling lives in town now.*	tânitê mêkwâc kâ-wîkiyit osîmisa awa? *Where does his/her younger sibling live now?*
okiskinwahamâkaniwiw nisîmis. *My younger sibling is a student.*	tânisi kâ-isi-atoskêyit osîmisa awa? *What does his/her younger sibling work at?*

NOTES ON OBVIATION: Obviation is the process that marks third person possessive nouns with a final "-a" and the 3' forms of verbs with a "-yiwa" for Indicative forms, a "-yit" for the Conjunct forms. The following appear in the exchange above:

   * wîtisâna – *his/her sibling* (NA-Possessive)
   ** isiyihkâsoyiwa – *his/her_____ is named*
   *** ê-akimimiht – *It is counted* (used when talking about a 3rd person's relative's data; "ê-akimiht" is the form used for everyone else's data).

QUESTIONS AND ANSWERS ABOUT PEOPLE'S VITAL STATISTICS

Q & A	NAME	AGE	BIRTH PLACE	BIRTHDAY	RAISED AT	SCHOOL AT	LIVES AT	WORK
Q in 2nd	tânisi kitisiyihkâson?	tânitahto-piponêyan?	tânitê kâ-kî-nihtâwikiyan?	tânispîhk mâna kâ-tipiskaman?	tânitê kâ-kî-pê-ohpikiyan?	tânitê kâ-kî-pê-kiskinwahamâkosiyan?	tânitê mêkwâc kâ-wîkiyan?	tânisi kâ-isi-atoskêyan?
A in 1st	(name) nitisiyihkâson.	(age) niti-tahto-piponân.	(place) nikî-nihtâwikin.	(date) ê-akimiht (month) mâna nitipiskên.	(place) nikî-pê-ohpikin?	(place) nikî-pê-kiskinwahamâkosin.	(place) mêkwâc niwîkin.	(occupation) niya.
Q in 3rd: Talking about someone else.	tânisi isiyihkâsow (kin)*?	tânitahto-piponêt (kin)?	tânitê kâ-kî-nihtâwikit (kin)?	tânispîhk mâna kâ-tipiskahk (kin)?	tânitê kâ-kî-pê-ohpikit (kin)?	tânitê kâ-kî-pê-kiskinwahamâkosit (kin)?	tânitê mêkwâc kâ-wîkit (kin)?	tânisi kâ-isi-atoskêt (kin)?
A in 3rd	(name) isiyihkâsow (kin)**.	(age) itahto-piponêw (kin).	(place) kî-nihtâwikiw (kin).	(date)*** ê-akimimiht (month) mâna tipiskam (kin).	(place) kî-pê-ohpikiw (kin).	(place) kâ-kî-pê-kiskinwahamâkosit (kin).	(place) mêkwâc wîkiw (kin).	(occupation) wiya (kin).
Q in 3' obviative: Talking about someone else's kin.	tânisi isiyihkâsoyiwa (kin)****?	tânitahto-piponêyit (kin)?	tânitê kâ-kî-nihtâwikiyit (kin)?	tânispîhk mâna kâ-tipiskamiyit (kin)?	tânitê kâ-kî-pê-ohpikiyit (kin)?	tânitê kâ-kî-pê-kiskinwahamâkosiyit (kin)?	tânitê mêkwâc kâ-wîkiyit (kin)?	tânisi kâ-isi-atoskêyit (kin)?
A in 3' obviative	(name) isiyihkâsoyiwa (kin).	(age) itahto-piponêyiwa (kin).	(place) kî-nihtâwikiyiwa (kin).	(date)*** ê-akimimiht (month) mâna tipiskamiyiwa (kin).	(place) kî-pê-ohpikiyiwa (kin).	(place) kî-pê-kiskinwahamâkosiyiwa (kin).	(place) mêkwâc wîkiyiwa (kin).	(occupation) wiya (kin).

* Kinship term is in the 2nd person form as in "kistês – *your older brother*."

** Kinship term is in the 1st person form as in "nistês – *my older brother*."

*** Note the extra 'im' in "ê-akimimiht" and the month ends in "wa."

**** Kinship term is in the obviative form as in "ostêsa – *her/his older brother*."

EXERCISE 4. KINSHIP FORMS

Complete the following chart, keeping in mind the process of obviation:

1ST PERSON	2ND PERSON	3RD PERSON
nohkom - *my grandmother*	kohkom–*your grandmother*	ohkoma–*his/her grandmother*
nimosôm–*my grandfather*	kimosôm–*your grandfather*	omosôma–*his/her grandfather*
ninîkihikwak–*my parents*		
nohtâwiy–*my father*		
nikâwiy–*my mother*		
nîtisân–*my sibling*		
nistês–*my older brother*		
nimis–*my older sister*		
nisîmis–*my younger sibling*		
niwâhkômâkan–*my relative*		
ninâpêm–*my husband*		
nitiskwêm–*my wife*		
niwîkimâkan–*my spouse*		
niwîcêwâkan–*my companion/partner*		
nitawâsimis–*my child*		
nikosis–*my son*		
nitânis–*my daughter*		
nôsisim–*my grandchild*		

EXERCISE 5. Check the best possible answer or fill in the most appropriate blank to the following questions:

1. tânisi?

    _____ namôya nânitaw, kiya mâka?

    _____ namôya nânitaw, niya mâka?

    _____ namoya nanitaw, kiya mâka?

2. *Solomon* nitisiyihkâson. kiya mâka, tânisi kitisiyihkâson?

    _____ kitisiyihkâson.

    _____ nitisiyihkason.

    _____ nitisiyihkâson.

3. *Stanley Mission* ohci niya. kiya mâka, tânitê ohci kiya?

    _____ ohci kiya.

    _____ ohci niya.

    _____ ochi niya.

4. *Regina* mêkwâc niwîkin. kiya mâka, tânitê mêkwâc kiwîkin?

    _____ mêkwâc kiwîkin.

    _____ mêkwâc niwîkin.

    _____ mêkwâc nîsta *Regina* niwîkin.

5. okiskinwahamâkêw niya. kiya mâka, okiskinwahamâkêw cî kiya?

    _____ âha, okiskinwahamâkêw niya.

    _____ namôya, namôya okiskinwahamâkêw niya.

    _____ namôya, okiskinwahamâkan niya.

CHAPTER TWO
• • • • • • • • • • • • •
NOUNS

2. ANIMACY

All nouns in Cree are viewed as alive (Animate), or not-alive (Inanimate). Other Cree texts refer to these distinctions as the Gender concept in Cree. We will call this concept "Animacy". Using the correct forms of verbs, demonstrative pronouns, and interrogative pronouns all depend on the Animacy of the noun under discussion.

Most nouns that are alive in the English way of thinking are Animate in Cree but there are exceptions. For instance, some clothing items are Animate and most body parts are Inanimate. There just is no logical way of explaining these, so the best way for a learner to know what is

Animate and what is Inanimate is simply by asking a Cree speaker how the person would say "*this is*" about a certain noun. The Cree speaker would use either "awa" following an Animate noun, or "ôma" following an Inanimate noun. We will follow the same process in this text: i.e., in asking you to do exercises where knowledge of Animacy is needed, I will include either "awa" or "ôma" to help you determine the Animacy of nouns.

Here is a list of some of these nouns that often baffle the student of Cree because the Animacy of the noun strays from the English view of the world:

ANIMATE NOUNS

mitâs	*a pair of pants*
asikan	*a sock*
astis	*a mitt/glove*
tâpiskâkan	*a scarf/tie*
maskasiy	*a fingernail/toenail*
ospwâkan	*a pipe*
asiniy	*a rock/stone*
êmihkwân	*a spoon*
askihk	*a pail*
apoy	*a paddle*
ahcâpiy	*a bow*
acos	*an arrow*
sêhkêpayîs	*a car*
sôminis	*a raisin*
ayôskan	*a raspberry*
oskâtâsk	*a carrot*
wîhkihkasikan	*a cake*

INANIMATE NOUNS

wâpikwaniy	*a flower*
maskosiy	*a piece of grass*
nîpiy	*a leaf*
maskihkiy	*medicine*
mêstakay	*a hair*
mîpit	*a tooth*
miskîsik	*an eye*
misit	*a foot*
miskât	*a leg*
mistikwân	*a head*
mitôn	*a mouth*
mihtawakay	*an ear*
micihciy	*a hand*
mitêhimin	*a strawberry*
iyinimin	*a blueberry*
misâskwatômin	*a saskatoon berry*
wîhkwaskwa	*sweetgrass (pl)*

There are no hard and fast rules in identifying which nouns are **Animate** or **Inanimate**, so students have to learn the above list. Explaining why things like pants, scarves, mitts, etc., are **Animate** is beyond most Cree speakers capabilities including this writer's. If a student wants to ask a fluent Cree speaker the **Animacy** of a noun it is best that you ask the Cree speaker which of the other **Grammatical** categories that speaker would use with the noun in question. For example, the **Demonstrative** pronouns and **Interrogative** pronouns listed below are useful to determine the animacy of nouns.

ENGLISH	USE for Animate Nouns	USE for Inanimate Nouns
This	awa	ôma
That	ana	anima
That (over there)	nâha	nêma
These	ôki	ôhi
Those	aniki	anihi
Those (over there)	nêki	nêhi
Where	tâniwâ	tâniwê
Where (for plural nouns)	tâniwêhkâk	tâniwêhâ

Understanding animacy, a way of looking at nouns in Cree, is central to the use of certain word formations in the language. All nouns in Cree are seen as either possessing a life force or lacking a life force: "living" nouns are animate, while "non-living" nouns are inanimate. Knowledge of a noun's animacy helps in using the correct plural forms, the right demonstrative and interrogative pronouns, the correct transitive verbs and the correct colour forms.

HOW ANIMACY WORKS

ANIMACY	PLURAL FORM	DEMONSTRATIVE PRONOUN	INTERROGATIVE PRONOUN	TRANSITIVE VERB	COLOUR FORM
Animate: atim *dog*	atimwak *dogs*	**Singular form:** awa atim *this dog* **Plural form:** ôki atimwak *these dogs*	**Singular form:** tâniwâ atim *Where is the dog?* **Plural form:** tâniwêhkâk atimwak? *Where are the dogs?*	**Singular form:** niwâpamâw atim. *I see a dog.* **Plural form:** niwâpamâwak atimwak. *I see dogs.*	**Singular form:** wâpiskisiw atim. *The dog is white.* **Plural form:** wâpiskisiwak atimwak. *The dogs are white.*
Inanimate: astotin *hat*	astotina *hats*	**Singular form:** ôma astotin *this hat* **Plural form:** ôhi astotina *these hats*	**Singular form:** tâniwê astotin? *Where is the hat?* **Plural form:** tâniwêhâ astotina? *Where are the hats?*	**Singular form:** niwâpahtên astotin. *I see a hat.* **Plural form:** niwâpahtên astotina. *I see hats.*	**Singular form:** wâpiskâw astotin. *The hat is white.* **Plural form:** wâpiskâwa astotina. *The hats are white.*

Refer to the previous chart, and place appropriate nouns in the blank spaces below.

Animacy	Number	Demonstrative	Interrogative	Transitive	Colour
Animate - singular	_____	awa _____	tâniwâ _____	niwâpamâw _____	wâpiskisiw _____
Animate - plural	_____**ak**	ôki _____**ak**	tâniwêhkâk _____**ak**	niwâpamâw**ak** _____**ak**	wâpiskisiw**ak** _____**ak**
Inanimate - singular	_____	ôma _____	tâniwê _____	niwâpahtên _____	wâpiskâw _____
Inanimate - plural	_____**a**	ôhi _____**a**	tâniwêhâ _____**a**	niwâpahtên _____**a**	wâpiskâw**a** _____**a**

ANIMACY AGREEMENT: Animacy applies to all units. If one unit is animate, then all units are animate; if one unit is inanimate, then all other units are inanimate.

NUMBER AGREEMENT: Number applies to all units except for transitive inanimate verbs ("niwâpahtên" above). If one unit is singular, then all units are singular; if one unit is plural, then all other units are plural.

2.1 NUMBER

Number refers to whether a noun is singular or plural. All animate nouns in their plural forms end in a "k" and all inanimate nouns in their plural forms end in an "a". Making the inflection from singular noun to plural noun depends on the ending of the singular noun as follows:

TABLE I

NOUN ENDINGS	ANIMATE PLURALS	INANIMATE PLURALS
Nouns ending in **k**: mistik–*a tree* (NA) mistik–*a log* (NI)	Add **wak**: mistikwak–*trees*	Add **wa**: mistikwa–*logs*
Nouns ending in **i**: ôsi–*boat* (NI) wâwi–*egg* (NI)	None with these endings.	Drop the **i** then add **a**: ôsa–*boats* wâwa - *eggs*
Nouns ending in **a**: mwâkwa–*loon* (NA)	Add **k**: mwâkwak–*loons*	None with these endings.
Some exceptional Nouns ending in **m**, **n**, or **s**: atim–*dog* (NA) wâpos–*rabbit* (NA)	Add **wak**: atimwak–*dogs* wâposwak–*rabbits*	Nouns ending in -êkin: e.g., pahkêkinwa–*hides*.
All other nouns not ending as those above:	Add **ak**.	Add **a**.

CLASSROOM ACTIVITY: NOUNS

DO: Have participants stand in a circle:

1. itwaha/itwah: Say 'itwaha' or 'itwah' depending on the animacy of the noun. The participants will point with you.

   CLASSROOM: Do classroom items first as you point to the object in the classroom.
   itwaha:

wâsênikan	asicâyihtak	wâsaskotênikan
iskwâhtêm	ispimihtak	wâsêpicikanis
têhtapiwin	mohcihtak	masinahikêwinâhtik
mîcisowinâhtik	kîhkêhtak	masinahikêwâpisk

   CLASSROOM ITEMS: Place items on a table then point to the objects or in the classroom as you say 'itwaha ____ NI ____' or 'itwah ____ NA ____'.

itwaha:	**itwah:**
masinahikan	nâpêw
masinahikanêkin	iskwêw
kâsîhikan	okiskinwahamâkêw
miskotâkay	okiskinwahamâkan
maskisin	masinahikanâhtik
astotin	masinahikanâpiskos
minihkwâcikan	masinahikêwasinîs
ayamâkanis	astis

2. nîpawi: Say 'nîpawi' with accompanying hand motions to indicate for the participant to stand up.

3. pê-itohtê: Say 'pê-itohtê' with accompanying hand motions to indicate for the participant to come toward you.

4. sâmina/sâmin: Say either 'sâmina' or 'sâmin' depending on the animacy of the noun you are touching. First the group leader touches the noun then indicate that the participant is to touch the noun: 'sâmina ____ NI ____' or 'sâmin ____ NA ____'.

sâmina:	**sâmin:**
masinahikan	nâpêw
masinahikanêkin	iskwêw
kâsîhikan	okiskinwahamâkêw
miskotâkay	okiskinwahamâkan
maskisin	masinahikanâhtik
astotin	masinahikanâpiskos
minihkwâcikan	masinahikêwasinîs
ayamâkanis	astis

5. nitawi-api: Say 'nitawi-api' with accompanying hand motions to indicate for the participant to go and sit down. Start 2-5 with the next participant and continue until all the participants have had a turn. Have each of the participants take a turn at being group leader.

EXERCISES

EXERCISE 1. Make plurals out of the following nouns (and demonstrative pronouns). Pay close attention to the demonstrative pronoun that follows the noun to determine the Animacy of the nouns. Make sure the demonstrative pronouns change to agree in number to the plural noun:

1. maskisin ôma. *This is a shoe.* _____

2. mitâs awa. *This is a pair of pants.* _____

3. astis awa. *This is a mitt.* _____

4. papakiwayân ôma. *This is a shirt.* _____

5. asikan awa. *This is a sock.* _____

6. astotin ôma. *This is a hat.* _____

7. tâpiskâkan awa. *This is a scarf.* _____

8. miskotâkay ôma. *This is a coat.* _____

9. wâpikwaniy ôma. *This is a flower.* _____

10. mîtos awa. *This is a tree (aspen).* _____

11. pîsim awa. *This is a sun.* _____

12. acâhkos awa. *This is a star.* _____

13. nipêwin ôma. *This is a bed.* _____

14. mîcisowinâhtik ôma. *This is a table.* _____

15. têhtapiwin ôma. *This is a chair.* _____

16. wâsênikan ôma. *This is a window.* _____

17. wâskahikan ôma. *This is a house.* _____

18. iskwâhtêm ôma. *This is a door.* _____

19. êmihkwân awa. *This is a spoon.* _____

20. môhkomân ôma. *This is a knife.* _____

EXERCISE 2. Complete the following, then write out the rule which applies:

1. a) acâhk (*star*) ➞ acâhkwak   b) akik (*mucus*) ➞ akikwak

   c) mistik (*tree*) ➞ _____   d) sikâk (*skunk*) ➞ _____

   RULE: _____

   _____

2. a) mwâkwa (*loon*) ➞ mwâkwak   b) kâkwa (*porcupine*) ➞ kâkwak

   c) maskwa (*bear*) ➞ _____

   d) môswa (*moose*) ➞ _____

   RULE: _____

   _____

3. a) mitâs (*pants*) ➞ mitâsak   b) sîsîp (*duck*) ➞ sîsîpak

   c) kohkôs (*pig*) ➞ _____

   d) astis (*mitt*) ➞ _____

   RULE: _____

   _____

4. a) mistik (*log*) ➞ mistikwa   b) mîcisowinâhtik (*table*) ➞ mîcisowinâhtikwa

   c) mîcisowikamik (*restaurant*) ➞ _____

   d) atâwêwikamik (*store*) ➞ _____

   RULE: _____

   _____

5. a) wâwi (*egg*) ➞ wâwa   b) ôsi (*boat*) ➞ ôsa

   c) wâti (*hole*) ➞ _____

   d) askipwâwi (*potato*) ➞ _____

   RULE: _____

   _____

6. a) masinahikan (*book*) → masinahikana

    b) maskisin (*shoe*) → maskisina

    c) cihcipayapisikanis (*bicycle*) → _____

    d) têhtapiwin (*chair*) → _____

    RULE: _____

    _____

EXERCISE 3. Check off the right answers in the following questions:

Polarity questions: In Cree we use "cî" for a type of question that requires a "yes" or "no" answer. These can be answered with "âha" for "yes", followed by stating part of the question, as in:

> **QUESTION:** "wâwi cî ôma? - *Is this an egg?*"
> **ANSWER:** "âha, wâwi anima. - *Yes, that is an egg.*"

A question needing a negative answer can be in two forms, as in answers A and B below:

> **QUESTION:** nîpiy cî ôma? - *Is this a leaf?*
> **ANSWER A:** namôya, namôya anima nîpiy. - *No, that is not a leaf.*
> **ANSWER B:** namôya, wâwi anima. - *No, that is an egg.*

nîpiy cî ôma?
_____ namôya, wâwi anima.
_____ âha, nîpiy anima.
_____ âha, nipiy anima.

wâwi cî ôma?
_____ namôya, nipiy anima.
_____ namôya, nîpiy anima.
_____ âha, wâwi anima.

cîstahâsêpon cî ôma?
_____ âha, cîstahâsêpon anima.
_____ âha, cîstahâsêpon ana.
_____ namôya, cîstahâsêpon anima.

minihkwâcikan cî ôma?
_____ âha, mihkwâkan anima.
_____ âha, minihkwâcikan anima.
_____ ahâ, minihkwâkan anima.

acâhkos cî awa?

_____ âha, acâhkos ana.

_____ âha, âcâhkos ana.

_____ namôya, masinahikanâhcikos ana.

wâpikwaniy cî ôma?

_____ âha, wâpikwaniy ana.

_____ âha, wâpikwaniya anihi.

_____ âha, wâpikwaniy anima.

masinahikanâhcikos cî awa?

_____ âha, masinahikanâhcikos ana.

_____ ahâ, masinahikanâhcikos ana.

_____ namôya, masinahikan anima.

masinahikan cî ôma?

_____ âha, masinahikanâhcikos ana.

_____ âha, masinahikan anima.

_____ namôya, masinahikanâhcikos ana.

papakiwayân cî ôma?

_____ namôya, miskotâkay anima.

_____ âha, papakiwayân anima.

_____ namôya, iskwêwasâkay anima.

iskwêwasâkay cî ôma?

_____ âha, iskwêwasakay anima.

_____ âha, iskwêwasâkay anima.

_____ namôya, papakiwayân anima.

astis cî awa?

_____ âha, mîtos ana.
_____ âha, mitâs ana.
_____ namôya, mitâs ana.

mitâs cî awa?

_____ âha, astis ana.
_____ namôya, astis ana.
_____ ahâ, astis ana.

mîcisowinâhtik cî ôma?

_____ ahâ, mîcisowinâhtik anima.
_____ âha, mîcisowinâhtik anima.
_____ namôya, têhtapiwin anima.

mîcisowinâhtik cî ôma?

_____ âha, mîcisowinâhtik anima.
_____ namôya, têhtapiwin anima.
_____ âha, cêhcapiwinis anima.

atim cî awa?

_____ âha, atim ana.
_____ âha, minôs ana.
_____ namôya, minôs ana.

minôs cî awa?

_____ âha, minôs ana.
_____ namôya, atim ana.
_____ âha, atim ana.

nâpêsis cî awa?

_____ âha, nâpêsis ana.
_____ namôya, nâpêw ana.
_____ âha, nâpêw ana.

nâpêw cî awa?

_____ âha, nâpêw ana.
_____ âha, nâpêsis ana.
_____ namôya, nâpêsis ana.

iskwêw cî awa?

_____ âha, iskwêsis ana.
_____ âha, iskwêw ana.
_____ namôya, iskwêsis ana.

iskwêsis cî awa?

_____ âha, iskwêsis ana.
_____ âha, iskwêw ana.
_____ namôya, iskwêw ana.

NOTE: The demonstrative pronouns in the questions are the ones used when the object is close to the speaker: awa – _this_ (for animates) and ôma – _this_ (for inanimates). Because the object is a little further from the one answering the questions, these demonstrative pronouns become ana – _that_ (for animates) and anima – _that_ (for inanimates).

2.1.A QUESTIONS AND ANSWERS

Work in pairs with the following:

Q. kîkwây ôma?
What is this?
A. iskwâhtêm anima.
That is a door.

Q. wâsênikan cî ôma?
Is this a window?

POSSIBLE ANSWERS:
1. namôya, iskwâhtêm anima.
2. namôya, namôya anima wâsênikan.
3. namôya, namôya anima wâsênikan, iskwâhtêm anima.

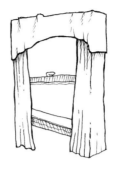

Q. kîkwây ôma?
What is this?
A. wâsênikan anima.
That is a window.

Q. iskwâhtêm cî ôma?
Is this a door?

POSSIBLE ANSWERS:
1. namôya, wâsênikan anima.
2. namôya, namôya anima iskwâhtêm.
3. namôya, namôya anima iskwâhtêm, wâsênikan anima.

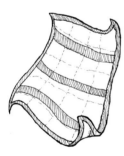

Q. kîkwây ôma?
What is this?
A. akohp anima.
That is a blanket.

Q. akohp cî ôma?
Is this a blanket?

POSSIBLE ANSWERS:
1 âha, akohp anima.
2. ahpô êtikwê.

Q. kîkwây ôma?
What is this?
A. wâwi anima.
That is an egg.

Q. wâwi cî ôma?
Is this an egg?

POSSIBLE ANSWERS:
1. âha, wâwi anima.
2. ahpô êtikwê.

Q. kîkwây ôma?
What is this?
A. mistik anima.
That is a log.

Q. tohtôsâpoy cî ôma?
Is this milk?

POSSIBLE ANSWERS:
1. namôya, mistik anima.
2. namôya, namôya anima tohtôsâpoy.
3. namôya, namôya anima tohtôsâpoy, mistik anima.

Q. kîkwây ôma?
What is this?
A. tohtôsâpoy anima.
That is milk.

Q. mistik cî ôma?
Is this a log?

POSSIBLE ANSWERS:
1. namôya, tohtôsâpoy anima.
2. namôya, namôya anima mistik.
3. namôya, namôya anima mistik, tohtôsâpoy anima.

Q. kîkwây ôma?
What is this?
A. môhkomân anima.
That is a knife.

Q. nîpiy cî ôma?
Is this a leaf?

POSSIBLE ANSWERS:
1. namôya, môhkomân anima.
2. namôya, namôya anima nîpiy.
3. namôya, namôya anima nîpiy, môhkomân anima.

Q. kîkwây ôma?
What is this?
A. nîpiy anima.
That is a leaf.

Q. môhkomân cî ôma?
Is this a knife?

POSSIBLE ANSWERS:
1. namôya, nîpiy anima.
2. namôya, namôya anima môhkomân.
3. namôya, namôya anima môhkomân, nîpiy anima.

Q. kîkwây ôma?
What is this?

A. minihkwâcikan anima.
That is a cup.

Q. minihkwâcikan cî ôma?
Is this a cup?

POSSIBLE ANSWERS:
1. âha, minihkwâcikan anima.
2. ahpô êtikwê.

Q. kîkwây ôma?
What is this?

A. cîstahâsêpon anima.
That is a fork.

Q. cîstahâsêpon cî ôma?
Is this a fork?

POSSIBLE ANSWERS:
1. âha, cîstahâsêpon anima.
2. ahpô êtikwê.

Q. kîkwây ôma?
What is this?

A. wâpikwaniy anima.
That is a flower.

Q. acâhkos cî awa?
Is this a star?

POSSIBLE ANSWERS:
1. namôya, wâpikwaniy anima.
2. namôya, namôya ana acâhkos.
3. namôya, namôya ana acâhkos,
   wâpikwaniy anima.

Q. kîkwây awa?
What is this?

A. acâhkos ana.
That is a star.

Q. wâpikwaniy cî ôma?
Is this a flower?

POSSIBLE ANSWERS:
1. namôya, acâhkos ana.
2. namôya, namôya anima wâpikwaniy.
3. namôya, namôya anima wâpikwaniy,
   acâhkos ana.

Q. kîkwây ôma?
What is this?

A. têhtapiwin anima.
That is a chair.

Q. masinahikanâhcikos cî awa?
Is this a pencil?

POSSIBLE ANSWERS:
1. namôya, têhtapiwin anima.
2. namôya, namôya ana masinahikanâhcikos.
3. namôya, namôya ana masinahikanâhcikos, têhtapiwin anima.

Q. kîkwây awa?
What is this?

A. masinahikanâhcikos ana.
That is a pencil.

Q. têhtapiwin cî ôma?
Is this a chair?

POSSIBLE ANSWERS:
1. namôya, masinahikanâhcikos ana.
2. namôya, namôya anima têhtapiwin.
3. namôya, namôya anima têhtapiwin, masinahikanâhcikos ana.

Q. kîkwây ôma?
What is this?

A. masinahikan anima.
That is a book.

Q. masinahikan cî ôma?
Is this a book?

POSSIBLE ANSWERS:
1. âha, masinahikan anima.
2. ahpô êtikwê.

Q. kîkwây awa?
What is this?

A. acosis ana.
That is an arrow.

Q. acosis cî awa?
Is this an arrow?

POSSIBLE ANSWERS:
1. âha, acosis ana.
2. ahpô êtikwê.

Q. kîkwây awa?
What is this?

A. atim ana.
That is a dog.

Q. miskotâkay cî ôma?
Is this jacket?

POSSIBLE ANSWERS:
1. namôya, atim ana.
2. namôya, namôya anima miskotâkay.
3. namôya, namôya anima miskotâkay,
   atim ana.

Q. kîkwây ôma?
What is this?

A. miskotâkay anima.
That is jacket.

Q. atim cî awa?
Is this a dog?

POSSIBLE ANSWERS:
1. namôya, miskotâkay anima.
2. namôya, namôya ana atim.
3. namôya, namôya ana atim,
   miskotâkay anima.

Q. kîkwây awa?
What is this?

A. astis ana.
That is a mitt.

Q. papakiwayân cî ôma?
Is this a shirt?

POSSIBLE ANSWERS:
1. namôya, astis ana.
2. namôya, namôya anima papakiwayân.
3. namôya, namôya anima papakiwayân,
   astis ana.

Q. kîkwây ôma?
What is this?

A. papakiwayân anima.
That is a shirt.

Q. astis cî awa?
Is this a mitt?

POSSIBLE ANSWERS:
1. namôya, papakiwayân anima.
2. namôya, namôya ana astis.
3. namôya, namôya ana astis,
   papakiwayân anima.

Q. kîkwây awa?
What is this?

A. mitâs ana.
That is a pair of pants.

Q. mitâs cî awa?
Is this a pair of pants?

POSSIBLE ANSWERS:
1. âha, mitâs ana.
2. ahpô êtikwê.

Q. kîkwây ôma?
What is this?

A. pakwâhtêhon anima.
That is a belt.

Q. pakwâhtêhon cî ôma?
Is this a belt?

POSSIBLE ANSWERS:
1. âha, pakwâhtêhon anima.
2. ahpô êtikwê.

Q. kîkwây awa?
What is this?

A. tâpiskâkan ana.
That is a scarf.

Q. astotin cî ôma?
Is this a hat?

POSSIBLE ANSWERS:
1. namôya, tâpiskâkan ana.
2. namôya, namôya anima astotin.
3. namôya, namôya anima astotin,
   tâpiskâkan ana.

Q. kîkwây ôma?
What is this?

A. astotin anima.
That is a hat.

Q. tâpiskâkan cî awa?
Is this a scarf?

POSSIBLE ANSWERS:
1. namôya, astotin anima.
2. namôya, namôya ana tâpiskâkan.
3. namôya, namôya ana tâpiskâkan,
   astotin anima.

Q. kîkwây awa?
What is this?
A. apoy ana.
That is a paddle.

Q. iskwêwasâkay cî ôma?
Is this a skirt?

POSSIBLE ANSWERS:
1. namôya, apoy ana.
2. namôya, namôya anima iskwêwasâkay.
3. namôya, namôya anima iskwêwasâkay, apoy ana.

Q. kîkwây ôma?
What is this?
A. iskwêwasâkay anima.
That is a skirt.

Q. apoy cî awa?
Is this a paddle?

POSSIBLE ANSWERS:
1. namôya, iskwêwasâkay anima.
2. namôya, namôya ana apoy.
3. namôya, namôya ana apoy, iskwêwasâkay anima.

Q. kîkwây awa?
What is this?
A. mîtos ana.
That is a tree.

Q. mîtos cî awa?
Is this a tree?

POSSIBLE ANSWERS:
1. âha, mîtos ana.
2. ahpô êtikwê.

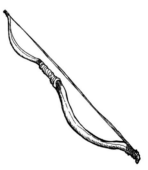

Q. kîkwây awa?
What is this?
A. ahcâpiy ana.
That is a bow.

Q. ahcâpiy cî awa?
Is this a bow?

POSSIBLE ANSWERS:
1. âha, ahcâpiy ana.
2. ahpô êtikwê.

Q. kîkwây awa?
What is this?

A. asiniy ana.
That is a rock.

Q. mîcisowinâhtik cî ôma?
Is this a table?

POSSIBLE ANSWERS:
1. namôya, asiniy ana.
2. namôya, namôya anima mîcisowinâhtik.
3. namôya, namôya anima mîcisowinâhtik, asiniy ana.

Q. kîkwây ôma?
What is this?

A. mîcisowinâhtik anima.
That is a table.

Q. asiniy cî awa?
Is this a rock?

POSSIBLE ANSWERS:
1. namôya, mîcisowinâhtik anima.
2. namôya, namôya ana asiniy.
3. namôya, namôya ana asiniy, mîcisowinâhtik anima.

Q. kîkwây awa?
What is this?

A. maskasiy ana.
That is a fingernail.

Q. maskosiy cî ôma?
Is this a blade of grass?

POSSIBLE ANSWERS:
1. namôya, maskasiy ana.
2. namôya, namôya anima maskosiy.
3. namôya, namôya anima maskosiy, maskasiy ana.

Q. kîkwây ôma?
What is this?

A. maskosiy anima.
That is a blade of grass.

Q. maskasiy cî awa?
Is this a fingernail?

POSSIBLE ANSWERS:
1. namôya, maskosiy anima.
2. namôya, namôya ana maskasiy.
3. namôya, namôya ana maskasiy, maskosiy anima.

Q. kîkwây awa?
What is this?
A. askihk ana.
That is a pail.

Q. askihk cî awa?
Is this a pail?

POSSIBLE ANSWERS:
1. âha, askihk ana.
2. ahpô êtikwê.

Q. kîkwây awa?
What is this?
A. êmihkwân ana.
That is a spoon.

Q. êmihkwân cî awa?
Is this a spoon?

POSSIBLE ANSWERS:
1. âha, êmihkwân ana.
2. ahpô êtikwê.

Q. kîkwây awa?
What is this?
A. pîswêhkasikan ana.
That is bread.

Q. minôs cî awa?
Is this a cat?

POSSIBLE ANSWERS:
1. namôya, pîswêhkasikan ana.
2. namôya, namôya ana minôs.
3. namôya, namôya ana minôs,
   pîswêhkasikan ana.

Q. kîkwây awa?
What is this?
A. minôs ana.
That is a cat.

Q. pîswêhkasikan cî awa?
Is this bread?

POSSIBLE ANSWERS:
1. namôya, minôs ana.
2. namôya, namôya ana pîswêhkasikan.
3. namôya, namôya ana pîswêhkasikan,
   minôs ana.

Q. kîkwây awa?
What is this?
A. ospwâkan ana.
That is a pipe.

Q. sôniyâw cî awa?
Is this money?

POSSIBLE ANSWERS:
1. namôya, ospwâkan ana.
2. namôya, namôya ana sôniyâw.
3. namôya, namôya ana sôniyâw, ospwâkan ana.

Q. kîkwây awa?
What is this?
A. sôniyâw ana.
That is money.

Q. ospwâkan cî awa?
Is this a pipe?

POSSIBLE ANSWERS:
1. namôya, sôniyâw ana.
2. namôya, namôya, ana ospwâkan.
3. namôya, namôya ana ospwâkan, sôniyâw ana.

Q. kîkwây awa?
What is this?
A. awâsisihkân ana.
That is a doll.

Q. awâsisihkân cî awa?
Is this a doll?

POSSIBLE ANSWERS:
1. âha, awâsisihkân ana.
2. ahpô êtikwê.

Q. kîkwây awa?
What is this?
A. pîsimohkân ana.
That is a clock.

Q. pîsimohkân cî awa?
Is this a clock?

POSSIBLE ANSWERS:
1. âha, pîsimohkân ana.
2. ahpô êtikwê.

Q. kîkwây awa?
What is this?

A. nâpêsis ana.
That is a boy.

Q. nâpêw cî awa?
Is this a man?

POSSIBLE ANSWERS:
1. namôya, nâpêsis ana.
2. namôya, namôya ana nâpêw.
3. namôya, namôya ana nâpêw,
   nâpêsis ana.

Q. kîkwây awa?
What is this?

A. nâpêw ana.
That is a man.

Q. nâpêsis cî awa?
Is this a boy?

POSSIBLE ANSWERS:
1. namôya, nâpêw ana.
2. namôya, namôya ana nâpêsis.
3. namôya, namôya ana nâpêsis,
   nâpêw ana.

Q. kîkwây ôma?
What is this?

A. kimiwanasâkay anima.
That is a raincoat.

Q. iskwêw cî awa?
Is this a woman?

POSSIBLE ANSWERS:
1. namôya, kimiwanasâkay anima.
2. namôya, namôya ana iskwêw.
3. namôya, namôya ana iskwêw,
   kimiwanasâkay anima.

Q. kîkwây awa?
What is this?

A. iskwêw ana.
That is a woman.

Q. kimiwanasâkay cî ôma?
Is this a raincoat?

POSSIBLE ANSWERS:
1. namôya, iskwêw ana.
2. namôya, namôya anima kimiwanasâkay.
3. namôya, namôya anima kimiwanasâkay,
   iskwêw ana.

Q. kîkwây ôma?
What is this?

A. nipêwin anima.
That is a bed.

Q. nipêwin cî ôma?
Is this a bed?

POSSIBLE ANSWERS:
1. âha, nipêwin anima.
2. ahpô êtikwê.

Q. kîkwây awa?
What is this?

A. iskwêsis ana.
That is a girl.

Q. iskwêsis cî awa?
Is this a girl?

POSSIBLE ANSWERS:
1. âha, iskwêsis ana.
2. ahpô êtikwê.

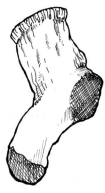

Q. kîkwây awa?
What is this?

A. asikan ana.
That is a sock.

Q. maskisin cî ôma?
Is this a shoe?

POSSIBLE ANSWERS:
1. namôya, asikan ana.
2. namôya, namôya anima maskisin.
3. namôya, namôya anima maskisin,
   asikan ana.

Q. kîkwây ôma?
What is this?

A. maskisin anima.
That is a shoe.

Q. asikan cî awa?
Is this a sock?

POSSIBLE ANSWERS:
1. namôya, maskisin anima.
2. namôya, namôya ana asikan.
3. namôya, namôya ana asikan,
   maskisin anima.

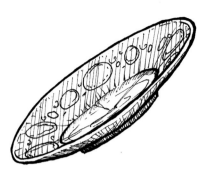

Q. kîkwây ôma?
What is this?
A. oyâkan anima.
That is a plate.

Q. piponasâkay cî ôma?
Is this a parka?

POSSIBLE ANSWERS:
1. namôya, oyâkan anima.
2. namôya, namôya anima piponasâkay.
3. namôya, namôya anima piponasâkay,
   oyâkan anima.

Q. kîkwây ôma?
What is this?
A. piponasâkay anima.
That is a parka.

Q. oyâkan cî ôma?
Is this a plate?

POSSIBLE ANSWERS:
1. namôya, piponasâkay anima.
2. namôya, namôya anima oyâkan.
3. namôya, namôya anima oyâkan,
   piponasâkay anima.

Q. kîkwây awa?
What is this?
A. môswa ana.
That is a moose.

Q. môswa cî awa?
Is this a moose?

POSSIBLE ANSWERS:
1. âha, môswa ana.
2. ahpô êtikwê.

Q. kîkwây ôma?
What is this?
A. masinahikanêkin anima.
That is a paper.

Q. masinahikanêkin cî ôma?
Is this a paper?

POSSIBLE ANSWERS:
1. âha, masinahikanêkin anima.
2. ahpô êtikwê.

Q. kîkwây awa?
What is this?
A. kâkwa ana.
That is a porcupine.

Q. piyêsîs cî awa?
Is this a bird?

POSSIBLE ANSWERS:
1. namôya, kâkwa ana.
2. namôya, namôya ana piyêsîs.
3. namôya, namôya ana piyêsîs,
   kâkwa ana.

Q. kîkwây awa?
What is this?
A. piyêsîs ana.
That is a bird.

Q. kâkwa cî awa?
Is this a porcupine?

POSSIBLE ANSWERS:
1. namôya, piyêsîs ana.
2. namôya, namôya ana kâkwa.
3. namôya, namôya ana kâkwa,
   piyêsîs ana.

PLURALS: The words in the above exercise will change when dealing with plurals as in the following:

ANIMATE NOUNS

INANIMATE NOUNS

Q. **kîkwâyak ôki?**
What are these?
A. kâkwak aniki.
Those are porcupine.

Q. **wâposwak cî ôki?**
A. i. namôya, kâkwak aniki.
   ii. namôya, namôya aniki wâposwak.
   iii. namôya, namôya aniki wâposwak,
      kâkwak aniki.

Q. **kîkwâya ôhi?**
What are these?
A. wâwa anihi.
Those are eggs.

Q. **wâwa cî ôhi?**
A. âha, wâwa anihi.

2.2 DIMINUTIVES

Diminutives are smaller counterparts of regular-sized nouns. Once again, the inflectional rules for going from a regular-sized noun to its smaller counterpart depends on the noun endings. A couple of points to remember before we get to the actual rules: every "t" must be changed to "c" and all diminutives end in an "s". To make plurals out of diminutives, simply add "ak" to Animate diminutives and add "a" to all Inanimate diminutives.

TABLE II

NOUN ENDINGS	DIMINUTIVES	RULES: every *t* changes to *c*, plus:
Nouns ending in "k": mistik – *log*	miscikos – *stick*	Add "os".
Nouns ending in "i": ôsi – *boat* wâwi – *egg*	ôcisis – *small boat* wâwisis – *a small egg*	Add "sis".
Nouns ending in "wa": mwâkwa – *loon*	mwâkosis – *small loon*	Drop "wa" then add "osis".
Nouns ending in "êw": nâpêw – *man* iskwêw – *woman*	nâpêsis – *boy* iskwêsis – *girl*	Drop "w" then add "sis".
Nouns ending in: "aw" – mêskanaw – *road* "ay"– miskotâkay – *coat* "âw" – sakâw – *bush*	mêskanâs – *a small road* miskocâkâs – *a small coat* sakâs – *a small bush*	Drop the "aw", the "ay" and the "âw" then add "âs".
Nouns ending in "iy" and "iw": maskosiy – *a blade of grass* pisiw – *lynx*	maskosîs – *a small blade of grass* pisîs – *a small lynx*	Drop the "iy" and "iw" then add "îs" or "îsis".
Nouns ending in "oy": tohtôsâpoy – *milk*	cohcôsâpôs – *a bit of milk (creamer)*	Drop "oy" then add "ôs".
Exceptional Nouns ending in "m", "n" or "s": atim – *dog* masinahikanêkin – *paper*	acimosis – *puppy or small dog* masinahikanêkinos – *small piece of paper*	Add "os(is)".
For all other nouns not ending in the above…		Add "is".

EXERCISES

EXERCISE 1. Make diminutives out of the following nouns. Then, using the demonstrative pronoun as a guide to Animacy, make plurals out of the diminutives:

NOUN	DIMINUTIVE	PLURAL
1. askihk awa. *This is a pail.*	_____	_____
2. apoy awa. *This is a paddle.*	_____	_____
3. mihtawakay ôma. *This is an ear.*	_____	_____
4. micihciy ôma. *This is a hand.*	_____	_____
5. sîwihtâkan ôma. *This is salt.*	_____	_____
6. miskîsik ôma. *This is an eye.*	_____	_____
7. pîswêhkasikan awa. *This is bread.*	_____	_____
8. sêhkêpayîs awa. *This is a car.*	_____	_____
9. picikwâs awa. *This is an apple.*	_____	_____
10. wâkâs awa. *This is a banana.*	_____	_____
11. pahkwêsikan awa. *This is bannock.*	_____	_____
12. masinahikan ôma. *This is a book.*	_____	_____
13. masinahikanêkin ôma. *This is paper.*	_____	_____
14. masinahikanâhcikos awa. *This is a pencil.*	_____	_____
15. maskasiy awa. *This is a finger-nail.*	_____	_____
16. sâkahikan ôma. *This is a lake.*	_____	_____
17. sakahikan ôma. *This is a nail.*	_____	_____
18. wâpamon ôma. *This is a mirror.*	_____	_____
19. oyâkan ôma. *This is a plate.*	_____	_____
20. minihkwâcikan ôma. *This is a cup.*	_____	_____

EXERCISE 2. Complete the following, then write out the rules that apply:

1.   a) âhkosîwikamik (*hospital*) ➔ âhkosîwikamikos   b) kinêpik (*snake*) ➔ kinêpikos

       c) kapêsiwikamik (*hotel*) ➔ _____   d) askihk (*pail*) ➔ _____

       RULE: _____

_____

2.   a) apoy (*paddle*) ➔ apôs   b) sîwâpoy (*pop*) ➔ sîwâpôs

       c) tohtôsâpoy (*milk*) ➔ _____   d) pihkahtêwâpoy (*coffee*) ➔ _____

       RULE: _____

_____

3.   a) maskasiy (*finger-nail*) ➔ maskasîs   b) asiniy (*stone*) ➔ asinîs

       c) nîpiy (*leaf*) ➔ _____   d) maskosiy (*blade of grass*) ➔ _____

       RULE: _____

_____

4.   a) mihtawakay (*ear*) ➔ mihcawakâs   b) mêskanaw (*road*) ➔ mêskanâs

       c) ôtênaw (*town*) ➔ _____   d) miskotâkay (*coat*) ➔ _____

       RULE: _____

_____

5.   a) nâpêw (*man*) ➔ nâpêsis   b) iskwêw (*woman*) ➔ iskwêsis

       c) ôcêw (*a fly*) ➔ _____   d) pihêw (*partridge/grouse*) ➔ _____

       RULE: _____

_____

6.   a) môswa (*moose*) ➔ môsosis   b) kâkwa (*porcupine*) ➔ kâkosis

       c) mwâkwa (*loon*) ➔ _____   d) maskwa (*bear*) ➔ _____

       RULE: _____

_____

EXERCISE 3. Fill in the chart from memory and transform the examples:

NOUN ENDINGS	DIMINUTIVES: examples	RULES: every t changes to c, plus:
Nouns ending in "k":	mistik _____	
Nouns ending in "i":	ôsi _____ wâwi _____	
Nouns ending in "wa":	maskwa _____	
Nouns ending in "êw":	nâpêw _____	
Nouns ending in: aw, ay, âw	ispatinaw _____ mihtawakay _____ sakâw _____	
Nouns ending in "iy" and "iw"	asiniy _____ mikisiw _____	
Nouns ending in "oy":	iskotêwâpoy _____	
Exceptional Nouns ending in "m", "n" or "s":	pîsim _____	
For all other nouns not ending in the above…	sâkahikan _____	

2.3 LOCATIVES

Locatives refer to the suffixes added to the noun to indicate location. For example, if you want to say "*at the lake*", you would use the noun "sâkahikan" and the locative suffix "ihk": sâkahikanihk – *at the lake*. Locative nouns can be translated as "*in the*", "*on the*", "*at the*", or "*to the*", depending on the situation. Most often, prepositions are also used with the locative nouns, and these prepositions are placed before the noun with its locative ending. Once again, the endings of the nouns determine which locative suffix to use:

TABLE III

NOUN ENDINGS	LOCATIVES	RULES
Nouns ending in "k": atâwêwikamik - *store*	atâwêwikamikohk – *to/at/in the store*	Add "ohk"
Nouns ending in "i" ôsi - *boat* wâwi - *egg*	ôsihk – *in the boat* wâwihk – *on the egg*	Add "hk"
Nouns ending in "aw", "ay" and "âw": mêskanaw - *road* miskotâkay - *coat* sakâw - *bush*	mêskanâhk – *on the road* miskotâkâhk – *in the coat* sakâhk – *in the bush*	Drop these endings, then add "âhk"
Nouns ending in "iy": maskosiy - *a blade of grass*	maskosîhk – *in the grass*	Drop the ending, then add "îhk"
Nouns ending in "oy": sîwâpoy - *juice/pop*	sîwâpôhk – *in the juice*	Drop the ending, then add "ôhk"
Nouns ending in "wa": mwâkwa - *loon*	mwâkohk – *on the loon**	Drop "wa", then add "ohk"
Exceptional nouns ending in "m", "n" or "s"	pîsimohk - *on the sun* pahkêkinohk - *on the hide*	Add "ohk"
For all others		Add "ihk"

*Please Note: Not all speakers will allow the locative to be added to animal or human nouns.

EXERCISES

EXERCISE 1. Make locatives out of the following nouns:

1. kihci-kiskinwahamâtowikamik - *University* _____

2. iskonikan - *reserve* _____

3. ôtênaw - *town* _____

4. ôsi - *boat* _____

5. mîcisowinâhtik - *table* _____

6. têhtapiwin - *chair* _____

7. âhkosîwikamik - *hospital* _____

8. mihtawakay - *ear* _____

9. mêtawêwikamik - *gym* _____

10. minihkwêwikamik - *bar* _____

11. sâkahikan - *lake* _____

12. sîpiy - *river* _____

13. ispatinaw - *hill* _____

14. wâyahcâw - *valley* _____

15. sakâw - *a bush* _____

16. kapêsiwikamik - *hotel/motel* _____

17. mîcisowikamik - *café* _____

18. sîwâpoy - *pop* _____

EXERCISE 2. Complete the following, then write out the rules that apply:

1. a) mistik (*tree*) ➔ mistikohk   b) sikâk (*skunk*) ➔ sikâkohk

    c) mîcisowinâhtik (*table*) ➔ _____   d) kapêsiwikamik (*hotel*) ➔ _____

    RULE: _____

2. a) ôsi (*boat*) ➔ ôsihk   b) wâwi (*egg*) ➔ wâwihk

    c) wîsti (*lodge*) ➔ _____   d) wâti (*hole/cave*) ➔ _____

    RULE: _____

3. a) mêskanaw (*road*) ➔ mêskanâhk   b) sakâw (*bush*) ➔ sakâhk

    c) ispatinaw (*hill*) ➔ _____   d) wâsâw (*bay*) ➔ _____

    RULE: _____

4. a) maskosiy (*grass*) ➔ maskosîhk   b) maskasiy (*fingernail*) ➔ maskasîhk

    c) asiniy (*stone*) ➔ _____   d) nipiy (*water*) ➔ _____

    RULE: _____

5. a) sîwâpoy (*pop*) ➔ sîwâpôhk   b) tohtôsâpoy (*milk*) ➔ tohtôsâpôhk

    c) mîcimâpoy (*soup*) ➔ _____   d) apoy (*paddle*) ➔ _____

    RULE: _____

6. a) kâkwa (*porcupine*) ➔ kâkohk   b) mwâkwa (*loon*) ➔ mwâkohk

    c) maskwa (*bear*) ➔ _____   d) môswa (*moose*) ➔ _____

    RULE: _____

7. a) maskisin (*shoe*) ➔ maskisinihk   b) astotin (*hat*) ➔ astotinihk

    c) mitâs (*pants*) ➔ _____   d) papakiwayân (*shirt*) ➔ _____

    RULE: _____

EXERCISE 3. Complete the following chart with examples:

NOUN ENDINGS	PLURALS	DIMINUTIVE	LOCATIVES
	DROP ENDING "-i"; then ADD:	DROP ENDINGS: "-i", "-w", "-iy", "iw" "-wa", "-aw", "-ay", "-âw", and "oy"; change "t" to "c"; then ADD:	DROP ENDINGS: "-i", "w", "iy", " iw", "-wa," "-aw", "-ay", "-âw", and "-oy"; then ADD:
-k (I)			
-k (A)			
-i			
-wa			
-aw			
-âw			
-êw			
-iw			
-iy			
-ay			
-oy			
-m -s -n (exceptional nouns only)			
All else			

2.4 CHAPTER TWO REVIEW

A. NOUNS

All nouns are either Animate or Inanimate. Endings of nouns determine the forms of plurals, diminutives, and locatives, as shown in the chart below:

Noun Ending	An. Plurals	In. Plurals	Diminutives	Locatives
-k askihk mistik	-wak askihk**wak** mistik**wak**	-wa mistik**wa**	-os askihk**os** mis**c**ik**os**	-ohk askihk**ohk** mistik**ohk**
-i ôsi wâwi		drop i; -a ôs**a** wâw**a**	-sis ôci**sis*** wâwi**sis**	-hk ôsi**hk** wâwi**hk**
-wa maskwa	-k maskwa**k**		drop wa; -osis mask**osis**	drop wa; -ohk mask**ohk**
-êw nâpêw iskotêw	-ak nâpêw**ak**	-a iskotêw**a**	drop w; -sis nâpê**sis** isko**c**ê**sis**	drop w; -hk/-nâhk nâpê**nâhk**** iskotê**hk**
-aw/âw mêskanaw môniyâw	-a môniyâw**ak**	-a mêskanaw**a**	drop aw/âw; -âs mêskan**âs** môniy**âs**	drop aw/âw; -âhk mêskan**âhk** môniy**ânâhk****
-ay mêstakay		-a mêstakay**a**	drop ay; -âs mês**c**ak**âs**	drop ay; -âhk mêstak**âhk**
-iy/iw maskosiy maskasiy mikisiw	-ak maskasiy**ak** mikisiw**ak**	-a maskosiy**a**	drop iy/iw; -îs maskos**îs** maskas**îs** mikis**îs**	drop iy/iw; -îhk maskos**îhk** maskas**îhk** mikis**înâhk****
-oy apoy tohtôsâpoy	-ak apoy**ak**	-a tohtôsâpoy**a**	drop oy; -ôs ap**ôs** coh**c**ôsâp**ôs**	drop oy; -ôhk ap**ôhk** tohtôsâp**ôhk**
-m/n/s*** atim	-wak atim**wak**		-osis a**c**im**osis**	-ohk atim**ohk**
all others	-ak	-a	-is	-ihk

--- "t" changes to "c" at all times for diminutives

* ôsi to ôcisis.

** Instead of adding the regular locative "-(i)hk" to nouns referring to humans or animals, an alternative distributive locative "-(i)nâhk" can be added; e.g., the locative for "nâpêw" is "nâpênâhk" and means *in the place of men*.

***Remember, only exceptional nouns like atim – *dog*, pîsim – *sun*, and a few others follow this pattern. Others, such as kinship terms nistim – *my niece* and nôsisim – *my grandchild*, take the regular endings.

B. Fill in the blanks for the plural, diminutives, and locatives.

DO: Note that the use of demonstrative pronouns "awa" and "ôma" will aid in determining the animacy of the nouns. Knowing the animacy of the nouns will help with making plurals.

NOUNS	PLURAL	DIMINUTIVE	LOCATIVE
mîcisowinâhtik ôma. *This is a table.*			
sikâk awa. *This is a skunk.*			
askipwâwi ôma. *This is a potato.*			
mwâkwa awa. *This is a loon.*			
ispatinaw ôma. *This is a hill.*			
sakâw ôma. *This is a bush.*			
mihtawakay ôma. *This is an ear.*			
iskwêw awa. *This is a woman.*			
nîpiy ôma. *This is a leaf.*			
maskasiy awa. *This is a fingernail.*			

c. Change the following nouns and demonstrative pronouns into their plural forms:

Examples:

ANIMATE NOUNS

a) nâpêw awa. ➔ nâpêwak ôki.
This is a man. ➔ *These are men.*

INANIMATE NOUNS

b) wâskahikan ôma. ➔ wâskahikana ôhi.
This is a house. ➔ *These are houses.*

1. mistik awa.
    This is a tree.   _____
                                              These are trees.

2. mîcisowinâhtik ôma.
    This is a table.   _____
                                              These are tables.

3. mitâs awa.
    This is a pair of pants.   _____
                                              These are pairs of pants.

4. papakiwayân ôma.
    This is a shirt.   _____
                                              These are shirts.

5. asikan awa.
    This is a sock.   _____
                                              These are socks.

6. maskisin ôma.
    This is a shoe.   _____
                                              These are shoes.

7. astis awa.
    This is a mitt.   _____
                                              These are mitts.

8. astotin ôma.
    This is a hat.   _____
                                              These are hats.

9. tâpiskâkan awa.
    This is a scarf.   _____
                                              These are scarves.

10. miskotâkay ôma.
    This is a coat.   _____
                                              These are coats.

CHAPTER THREE

PREPOSITIONS AND PRONOUNS

3. LOCATION WORDS

In the previous chapter we saw the addition of suffixes to nouns to indicate location. These suffixes to nouns form locatives. Nouns with locative suffixes can be translated to mean "to/at/in/on the particular noun" depending on the context of the utterance. In addition to the locatives, Cree also has other grammatical units that help in identifying the location of whatever it is that is being talked about. These grammatical units include prepositions, demonstrative pronouns, and directions. It is common to use a preposition and a locative together, with the preposition preceding the locative noun. Every utterance using these units in Cree indicates the spatial relationship the speaker has with his or her surroundings. Let's have a look at these units, beginning with prepositions.

3.1 PREPOSITIONS

A preposition expresses a locative relation to another word, usually a noun or a pronoun, and is very rarely used on its own. In speaking Cree, people often use the prepositions with nouns that include locative endings. Following is a list of Cree prepositions:

wayawîtimihk	– outside		pîhcâyihk	– inside
wayawîtimiskwâht	– just outside the door		pîhtokamihk	– indoors
nohcimihk	– inland		nâsipêtimihk	– at the shore
asicâyihk	– beside/against		ispimihk	– up/upstairs
mohcihk	– down/on the ground		nîhcâyihk	– down/downstairs
atâmihk	– beneath/under		sîpâ/sîpâyihk	– under
atâmipîhk	– underwater		capasis	– below
tahkohc	– on top		capasîs	– lower down
sisonê	– along		wâsakâm	– around
wâhyaw	– far		cîki	– near
wâhyawês	– a bit of a ways		kisiwâk	– nearby
tâwâyihk	– in the middle		tastawâyihk	– in between
âyîtawâyihk	– on either side		âpihtawanohk	– halfway
kisipanohk	– at the end		iskwêyânihk	– at the last place
namahcîhk	– to the left		kihciniskêhk	– to the right

Other common words that show location include the following directions:

    kîwêtinohk – *north*   sâkâstênohk – *east*

    sâwanohk – *south*   pahkisimotâhk – *west*

These particles also indicate location or a change in movement:

    isko – *as far as/up to*   isi – *toward/manner in which something is done*

    ohci – *from*   pê- – *come/in this direction*

EXERCISES

EXERCISE 1. Answer the following questions:

1. tâniwâ nâha minôs?
   Where is that cat over there?

_____

_____

2. tâniwâ awa ayîkis?
   Where is this frog?

_____

_____

3. tâniwâ awa minôs?
   Where is this cat?

_____

4. tâniwêhkâk ôki okiskinwahamâkanak?
   Where are these students?

_____

EXERCISE 2. Translate the sentences below using the following words:

NOUNS
minôs (*cat*)
atim (*dog*)
mistik (*tree*)
iskwêw (*woman*)
sîsîp (*duck*)
nipiy (*water*)
môswa (*moose*)
sîpiy (*river*)
mêtawêwikamik (*gym*)
mîcisowinâhtik (*table*)

PREPOSITIONS
asicâyihk (*against/beside*)
sîpâ (*under*)

TABLE IV

NUMBER	USE WITH INANIMATE	USE WITH ANIMATE
SINGULAR	astêw = *it is there*	ayâw = *s/he is there*
PLURAL	astêwa = *they are there*	ayâwak = *they are there*

1. The cat is under the table.

   _____

2. The dog is beside the tree.

   _____

3. The ducks are on the water.

   _____

4. The moose is in the river.

   _____

5. The woman is at the gym.

   _____

EXERCISE 3. PREPOSITIONS AND LOCATIVES

Prepositions and **locatives** usually go together. In the exercises below, make the nouns following the prepositions into locatives to match the translation. Some prepositions operate without a locative noun; in those cases, make the nouns and form of the verb "to be" (from **TABLE IV** above) agree in number. The first two are done for you:

1. atim ayâw sîpâ mîcisowinâhtik. (*The dog is under the table.*)
    atim ayâw sîpâ mîcisowinâhtikohk.
    _____

2. kinêpik ayâw atâmihk asiniy. (*The snake is under the rock.*)
    kinêpik ayâw atâmihk asinîhk.
    _____

3. apoy ayâw asicâyihk têhtapiwin. (*The paddle is against the chair.*)
    _____

4. maskwa ayâw nohcimihk sakâw. (*The bear is inland in the bush.*)
    _____

5. nipêwin astêw ispimihk wâskahikan. (*The bed is upstairs in the house.*)
    _____

6. atimwak ayâw nîhcâyihk wâskahikanihk. (*The dogs are downstairs in the house.*)
    _____

7. astisak ayâw mohcihk. (*The mitts are on the ground.*)
    _____

8. masinahikana astêw kisiwâk. (*The books are nearby.*)
    _____

9. awâsis ayâwak wayawîtimihk. (*The children are outside.*)
    _____

10. kinosêwak ayâw atâmipîhk. (*The fish are underwater.*)
    _____

11. cêhcapiwinis astêw capasis wâsênikan. (*The small chair is below the window.*)

_____

12. ayîkis ayâw tahkohc mistik. (*The frog is on top of the log.*)

_____

13. mahihkan ayâw sisonê sâkahikan. (*The wolf is along the lake.*)

_____

14. kihiwak ayâw wâhyawês. (*The eagle is a little ways off.*)

_____

15. nitôtêm ayâwak wâhyaw. (*My friends are far away.*)

_____

16. minôs ayâw cîki iskwâhtêm. (*The cat is near the door.*)

_____

17. têhtapiwin astêw tâwâyihk mistik. (*The chair is in the middle of the trees.*)

_____

18. mistikwak ayâwak âyîtawâyihk têhtapiwin. (*The trees are on either side of the chair.*)

_____

19. masinahikan astêwa kihciniskêhk. (*The books are to the right.*)

_____

20. maskisina astêw namahcîhk. (*The shoes are to the left.*)

_____

3.2 PRONOUNS

There are various types of pronouns in Cree. These pronouns include the demonstrative pronouns, the interrogative pronouns, the personal pronouns, and the emphatic pronouns. Let's look at these pronouns in separate sections.

3.2.A DEMONSTRATIVE PRONOUNS

Demonstrative pronouns show location of nouns. The correct usage of some of these pronouns depends on the animacy and number of the nouns as well as the distance the noun under discussion is from the speaker.

USE THESE DEMONSTRATIVE PRONOUNS WITH ANIMATE NOUNS:

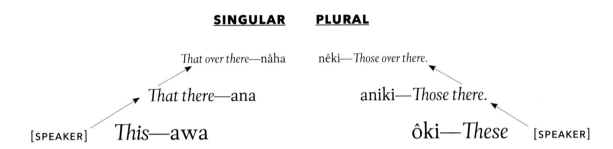

Use "awa" for singular Animate nouns and "ôki" for plural Animate nouns when the speaker is close to the noun being talked about. Use "ana" for singular Animate nouns and "aniki" for plural Animate nouns when the object is a little ways from the speaker. Use "nâha" for singular Animate nouns and "nêki" for plural Animate nouns when the object is quite a ways from the speaker.

USE THESE DEMONSTRATIVE PRONOUNS WITH INANIMATE NOUNS:

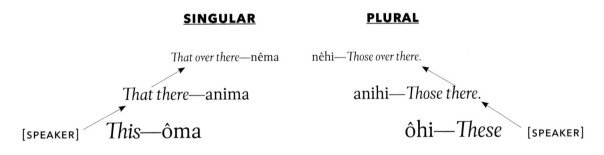

Use "ôma" for singular Inanimate nouns and "ôhi" for plural Inanimate nouns when the speaker is close to the noun being discussed. Use "anima" for singular Inanimate nouns and "anihi" for plural Inanimate nouns when the object is a little ways from the speaker. Use "nêma" for singular Inanimate nouns and "nêhi" for plural Inanimate nouns when the object is quite a ways from the speaker.

NOTE: When the demonstrative pronoun is said before the noun as in "awa atim" then the statement is simply saying: "*This dog* (or whatever noun)." When the demonstrative pronoun comes after the noun as in "atim awa" then the translation includes the verb "*to be*" as in the following: "*This is a dog* (or whatever noun)."

TABLE V

ENGLISH	Use with Animate nouns	Use with Inanimate nouns
This	awa	ôma
That	ana	anima
That over there	nâha	nêma
These	ôki	ôhi
Those	aniki	anihi
Those over there	nêki	nêhi

The use of the right demonstrative pronoun with a noun depends on the animacy of the noun, its number, and the distance the noun is from the speakers as in the example below.

kâkwa nâha.
That is a porcupine over there.

kâkwak nêki.
Those are porcupines over there.

kâkwa ana.
That is a porcupine.

kâkwak aniki.
Those are porcupines.

kâkwa awa
This is a porcupine.

SPEAKERS ARE CLOSE TO THE NOUNS HERE

kâkwak ôki.
These are porcupines.

EXERCISES WITH NOUNS AND DEMONSTRATIVE PRONOUNS
(Bring items you want to work with to class and do the following exercises with the students.)

a) Say the Cree word for items in this exercise as you place them around the classroom, saying "awa" after each Animate noun and "ôma" after each Inanimate noun: have one row of Animate nouns and one row of Inanimate nouns.

b) Have a student stand at the foot of Animate nouns and another student at the foot of the Inanimate nouns.

c) Group leader will start at the foot of the Animate nouns, asking the other student for a "yes" response to that item, then will move on to the next item in the same row, then on to the last item, asking the last question in that row. Repeat the process for the inanimate nouns.

SINGULAR NOUNS:

ANIMATE NOUNS

GROUP LEADER	STUDENT RESPONSE

1) Item is close to both the group leader and the student responding:

astis cî awa?	âha, astis awa.
Is this a mitt?	*Yes, this is a mitt.*

2) Group leader moves on to the second item, but student responding *stays* by the first item:

mitâs cî awa?	âha, mitâs ana.
Is this a pair of pants?	*Yes, that is a pair of pants there.*

3) Group leader moves to the last item in the row, and again the student *remains* by the first item:

asikan cî awa?	âha, asikan (ana) nâha.
Is this a sock?	*Yes, that is a sock over there.*

INANIMATE NOUNS

GROUP LEADER	STUDENT RESPONSE

1) Item is close to both the group leader and the student responding:

astotin cî ôma?	âha, astotin ôma.
Is this a hat?	*Yes, this is a hat.*

2) Group leader moves on to the second item, but student responding *stays* by the first item:

papakiwayân cî ôma?	âha, papakiwayân anima.
Is this a shirt?	*Yes, that is a shirt there.*

3) Group leader moves to the last item in the row, and again the student *remains* by the first item:

maskisin cî ôma?
Is this a shoe?

âha, maskisin (anima) nêma.
Yes, that is a shoe over there.

Have each student take a turn at being group leader as well as being the one answering the questions.

ANIMATE NOUNS

GROUP LEADER	STUDENT RESPONSE

1) Item is close to both the group leader and the student responding:

asikan cî awa?
Is this a sock?

namôya, astis awa.
No, this is a mitt.

2) Group leader moves on to the second item, but student responding *stays* by the first item:

astis cî awa?
Is this a mitt?

namôya, mitâs ana.
No, that is a pair of pants there.

3) Group leader moves to the last item in the row, and again the student *remains* by the first item:

mitâs cî awa?
Is this a pair of pants?

namôya, asikan (ana) nâha.
No, that is a sock over there.

INANIMATE NOUNS

GROUP LEADER	STUDENT RESPONSE

1) Item is close to both the group leader and the student responding:

papakiwayân cî ôma?
Is this a shirt?

namôya, astotin ôma.
No, this is a hat.

2) Group leader moves on to the second item, but student responding *stays* by the first item:

maskisin cî ôma?
Is this a shoe?

namôya, papakiwayân anima.
No, that is a shirt there.

3) Group leader moves to the last item in the row, and again the student *remains* by the first item:

astotin cî ôma?
Is this a hat?

namôya, maskisin (anima) nêma.
No, that is a shoe over there.

PLURAL NOUNS:

ANIMATE NOUNS

GROUP LEADER	STUDENT RESPONSE

1) Item is close to both the group leader and the student responding:

astisak cî ôki? âha, astisak ôki.
Are these mitts? *Yes, these are mitts.*

2) Group leader moves on to the second item, but student responding *stays* by the first item:

mitâsak cî ôki? âha, mitâsak aniki.
Are these pairs of pants? *Yes, those are pairs of pants there.*

3) Group leader moves to the last item in the row, and again the student *remains* by the first item:

asikanak cî ôki? âha, asikanak (aniki) nêki.
Are these socks? *Yes, those are socks over there.*

INANIMATE NOUNS

GROUP LEADER	STUDENT RESPONSE

1) Item is close to both the group leader and the student responding:

astotina cî ôhi? âha, astotina ôhi.
Are these hats? *Yes, these are hats.*

2) Group leader moves on to the second item, but student responding *stays* by the first item:

papakiwayâna cî ôhi? âha, papakiwayâna anihi.
Are these shirts? *Yes, those are shirts there.*

3) Group leader moves to the last item in the row, and again the student *remains* by the first item:

maskisina cî ôhi? âha, maskisina (anihi) nêhi.
Are these shoes? *Yes, those are shoes over there.*

Have each student take a turn at being group leader as well as being the one answering the questions.

ANIMATE NOUNS

GROUP LEADER	STUDENT RESPONSE

1) Item is close to both the group leader and the student responding:

asikanak cî ôki?
Are these socks?

namôya, astisak ôki.
No, these are mitts.

2) Group leader moves on to the second item, but student responding *stays* by the first item:

astisak cî ôki?
Are these mitts?

namôya, mitâsak aniki.
No, those are pairs of pants there.

3) Group leader moves to the last item in the row, and again the student *remains* by the first item:

mitâsak cî ôki?
Are these pairs of pants?

namôya, asikanak (aniki) nêki.
No, those are socks over there.

INANIMATE NOUNS

GROUP LEADER	STUDENT RESPONSE

1) Item is close to both the group leader and the student responding:

papakiwayâna cî ôhi?
Are these shirts?

namôya, astotina ôhi.
No, these are hats.

2) Group leader moves on to the second item, but student responding *stays* by the first item:

maskisina cî ôhi?
Are these shoes?

namôya, papakiwayâna anihi.
No, those are shirts there.

3) Group leader moves to the last item in the row, and again the student *remains* by the first item:

astotina cî ôhi?
Are these hats?

namôya, maskisina (anihi) nêhi.
No, those are shoes over there.

3.2.B INTERROGATIVE PRONOUNS

Interrogative pronouns are used in asking content questions. As opposed to the polarity question indicator "cî" that requires a "yes – âha" or "no – namôya" answer, these content questions ask for specific information. Most of these content question words in Cree begin with "tân" so many people refer to them as the "tân words." However, there are a few content question indicators that do not begin with "tân" and these include the following:

kîkwây ôma?	– *what is this?* (for singular inanimate nouns)
kîkwâya ôhi?	– *what are these?* (for plural inanimate nouns)
kîkwây awa?	– *what is this?* (for singular animate nouns)
kîkwâyak ôki?	– *what are these?* (for plural animate nouns)
awîna	– *who* (for singular animate)
awîniki	– *who* (for plural animate)
kêko	– *which/what kind*

All other interrogative pronouns can be rightly called the "tân words." Some of these "tân" words depend on the animacy and the number of the noun being discussed. These interrogative pronouns include the following:

tâniwâ	– *where is* (singular animate)
tâniwêhkâk	– *where are* (plural animate)
tâniwê	– *where is* (singular inanimate)
tâniwêhâ	– *where is* (plural inanimate)
tâna	– *which* (singular animate)
tâniki	– *which* (plural animate)
tânima	– *which* (singular inanimate)
tânihi	– *which* (plural inanimate)

The above pronouns can be set in a chart like the following for easier access:

TABLE VI: INTERROGATIVE PRONOUNS THAT DEPEND ON ANIMACY AND NUMBER

NUMBER	ENGLISH	ANIMATE	INANIMATE
SINGULAR	Where	tâniwâ	tâniwê
	Which	tâna	tânima
	What	kîkwây	kîkwây
	Who	awîna	–
PLURAL	Where	tâniwêhkâk	tâniwêhâ
	Which	tâniki	tânihi
	What	kîkwâyak	kîkwâya
	Who	awîniki	–

Some interrogative pronouns do not depend on the animacy or the number of the noun for correct usage. These include the following:

tânisi	- *How / How are you?*	tânêhki	- *Why? How come?*
tânispîhk	- *When?*	tânita	- *Where abouts?*
tânitê	- *Where* (in general)	tânitahto	- *How many?*
tânitahtwâw	- *How many times?*	tâniyikohk	- *How much?*
tânitowahk	- *What kind?*	tânimayikohk	- *How much?*

EXERCISES

EXERCISE 1. DEMONSTRATIVE PRONOUNS AND INTERROGATIVE PRONOUNS. Using the English as a guide, correct as needed to get the units below to agree in animacy and in number:

1. tâniwêhâ aniki iskwêwak? (*Where are those women?*)

2. tâniwêhkâk anihi masinahikana? (*Where are those books?*)

3. tânihi minôsak? (*Which cats?*)

4. tâniki maskisina? (*Which shoes?*)

5. tânima astis? (*Which mitt?*)

6. tâna astotin? (*Which hat?*)

7. tâniwê ana tâpiskâkan? (*Where is that scarf?*)

8. tâniwâ anima miskotâkay? (*Where is that coat?*)

9. awîna aniki nêki? *(Who are those over there?)*

_____

10. kîkwây anihi nêhi? *(What are those over there?)*

_____

EXERCISE 2. Demonstrative pronouns and Interrogative pronouns must agree in Number and Animacy to the nouns they modify. Correct the Number or Animacy of the following sentences:

1. tâniwâ atimwak? _____

2. tâniwêhâ maskisin? _____

3. tâniwêhkâk iskwêw? _____

4. tâniwê masinahikana? _____

5. tâna nâpêwak? _____

6. tânima iskwâhtêma? _____

7. tâniki nâpêsis? _____

8. tânihi oyâkan? _____

9. awa sîsîpak. _____

10. ôma astotina. _____

11. ôki iskwêsis. _____

12. ôhi maskosiy. _____

13. nâha misatimwak. _____

14. nêma wâskahikana. _____

15. nêki kohkôs. _____

16. nêhi wâsênikan. _____

17. awîna aniki? _____

18. awîniki ana? _____

19. kîkwây ôhi? _____

20. kîkwâya ôma? _____

Other Demonstrative pronouns that do not depend on animacy include:

ôta	– *here*	anita	– *there*
nêtê	– *over there*	êkota	– *there*
êkotê	– *over there*	êwako	– *that one*

EXERCISE 3. ANIMACY AND NUMBER AGREEMENT. The animacy or number agreements of nouns and demonstrative pronouns in the following need changing:

1. atimwak ôhi. _____ *These are dogs.*

2. astotina anima. _____ *That is a hat.*

3. mîcisowinâhtik anihi. _____ *Those are tables.*

4. nêhi mistik. _____ *Those logs over there.*

5. nêki mistik. _____ *Those trees over there.*

6. aniki maskisina. _____ *Those shoes there.*

7. ana minôsak. _____ *Those cats there.*

8. ôma miskotâkaya. _____ *This coat.*

9. awa tâpiskâkanak. _____ *These scarves.*

10. ôki masinahikana. _____ *These books.*

11. astis nêma. _____ *That is a mitt.*

12. mitâsak nâha. _____ *That is a pair of pants over there.*

13. papakiwayâna anima. _____ *That is a shirt.*

14. nâha masinahikanâhcikosak. _____ *Those pencils.*

15. asikan aniki. _____ *Those are socks.*

3.2.C PERSONAL PRONOUNS

There are seven personal pronouns in Cree as listed below:

1 niya – *I/me*

2 kiya – *you*

3 wiya – *he/she*

1P niyanân – *us/we* (excludes the one spoken to)

21 kiyânaw – *us/we* (includes the one spoken to)

2P kiyawâw – *you* (plural)

3P wiyawâw – *they*

The above numerical notations refer to the "person" and the same numerical notations are used in setting up the paradigms for the emphatic pronouns as well as the various verbs we use in Cree. English has the personal pronouns "he" and "she" for the third person, but we only have the term "wiya" for these, so it is not surprising to hear a Cree speaker using "she" when talking about a male in English!

3.2.D EMPHATIC PRONOUNS

Emphatic pronouns follow the same numerical system as the personal pronouns. Emphatic pronouns are inclusive indicators as in "me too" or "me also", etc. Consider the following segment of dialogue:

A. nêhiyaw ôma niya. – *I am a Cree….*(uses the personal pronoun "niya")

B. nêhiyaw ôma nîsta. – *I am a Cree too…*(uses the emphatic pronoun "nîsta")

The following lists the emphatic pronouns using the same numerical notation:

1 nîsta – *me too*

2 kîsta – *you too*

3 wîsta – *she/he too*

1P nîstanân – *us too* (excludes the one spoken to)

21 kîstanaw – *us too* (includes the one spoken to)

2P kîstawâw – *you* (plural) *too*

3P wîstawâw – *they too*

As mentioned, the numerical notation identifies the "person" speaking, being spoken to, or being spoken about, as outlined below:

1 This refers to the speaker: known as the first person singular form "I".

2 This refers to the one being spoken to: known as the second person singular form "you".

3 This refers to the one being spoken about: known as the third person singular form "she" or "he".

1P This refers to the speaker and others but excludes the one spoken to: known as the first person plural exclusive form "we".

21 This refers to the speaker and others including the one spoken to: known as the first person plural inclusive form "we".

2P This refers to the ones spoken to: known as the second person plural form "you".

3P This refers to the ones being spoken about: known as the third person plural form "they".

EXERCISES

EXERCISE 1. Answer the following questions:

1. nêhiyaw cî kiya? *Are you a Cree?*

_____

2. nêhiyaw cî kîsta? *Are you a Cree too?*

_____

3. nêhiyawak cî kiyawâw? *Are you (plural) Cree?*

_____

4. nêhiyawak cî kîstawâw? *Are you (plural) Cree too?*

_____

5. nêhiyaw cî wiya? *Is she/he Cree?*

_____

6. nêhiyaw cî wîsta? *Is she/he Cree too?*

_____

7. nêhiyawak cî wiyawâw? *Are they Cree?*

_____

8. nêhiyawak cî wîstawâw? *Are they Cree too?*

_____

9. kinêhiyawân cî kiya? *Do you speak Cree?*

_____

10. kîsta cî kinêhiyawân? *Do you speak Cree too?*

_____

11. kinêhiyawânâwâw cî kiyawâw? *Do you (plural) speak Cree?*

_____

12. kîstawâw cî kinêhiyawânâwâw? *Do you (plural) speak Cree too?*

_____

13. nêhiyawêw cî wiya kitôtêm? *Does your friend speak Cree?*

_____

14. wîsta cî kitôtêm nêhiyawêw? *Does your friend speak Cree too?*

_____

15. nêhiyawêwak cî wiyawâw? *Do they speak Cree?*

_____

16. wîstawâw cî nêhiyawêwak? *Do they speak Cree too?*

_____

3.3 DIALOGUE FOUR

A: tânisi (name)

B: tânisi (name)

A: anohc nitipiskên!

B: kah, tânitahtopiponêyan êkwa?

A: nîsitanaw pêyakosâp nititahtopinonân.
kiya mâka, tânitahtopiponêyan?

B: kêkâ-nîsitanaw niya nititahtopiponân.

A: tânispîhk kâ-tipiskaman?

B: kêkâ-nistomitanaw ê-akimiht mikisiwi-pîsim.

A: *Hello (name)*

B: *Hello (name)*

A: *Today is my birthday!*

B: *Oh, so how old are you now?*

A: *I am twenty-one years old.*
How about you, how old are you?

B: *I am nineteen years old.*

A: *When is your birthday?*

B: *On February 29th.*

VOCABULARY

anohc – *today*
kah – *oh*
êkwa – *now*
tânispîhk – *when*
kêkâ-nîsitanaw – *nineteen*
kêkâ-nistomitanaw – *twenty-nine*
mikisiwi-pîsim – *February*

nitipiskên – *I have a birthday.*
tânitahtopiponêyan – *How old are you?*
nîsitanaw pêyakosâp – *twenty-one*
nititahtopinonân – *I am of that age.*
kâ-tipiskaman – *(when) you have a birthday*
ê-akimiht – *it is counted*
kititahtopiponân – *You are of that age.*

NOTES

1) The greeting "tânisi" can be answered in a variety of ways: it can mean "*How are you?*" to which you can answer "namôya nânitaw" meaning "*I am fine*" or it can mean "*hello*" to which you can answer as in the above dialogue "tânisi – *hello*".

2) The phrase "nitipiskên", meaning "*I have a birthday*", is the first person indicative mood form of the transitive inanimate verb-class 1 (VTI-1) "tipiska – *have a birthday*". The same verb appears on the second last line in the above dialogue in a relative clause (conjunct mood), second person form, as "kâ-tipiskaman". The last "a" in the verb stem "tipiska" changes to "ê" for the first and second person forms of the indicative mood. This rule applies to all VTI-1 in the indicative mood and 21 of the Imperative.

3) The formula for saying the date is to say the date first, then the phrase meaning "*It is counted.* – ê-akimiht", followed by the month as in the above dialogue:"kêkâ-nistomitanaw ê-akimiht mikisiwi-pîsim."

DO: the above dialogue with a classmate and substitute the phrase for age and the phrase "kêkâ-nistomitanaw ê-akimiht mikisiwi-pîsim" with your own birthdate.

3.4 CHAPTER THREE REVIEW

DEMONSTRATIVE PRONOUNS

ENGLISH	Use with Animate nouns	Use with Inanimate nouns
This	awa	ôma
That	ana	anima
That over there	nâha	nêma
These	ôki	ôhi
Those	aniki	anihi
Those over there	nêki	nêhi

INTERROGATIVE PRONOUNS THAT DEPEND ON ANIMACY AND NUMBER

NUMBER	ENGLISH	ANIMATE	INANIMATE
SINGULAR	Where	tâniwâ	tâniwê
	Which	tâna	tânima
	What	kîkwây	kîkwây
	Who	awîna	_____
PLURAL	Where	tâniwêhkâk	tâniwêhâ
	Which	tâniki	tânihi
	What	kîkwâyak	kîkwâya
	Who	awîniki	_____

RULES FOR PLURALS

NOUN ENDINGS	ANIMATE PLURALS	INANIMATE PLURALS
_____k	Add **wak**	Add **wa**
_____i	NONE HERE	Drop **i** then add **a**
_____wa	Add **k**	NONE HERE
(rare) _____m/n/s	Add **wak**	Add **wa**
ALL OTHERS	Add **ak**	Add **a**

A. DIMINUTIVES AND DEMONSTRATIVE PRONOUNS. Make the nouns below into diminutives, and make sure the demonstrative pronouns correspond with the English meaning:

1. atimwak ana. _____ *Those are puppies.*

2. astotin anihi. _____ *That is a small hat.*

3. mîcisowinâhtik anima. _____ *Those are small tables.*

4. nâha mistik. _____ *That little tree.*

5. nêma tohtôsâpoy. _____ *That small milk over there.*

6. nêhi mêskanaw. _____ *Those small roads there.*

7. awa mikisiw. _____ *That eaglet over there.*

8. ôhi miskotâkaya. _____ *This small coat.*

9. aniki maskasiyak. _____ *These small fingernails.*

10. ôma ôsi. _____ *These small boats.*

11. nâpêw ana. _____ *That is a boy over there.*

12. mwâkwa nâha. _____ *That is a small loon.*

RULES FOR DIMINUTIVES. Change every "t" to "c" and then:

NOUN ENDINGS	RULES
_____ k	Add **os**
_____ i	Drop **i**, then add **is(is)**
_____ wa	Drop **wa**, then add **osis**
_____ êw	Drop **w**, then add **sis**
_____ aw _____ ay _____ âw	Drop endings **aw**, **ay** and **âw**, then add **âs**
_____ iy _____ iw	Drop endings **iy** and **iw**, then add **îs**
_____ oy	Drop ending **oy**, then add **ôs**
(rare) _____ m/n/s	Add **osis**
ALL OTHERS	Add **is**

B. ANIMACY AND NUMBER AGREEMENT. The animacy or number agreements of nouns and the verb "be" in the following need changing:

1. nohcimihk ayâw maskwak. _____

2. astotina astêw tahkohc mîcisowinâhtik. _____

3. ispimihk mistik ayâwak minôs. _____

4. wayawîtimihk astêw maskisina. _____

5. cîki sâkahikan ayâw môswak. _____

6. atâmipîhk ayâwak kinosêw. _____

7. sîpâ asiniy ayâw kinêpikwak. _____

8. sisonê mêskanaw ayâwak minôsis. _____

9. atâmihk miskotâkay astêw masinahikana. _____

THE VERB "BE"

ENGLISH	USE WITH ANIMATE NOUNS	USE WITH INANIMATE NOUNS
(It) is there.	ayâw	astêw
(They) are there.	ayâwak	astêwa

RULES FOR LOCATIVES

NOUN ENDINGS	RULES
_____k	Add **ohk**
_____i	Drop ending, then add **ihk**
_____aw _____ay _____âw	Drop ending, then add **âhk**
_____iy _____iw	Drop ending, then add **îhk**
_____wa	Drop **wa**, then add **ohk**
_____oy	Drop ending, then add **ôhk**
(rare) _____m/n/s	Add **ohk**
ALL OTHERS	Add **ihk**

C. Make plurals out of the following nouns and demonstrative pronouns:

e.g., atim awa. → atimwak ôki.   *This is a dog.* → *These are dogs.*

1. sikâk awa (*This is a skunk*).   _____

2. mîcisowinâhtik ôma (*This is a table*).   _____

3. niska awa (*This is a goose*).   _____

4. wâwi ôma (*This is an egg*).   _____

5. wâti ôma (*This is a cave*).   _____

6. pîsim awa (*This is a sun*).   _____

7. maskwa awa (*This is a bear*).   _____

8. sîsîp awa (*This is a duck*).   _____

9. môhkomân ôma (*This is a knife*).   _____

10. misit ôma (*This is a foot*).   _____

D. Make diminutives out of the following nouns:

1. miskîsik (*an eye*)   _____

2. ôsi (*a boat*)   _____

3. kâkwa (*a porcupine*)   _____

4. iskwêw (*a woman*)   _____

5. mihtawakay (*an ear*)   _____

6. ispatinaw (*a hill*)   _____

7. môniyâw (*a Caucasian*)   _____

8.   sîwâpoy (*a soda pop*)   _____

9. atim (*a dog*)   _____

10. maskasiy (*a fingernail*)   _____

E. Make locatives out of the following nouns:

1. âhkosîwikamik (*a hospital*) _____

2. wâti (*a cave*) _____

3. mêskanaw (*a road*) _____

4. piponasâkay (*a parka*) _____

5. sakâw (*a bush*) _____

6. nipiy (*water*) _____

7. tohtôsâpoy (*milk*) _____

8. mistikowat (*box*) _____

9. mistik (*tree*) _____

10. akocikan (*shelf*) _____

F. Put locative endings to the nouns following prepositions, and make sure there is number agreement between the nouns and the verb "be" in the following:

1. tahkohc têhtapiwin ayâw minôsak. (*The cat is on top of the chair*).

   _____

2. sisonê mêskanaw astêwa maskisin. (*The shoes are along the road*).

   _____

3. nipiy ayâwak sîsîp. (*The ducks are in the water*).

   _____

4. ispimihk mistik ayâwak kâkwa. (*The porcupines are up the tree*).

   _____

5. pîhcâyihk mistikowat astêw môhkomâna. (*The knives are inside the box*).

   _____

G. Correct the number agreement in the following sentences, using the correct demonstrative pronouns and/or the correct interrogative pronouns:

1. tâniwâ maskwak? (*Where are the bears?*) _____

2. tâniwêhkâk nâpêsis? (*Where is the boy?*) _____

3. tâniwêhâ maskisin? (*Where are the shoes?*) _____

4. tâniwê piponasâkaya? (*Where are the parkas?*) _____

5. awîna aniki? (*Who are those?*) _____

6. awîniki ana? (*Who is that?*) _____

7. kîkwâya ôma? (*What is this?*) _____

8. kîkwây ôhi? (*What are these?*) _____

9. tâna nâpêwak? (*Which men?*) _____

10. tâniki iskwêw? (*Which woman?*) _____

H. Translate the following, using words from the previous exercises:

1. *The dogs are in the bush.* _____

2. *The pop is on the table.* _____

3. *The skunks are along the road.* _____

4. *The bear is in the cave.* _____

5. *The parka is on top of the shoes.* _____

6. *Where is your book?* _____

7. *Where are your mitts?* _____

8. *Where are your shoes?* _____

9. *Where is your scarf?* _____

10. *Who are you?* _____

I. NOUNS (ANIMACY AND NUMBER): Make plurals out of the following nouns (the demonstratives indicate animacy) and demonstrative pronouns:

1. maskosiy ôma (*This is a blade of grass*). _____

2. maskasiy awa (*This is a fingernail*). _____

3. mistik ôma (*This is a log*). _____

4. mistik awa (*This is a tree*). _____

5. ôsi ôma (*This is a boat*). _____

6. atim awa (*This is a dog*). _____

7. môswa awa (*This is a moose*). _____

8. nîpiy ôma (*This is a leaf*). _____

9. mitâs awa (*This is a pair of pants*). _____

10. wâpikwaniy ôma (*This is a flower*). _____

J. NOUNS (DIMINUTIVES): Make diminutives out of the following:

1. asiniy (*a stone*) _____

2. piponasâkay (*a parka*) _____

3. miskâhtik (*a forehead*) _____

4. maskwa (*a bear*) _____

5. iskwêw (*a woman*) _____

6. mistatim (*a horse*) _____

7. nêhiyaw (*a Cree*) _____

8. môniyâw (*a Caucasion*) _____

9. tohtôsâpoy (*milk*) _____

10. nipiy (*water*) _____

K. NOUNS (LOCATIVES): Make locatives out of the following nouns:

1.   mîcisowikamik (*a café*) _____

2.   ôsi (*a boat*) _____

3.   ispatinaw (*a hill*) _____

4.   miskotâkay (*a coat*) _____

5.   sakâw (*a bush*) _____

6.   nîpiy (*a leaf*) _____

7.   sîwâpoy (*a soda-pop*) _____

8.   sîpiy (*a river*) _____

9.   nipiy (*a water*) _____

10. wâti (*a cave*) _____

L. PREPOSITIONS, LOCATIVES AND THE VERB "TO BE": Add the necessary endings to the nouns that need to change, and make sure there is number agreement between the nouns and the verb "to be":

1.   maskasiy ayâwak tahkohc mîcisowinâhtik (*The fingernails are on top of the table*).

_____

2.   mwâkwak ayâw sâkahikan (*The loons are in the lake*).

_____

3.   sikâk ayâwak nohcimihk sakâw (*The skunk is inland in the bush*).

_____

4.   maskosiya astêw tahkohc mêskanaw (*The grasses are on top of the road*).

_____

5.   ôsi astêwa tahkohc mistik (*The boat is on top of the log*).

_____

M. Translate the following Cree to English:

1. nâha mwâkwa. _____

2. sikâk awa. _____

3. ana iskwêw. _____

4. mîcisowinâhtik anima. _____

5. nêma ôsi. _____

6. wâpikwaniy ôma. _____

7. ôki maskasiyak. _____

8. iskwêsisak aniki. _____

9. nêhi mêskanawa. _____

10. mistikwa anihi. _____

N. Make sure the interrogative pronouns agree in number to the nouns and/or demonstrative pronouns:

1. tâniwâ aniki nâpêwak. (*Where are those men?*)

   _____

2. tâniwêhkâk ana iskwêsis. (*Where is that girl?*)

   _____

3. tâna iskwêsisak. (*Which girls?*)

   _____

4. tâniki iskwêw. (*Which woman?*)

   _____

5. tâniwê anihi wâpikwaniya. (*Where are those flowers?*)

   _____

6. tâniwêhâ anima mêskanaw. (*Where is that road?*)

   _____

7. tânihi mistik. (*Which log?*)

_____

8. tânima mîcisowinâhtikwa. (*Which tables?*)

_____

9. awîniki ana nâha. (*Who is that over there?*)

_____

10. kîkwâya anima nêma. (*What is that over there?*)

_____

o. Fill in the following charts with the correct rules:

THE VERB "BE"

ENGLISH	USE WITH ANIMATE NOUNS	USE WITH INANIMATE NOUNS
(It) is there.		
(They) are there.		

RULES FOR PLURALS

NOUN ENDINGS	ANIMATE PLURALS	INANIMATE PLURALS
_____ k		
_____ i		
_____ wa		
(rare) _____ m/n/s		
ALL OTHERS		

RULES FOR DIMINUTIVES: change every ———————— to ————————

NOUN ENDINGS	RULES
_____k	
_____i	
_____wa	
_____êw	
_____aw	
_____ay	
_____âw	
_____iy/iw	
_____oy	
(rare) _____m/n/s	
ALL OTHERS	

RULES FOR LOCATIVES

NOUN ENDINGS	RULES
_____k	
_____i	
_____aw	
_____ay	
_____âw	
_____wa	
_____iy/iw	
_____oy	
_____im	
ALL OTHERS	

DEMONSTRATIVE PRONOUNS

ENGLISH	Use with Animate nouns	Use with Inanimate nouns
This		
That		
That over there		
These		
Those		
Those over there		

INTERROGATIVE PRONOUNS THAT DEPEND ON ANIMACY AND NUMBER
DEMONSTRATIVE PRONOUNS

ENGLISH	Use with Animate nouns	Use with Inanimate nouns
SINGULAR		
Where		
Which		
What		
Who		
PLURAL		
Where		
Which		
What		
Who		

CHAPTER FOUR
. . . .
ANIMATE INTRANSITIVE VERBS

4. ANIMATE INTRANSITIVE VERBS

Animate Intransitive verbs (VAI) are verbs that are of a common occurrence which have Animate actors and take no objects. These verbs can be in various forms: *Imperatives, Negative Imperatives, Delayed Imperatives, Indicative,* and *Conjunct (Subjunctive).*

4.1 IMPERATIVES

Imperatives are orders to do something. Orders can be given to one person (2 in charts below), to two or more persons (2P), and to one or more persons invited by the speaker to do something (21). Negative Imperatives are orders given asking others to not do something. Delayed Imperatives are orders given to be carried out at a later time. Here are the paradigms for all three forms of Imperatives:

IMPERATIVES – ORDERS TO DO	NEGATIVE IMPERATIVES – ORDERS TO NOT DO	DELAYED IMPERATIVES – ORDERS TO DO LATER
2 verb stem	**2** êkâwiya verb stem	**2** verb stem hkan
2P verb stem k	**2P** êkâwiya verb stem k	**2P** verb stem hkêk
21 verb stem tân	**21** êkâwiya verb stem tân	**21** verb stem hkahk

Let's put the verb "mîciso – *eat*" in the above boxes to clarify how these work:

IMPERATIVES – ORDERS TO DO	NEGATIVE IMPERATIVES – ORDERS TO NOT DO	DELAYED IMPERATIVES – ORDERS TO DO LATER
2 mîciso – *Eat*	**2** êkâwiya mîciso – *Don't eat.*	**2** mîciso hkan – *Eat later.*
2P mîciso k – *Eat*	**2P** êkâwiya mîciso k – *Don't eat.*	**2P** mîciso hkêk – *Eat later.*
21 mîciso tân – *Let's eat*	**21** êkâwiya mîciso tân – *Let's not eat.*	**21** mîciso hkahk – *Let's eat later.*

Note that the verb stem "mîciso" does not change in any of the forms above. Let's have a look at this verb stem in the following forms:

1. Present tense, Indicative: *I eat.* – ni**mîciso**n.
2. Past tense, Indicative: *I ate.* – nikî-**mîciso**n.
3. Future intentional tense, Indicative: *I am going to eat.* – niwî-**mîciso**n.
4. Future definite tense, Indicative: *I will eat.* – nika-**mîciso**n.
5. Present tense, with preverb "nôhtê", Indicative: *I want to eat.* – ninôhtê-**mîciso**n.
6. Past tense, with preverb "nôhtê", Indicative: *I wanted to eat.* – nikî-nôhtê-**mîciso**n.

More on these forms later, but for now: notice how the verb stem "**mîciso**" stays in its position next to the final "n" in all the structures from 1-6.

DO: Write the 2, 2P, and 21 forms of the following verb stems in a) imperative, b) negative imperative, and c) delayed imperative:

nipâ – *sleep*	waniskâ – *wake/get up*	kâkîsimo – *pray (traditionally)*
kistâpitêho – *brush teeth*	kâsîhkwê – *wash face*	sîkaho – *comb hair*
postayiwinisê – *dress*	kîsitêpo – *cook*	api – *sit/be at home*
mîciso – *eat*	minihkwê – *drink*	pasikô – *get up/stand up*
wayawî – *go out*	pimohtê – *walk*	pôsi – *get on board*
pimipayi – *drive*	kapâ – *get out (of water)*	atoskê – *work*
masinahikê – *write*	ayamihcikê – *read*	nîmihito – *dance*
nikamo – *sing*	mâto – *cry*	pâhpi – *laugh*
sêsâwî – *exercise*	pimipahtâ – *run*	kîwê – *go home*
pîhtokwê – *enter*	nôhtêhkatê – *be hungry*	kisîpêkiyâkanê – *wash dishes*
kâsîyâkanê – *dry dishes*	nôhtêhkwasi – *be sleepy*	kêtayiwinisê – *undress*
kisîpêkinastê – *bathe*	kawisimo – *lay down*	matwêhkwâmi – *snore*

NOTES ON IMPERATIVES

2–All the foregoing are orders said to one person taken from the 2 — second person singular — form of the Imperative mood.

2P–To say orders to two or more people (the 2P — second person plural — form of the Imperative mood), we would add a "k" to the end of the above forms.

21–To say orders in the form of an invitation (the 21 of the Imperative), we would add "tân" to the end of the above forms.

The Animate Intransitive verbs (VAI) are common everyday actions, or states of being, that do not transfer action from one person to another. The VAIs we've encountered thus far include the following in their verb stem form:

isiyihkâso – *be called/named*
wîki – *reside/live*
ohpiki – *grow up*

itahtopiponê – *be of a certain age*
kiskinwahamâkosi – *go to school/learn*
ohcî – *be from someplace*

All the above are in the verb stem form and are normally used when giving orders to one person. Orders are known as Imperatives.

4.1.A 2 - SECOND PERSON SINGULAR

The form of Imperative known as the second person singular, identified by the "2" notation in conjugation, is a command said to one person. All the above verbs are in the second person singular form with the subject of the verb being understood to be "*you* (singular)". In other words, when giving orders, the "*you*" is rarely said but is understood to be there. The verb stems for the conjugation of all verbs comes from the second person singular form of the Imperative.

4.1.B 2P - SECOND PERSON PLURAL

Orders given to two or more people are identified in conjugation by the "2P" notation and are known as the second person plural forms of the Imperative, meaning "*you all*." To make second person plural forms, we simply add a "**k**" to the verb stem as shown below:

nipâ**k** – *sleep*
sîkaho**k** – *comb (your) hair*
kîsitêpo**k** – *cook*
kâkîsimo**k** – *pray (traditionally)*
mîciso**k** – *eat*

waniskâ**k** – *get (wake) up*
pasikô**k** – *stand up*
pimohtê**k** – *walk*
api**k** – *sit (be at home)*
minihkwê**k** – *drink*

The subject of the above form is understood as being "*you* (plural)".

4.1.C 21 - THE IMPERATIVE INCLUSIVE

Orders can also be given as an invitation by the speaker for one or more people to do an action together. This form of the Imperative is known as the inclusive form and is identified by the "21" notation in conjugation. To make the inclusive Imperative, we simply add "**tân**" to the verb stem as shown in the examples below:

pîhtokwê**tân** – *Let's go inside*
wayawî**tân** – *Let's go outside*
pimipahtâ**tân** – *Let's run*
sipwêhtê**tân** – *Let's leave*

pwâtisimo**tân** – *Let's dance pow-wow*
sêsâwipahtâ**tân** – *Let's jog*
itohtê**tân** – *Let's go (somewhere)*
pimohtê**tân** – *Let's walk*

The subjects, actors, of the 21 form of the Imperative are the "*you*" (the one spoken to) and the "*I*" (the one speaking), while using the "*let us*" to express an intention, a proposal, or instructions and, as is in this case, to convey an invitation.

To recap, then, all the foregoing are Imperative, or orders, given to others to carry out an action immediately. The orders known as Negative Imperative are given to people telling them not to do something. To use Negative Imperative, simply add "**êkâwiya**" in front of all the foregoing forms. Yet another form of Imperative are the orders to be carried out at a later time. These orders are known as the Delayed Imperative. Delayed Imperatives have suffixes that are placed after the verb stem.

4.1.D CONJUGATION CHART FOR IMPERATIVES

The above imperatives can be placed in the following conjugation chart with the blank showing where the verb stem goes:

Imperatives		Negative Imperatives	Delayed Imperatives
2 _____		**2** êkâwiya _____	**2** _____ hkan
2P _____ k		**2P** êkâwiya _____ k	**2P** _____ hkêk
21 _____ tân		**21** êkâwiya _____ tân	**21** _____ hkahk

4.1.E DELAYED IMPERATIVES

Recall that the Imperative Mood is the form verbs take for giving orders for others to do something and that the Negative Imperatives are orders for **not** to do something. Both these forms require the person being ordered to perform that task right away. The Delayed Imperatives, on the other hand, give orders that are to be carried out at a later time. Things like "*come see me tomorrow*" and "*let's dance pow-wow on Saturday*" are **Delayed Imperatives**. Another Delayed Imperative most of you have heard is "*Do your homework tonight*".

While the Delayed Imperative in English is marked by words like "*tomorrow*", "*tonight*", and "*on Saturday*", with no change in the verb structure, this is not the case in Cree. In Cree, the verb structure changes to signal a Delayed Imperative, as well has having the markers such as "*tomorrow*", etc., in the Future Conditional form.

For now, concentrate on the VAI Delayed Imperative:

IMPERATIVE		DELAYED IMPERATIVE	
2	mîciso	**2**	mîciso**hkan**
2P	mîcisok	**2P**	mîciso**hkêk**
21	mîcisotân	**21**	mîciso**hkahk**

In comparing the two, one will notice that the Delayed Imperative is derived by simply adding certain endings to the verb stem (which you will recall is taken from 2 of the Imperative mood). Here are those endings (the blanks are where the verb stem goes).

DELAYED IMPERATIVE	
2	_____hkan
2P	_____hkêk
21	_____hkahk

One can place all VAI verb stems in the above chart: they all give orders for doing something at a later time than when they were issued.

EXERCISES

EXERCISE 1. Put the first verb (which is the Imperative mood) into the Delayed Imperative. The second verb (includes time of day and days of the week) is in the Future Conditional form.

1. nitawi-pwâtisimotân nikotwâso-kîsikâki. (*Let's go dance pow-wow on Saturday.*)

2. pê-itohtêk nîso-kîsikâki. (*Come over on Tuesday.*)

3. pêci-pîhtokwê ati-kimiwahki. (*Come inside when/if it begins to rain.*)

4. ati-kîwêk pôni-sîkipêstâki. (*Begin to go home when/if it stops pouring rain.*)

5. mîcisotân otâkosiki. (*Let's eat this evening.*)

6. sôhki-atoskêk pôni-âpihtâ-kîsikâki. (*Work hard this afternoon.*)

7. sêsâwipahtâ kîkisêpâki. (*Jog in the morning.*)

8. ayamihcikê wâpahki. (*Read tomorrow.*)

9. ayamihcikêk tipiskâki. (*Read tonight.*)

10. itohtêtân iskonikanihk ayamihêwi-kîsikâki. (*Let's go to the reserve on Sunday.*)

WORDS FROM ABOVE:

nikotwâso-kîsikâki – *on Saturday*
ati-kimiwahki – *when/if it begins to rain*
otâkosiki – *this evening*
kîkisêpâki – *in the morning*
tipiskâki – *tonight*

nîso-kîsikâki – *on Tuesday*
pôni-sîkipêstâki – *when/if it stops pouring rain*
pôni-âpihtâ-kîsikâki – *this afternoon*
wâpahki – *tomorrow*
ayamihêwi-kîsikâki – *on Sunday*

EXERCISE 2. Translate the sentences:

1. *Let's go to the store this afternoon.* _____

2. *Walk (2P) along the lake this evening.* _____

3. *Let's jog in the morning.* _____

4. *Go to work tonight.* _____

5. *Let's go eat at the restaurant this evening.* _____

6. *Let's go to the lake on Tuesday.* _____

7. *Work tomorrow.* _____

8. *Come (2P) on Saturday.* _____

9. *Let's go to school tomorrow.* _____

10. *Leave early tomorrow.* _____

DELAYED IMPERATIVES usually go with **FUTURE CONDITIONALS** but can also be used in conjunction with these other temporal words:

mwêstas – *later*
pâcimâsîs – *a little while from now*
awasi-wâpahki – *the day after tomorrow*

pâtimâ – *at a later time*
kotak ispayiki – *next week*

EXERCISE 3. Translate the following using the above words and the following verb stems and preverbs:

masinahikê – *write* (VAI)
mîciso – *eat* (VAI)
nitawi- – *go and* (PV)

kîwê – *go home* (VAI)
atoskê – *work* (VAI)
ati- – *begin to* (PV)

kiyokê – *go visit* (VAI)
kakwê- – *try to* (PV)
pê- – *come* (PV)

1. nitawi-mîcisohkan mwêstas. _____

2. kîwêhkêk pâtimâ. _____

3. ati-atoskêhkahk pâcimâsîs. _____

4. pê-kiyokêhkêk kotakispayiki. _____

5. kakwê-masinahikêhkan awasi-wâpahki. _____

4.2 INDICATIVE MOOD

The Indicative mood is used in independent sentences. They are often statements and/or declarative statements. These forms can be in various tenses and can use preverbs (verb-modifiers). The standard verb structure then is as follows:

Person indicator	Tense indicator	Preverb	Verb stem	Ending

The person indicator and verb endings are as follows:

1 ni ⟨tense⟩-⟨preverb⟩-⟨verb stem⟩ n
2 ki ⟨tense⟩-⟨preverb⟩-⟨verb stem⟩ n
3 ⟨tense⟩-⟨preverb⟩-⟨verb stem⟩ w
3' ⟨tense⟩-⟨preverb⟩-⟨verb stem⟩ yiwa

1P ni ⟨tense⟩-⟨preverb⟩-⟨verb stem⟩ nân
21 ki ⟨tense⟩-⟨preverb⟩-⟨verb stem⟩ naw
2P ki ⟨tense⟩-⟨preverb⟩-⟨verb stem⟩ nâwâw
3P ⟨tense⟩-⟨preverb⟩-⟨verb stem⟩ wak
3'P ⟨tense⟩-⟨preverb⟩-⟨verb stem⟩ yiwa

The numbers in the chart indicate the subject of the verb:

1 is the first person singular ("I" as subject) and has "ni" at the beginning as the person indicator and ends in "n";

2 is the second person singular ("you" as subject) and has "ki" at the beginning as the person indicator and ends in "n";

3 is the third person singular ("she/he/it" as subject) and has no person indicator at the beginning and ends in "w";

3' is the third person obviative (someone's relative, friend or pet as subject) and has no person indicator at the beginning and ends in "yiwa";

1P is the first person plural exclusive ("we" as subject but excludes the one spoken to) and has the "ni" as the person indicator at the beginning and ends in "nân";

21 is the first person plural inclusive ("we" as subject and includes the one spoken to) and has the "ki" as the person indicator at the beginning and ends in "naw";

2P is the second person plural (the plural "you" as subject) and has the "ki" as the person indicator at the beginning and ends in "nâwâw";

3P is the third person plural ("they" as subject) and has no person indicator at the beginning and ends in "wak";

3'P is the third person obviative plural (their relative, friend, or pet as subject) and has no person indicator at the beginning and ends in "yiwa". [**Note**: this is always identical to 3' forms and so is not always included in conjugation patterns.]

The verb conjugation pattern is similar to the conjugation pattern of the personal and emphatic pronouns, which we saw in the last chapter.

Examples of indicative mood using "nêhiyawê – *speak Cree*":

A. Present tense with verb stem "**nêhiyawê** – *speak Cree*":

1	1st person singular	ni**nêhiyaw**án	*I speak Cree.*
2	2nd person singular	ki**nêhiyawâ**n	*You speak Cree.*
3	3rd person singular	**nêhiyawê**w	*She/he speaks Cree.*
3'	3rd person obviative	**nêhiyawê**yiwa	*Her/his friend(s) speak(s) Cree.*
1P	1st person plural (excl)	ni**nêhiyawâ**nân	*We speak Cree (exclude listener).*
21	1st person plural (incl)	ki**nêhiyawâ**naw	*We speak Cree (include listener).*
2P	2nd person plural	ki**nêhiyawâ**nâwâw	*You (plural) speak Cree.*
3P	3rd person plural	**nêhiyawê**wak	*They speak Cree.*

B. Present tense with verb stem "**nêhiyawê** – *speak Cree*" and preverb "**nôhtê** – *want to*":

1	1st person singular	ni**nôhtê**-nêhiyawân	*I want to speak Cree.*
2	2nd person singular	ki**nôhtê**-nêhiyawân	*You want to speak Cree.*
3	3rd person singular	**nôhtê**-nêhiyawêw	*She/he wants to speak Cree.*
3'	3rd person obviative	**nôhtê**-nêhiyawêyiwa	*Her/his friend(s) want(s) to speak Cree.*
1P	1st person plural (excl)	ni**nôhtê**-nêhiyawânân	*We want to speak Cree (excluvise).*
21	1st person plural (incl)	ki**nôhtê**-nêhiyawânaw	*We want to speak Cree (inclusive).*
2P	2nd person plural	ki**nôhtê**-nêhiyawânâwâw	*You (plural) want to speak Cree.*
3P	3rd person plural	**nôhtê**-nêhiyawêwak	*They want to speak Cree.*

C. Past tense **kî** with verb stem "**nêhiyawê** – *speak Cree*":

1	1st person singular	ni**kî**-nêhiyawân	*I spoke Cree.*
2	2nd person singular	ki**kî**-nêhiyawân	*You spoke Cree.*
3	3rd person singular	**kî**-nêhiyawêw	*She/he spoke Cree.*
3'	3rd person obviative	**kî**-nêhiyawêyiwa	*Her/his friend(s) spoke Cree.*
1P	1st person plural (excl)	ni**kî**-nêhiyawânân	*We spoke Cree (exclusive).*
21	1st person plural (incl)	ki**kî**-nêhiyawânaw	*We spoke Cree (inclusive).*
2P	2nd person plural	ki**kî**-nêhiyawânâwâw	*You (plural) spoke Cree.*
3P	3rd person plural	**kî**-nêhiyawêwak	*They spoke Cree.*

D. Past tense **kî** with verb stem "**nêhiyawê** – *speak Cree*" and preverb "**nôhtê** – *want to*":

1	1st person singular	ni**kî-nôhtê-nêhiyawâ**n	*I wanted to speak Cree.*
2	2nd person singular	ki**kî-nôhtê-nêhiyawâ**n	*You wanted to speak Cree.*
3	3rd person singular	**kî-nôhtê-nêhiyawê**w	*She/he wanted to speak Cree.*
3'	3rd person obviative	**kî-nôhtê-nêhiyawê**yiwa	*Her friend(s) wanted to speak Cree.*
1P	1st person plural (excl)	ni**kî-nôhtê-nêhiyawâ**nân	*We wanted to speak Cree (exclusive).*
21	1st person plural (incl)	ki**kî-nôhtê-nêhiyawâ**naw	*We wanted to speak Cree (inclusive).*
2P	2nd person plural	ki**kî-nôhtê-nêhiyawâ**nâwâw	*You (plural) wanted to speak Cree.*
3P	3rd person plural	**kî-nôhtê-nêhiyawê**wak	*They wanted to speak Cree.*

NOTE: In the foregoing examples we can see the basic verb structure for all verbs. The person indicator (if any) always comes first, followed by the tense indicator (if any), followed by the preverb (if any), followed by the verb stem, followed by the verb ending that corresponds with the person (subject) indicator. Not all units are present at all times. However, when there is a tense indicator, then that indicator connects to the person indicator followed by a hyphen; if the tense indicator is absent, then the person indicator connects to the next unit without a hyphen.

Using the verb stem "nêhiyawê – *speak Cree*", here is how the structure looks like in various forms:

PRESENT TENSE: ninêhiyawân – *I speak Cree*

Person indicator ni	Verb stem nêhiyawê	Ending n

PRESENT TENSE WITH PREVERB: ninôhtê-nêhiyawân – *I want to speak Cree.*

Person indicator ni	Preverb nôhtê-	Verb stem nêhiyawê	Ending n

PAST TENSE WITH PREVERB: nikî-nôhtê-nêhiyawân – *I wanted to speak Cree.*

Person indicator ni	Tense indicator kî-	Preverb nôhtê-	Verb stem nêhiyawê	Ending n

RULES: there are two rules that come into play in the Indicative mood:

1) t-connection: if the verb stem or preverb begins with a vowel, then the person indicator is followed by a **t** to connect it to the verb stem or preverb. This rule applies *only* in the present tense of the Indicative.

2) If the verb stem ends with an **ê**, then that **ê** changes to **â** for the following persons of the indicative mood: 1, 2, 1P, 21, and 2P. Again, this applies only for the Indicative.

EXAMPLES:
1. t-connection and "**ê** to **â**" rule together: given the preverb "ati – *begin*" and the verb stem "nêhiyawê – *speak Cree,*" provide the correct Cree translation for the following:

   a) *I begin to speak Cree.* _____

   b) *I began to speak Cree.* _____

4.2.A ANIMATE INTRANSITIVE VERB PATTERNS

IMPERATIVE		NEGATIVE IMPERATIVE		DELAYED IMPERATIVE	
2	_____	**2** êkâwiya _____		**2** _____ hkan	
2P	_____ k	**2P** êkâwiya _____ k		**2P** _____ hkêk	
21	_____ tân	**21** êkâwiya _____ tân		**21** _____ hkahk	

INDICATIVE:

PRESENT:

1	ni _____ n	**1P**	ni _____ nân
2	ki _____ n	**21**	ki _____ naw
3	_____ w	**2P**	ki _____ nâwâw
3'	_____ yiwa	**3P**	_____ wak
3'P	_____ yiwa		

PAST: use "**kî-**"

1	ni**kî-** _____ n	**1P**	ni**kî-** _____ nân
2	ki**kî-** _____ n	**21**	ki**kî-** _____ naw
3	**kî-** _____ w	**2P**	ki**kî-** _____ nâwâw
3'	**kî-** _____ yiwa	**3P**	**kî-** _____ wak
3'P	**kî-** _____ yiwa		

FUTURE INTENTIONAL: use "**wî-** – _going to_"

1	ni**wî-** _____ n	**1P**	ni**wî-** _____ nân
2	ki**wî-** _____ n	**21**	ki**wî-** _____ naw
3	**wî-** _____ w	**2P**	ki**wî-** _____ nâwâw
3'	**wî-** _____ yiwa	**3P**	**wî-** _____ wak
3'P	**wî-** _____ yiwa		

FUTURE DEFINITE: use "**ka-**" for first and second persons and "**ta-**" for third persons – "_will_"

1	ni**ka-** _____ n	**1P**	ni**ka-** _____ nân
2	ki**ka-** _____ n	**21**	ki**ka-** _____ naw
3	**ta-** _____ w	**2P**	ki**ka-** _____ nâwâw
3'	**ta-** _____ yiwa	**3P**	**ta-** _____ wak
3'P	**ta-** _____ yiwa		

RULES FOR INDICATIVE ONLY:

1) If verb stem ends in **ê**, change the **ê** to **â** for first and second persons;

2) In present tense only, if verb stem or preverb begins with a vowel, use a **t** between the person indicator and verb stem or preverb.

STANDARD VERB STRUCTURE

Person indicator	Tense indicator	Preverb	Verb stem	Ending

A. Take any verb and put it in the following charts:

IMPERATIVE

2 _____

2P _____

21 _____

NEGATIVE IMPERATIVE

2 _____

2P _____

21 _____

DELAYED IMPERATIVE

2 _____

2P _____

21 _____

INDICATIVE:

PRESENT:

1 _____   1P _____

2 _____   21 _____

3 _____   2P _____

3' _____   3P _____

3'P _____

PAST:

1 _____   1P _____

2 _____   21 _____

3 _____   2P _____

3' _____   3P _____

3'P _____

FUTURE INTENTIONAL:

1 _____   1P _____

2 _____   21 _____

3 _____   2P _____

3' _____   3P _____

3'P _____

FUTURE DEFINITE:

1 _____   1P _____

2 _____   21 _____

3 _____   2P _____

3' _____   3P _____

3'P _____

RULES:

1) ê to â: _____   2) t-connection: _____

TENSES:

1) Past: _____   2) Future Intentional: _____

3) Future Definite: _____ for first and second person verbs

_____ for third person verbs

DO: Use the vocabulary from the chart below to make ten sentences.

SUBJECT	TENSE	PREVERB	VERB STEMS	ENDINGS
INDICATIVE: ni (1,1P) ki (2, 21, 2P) There's no person indicator for 3, 3', 3P, 3'P	**kî-** past **wî-** future intentional **ka-** "will" for: (1, 2, 1P, 21, 2P) **ta-** "will" for: (3, 3', 3P, 3'P). **ka-kî-** is the modal indicator for "can/ could/ should"	kakwê- *(try to)* nitawi- *(go and)* nôhtê- *(want to)* nihtâ- *(ability to)* mâci- *(begin)* pêyako- *(alone)* pôni- *(stop)* ati- *(start)* pê- *(come)* pêci- *(come)* sâpo- *(through(* papâsi- *(hurriedly)* nisihkâci- *(slowly)*	nipâ *(sleep)* waniskâ *(get up)* kâkîsimo *(pray)* kâsîhkwê *(wash face)* sîkaho *(comb hair)* kistâpitêho *(brush teeth)* kisîpêkinastê *(bathe)* kisîpêkiyâkanê *(wash dishes)* postayiwinisê *(dress)* kêtayiwinisê (undress) pimohtê *(walk)* pimipahtâ *(run)* kîsitêpo *(cook)* mîciso *(eat)*	**INDICATIVE** n (1, 2) w (3) yiwa (3', 3'P) nân (1P) naw (21) nâwâw (2P) wak (3P)
CONJUNCT: **There are three forms of conjuncts in Cree but these three will share the same endings.** **ê-** Is used in all subordinate clause inflections followed by the units to the right. **kâ-** is used in adjectivial or relational clauses. **ta-** is used for the infinitive clauses.	-present tense has no tense indicator. **RULES, ONLY FOR INDICATIVE:** **1.** Use "t" as a connector if VS or PV begins with a vowel but only in the present tense for: 1, 2, 1P, 21, 2P. 2. In all tenses if VS ends in an "ê" change that to "â" for 1, 2, 1P, 21, 2P. _____ **Only the past and future intentional indicators are used in Conjunct.**	miyo- *(good)* pêyâhtaki- *(carefully)* mâyi- *(bad)* maci- *(evil)* sôhki- *(hard)* pisci- *(accidently)*	minihkwê *(drink)* pasikô *(get up)* ayamihcikê *(read)* masinahikê *(write)* pôsi *(board)* kapâ *(get off)* mâto *(cry)* pâhpi *(laugh)* nêhiyawê *(speak Cree)* âkayâsîmo *(speak English)* wayawî *(go out)* pîhtokwê *(go in)* pimipayi *(drive)* atoskê *(work)* nîmihito *(dance)* nikamo *(sing)* sêsâwî *(exercise)* kîwê *(go home)* api *(sit)* nôhtêhkatê *(be hungry)* nôhtêhkwasi *(be sleepy)* kawisimo *(lay down)* kâsîyâkanê *(dry dishes)*	**CONJUNCT** yân (1) yan (2) t (3) yit (3', 3'P) yâhk (1P) yahk (21) yêk (2P) cik (3P)

4.3 THE VAI INDICATIVE MOOD AND CONJUNCT MOOD

The Indicative Mood is the form the verbs take when making simple statements, as well as appearing in independent clauses of complex sentences. For example, a simple declarative sentence would be in the statement "*I got up early this morning* – nikî-waniskân wîpac kîkisêp." A complex sentence would include a verb in the Indicative mood in an independent clause and another verb in the Conjunct mood in a subordinate clause as in the following:

(SUBORDINATE CLAUSE) [INDEPENDENT CLAUSE]
(Although I got up early this morning) *[I did not brush my teeth]*.
(âta wîpac kîkisêp ê-kî-waniskâyân) [namôya nikî-kistâpitêhon].

Verbs in the Indicative mood can stand on their own to complete full sentences. They can be statements about doing an action: "nikî-kistâpitêhon – *I brushed my teeth*." Or they can be statements about not doing something: "namôya nikî-kistâpitêhon – *I did not brush my teeth*." To make a negative statement we simply include a "namôya – *no/not*" in front of the complete affirmative verb form as in the foregoing example.

All verbs in the Indicative and Conjunct forms can have nine possible agents/subjects carrying out the action, identified in the conjugation pattern by the following numeric system:

NO.	SUBJECT/AGENT	INDICATIVE MOOD	CONJUNCT MOOD
1	1st person singular '*I*'	ni _____ n	ê- _____ yân
2	2nd person singular '*you*'	ki _____ n	ê- _____ yan
3	3rd person singular '*s/he/it*'	_____ w	ê- _____ t
3'	3rd person obviative '*her friend*'	_____ yiwa	ê- _____ yit
1P	1st person plural '*we*' (excl.)	ni _____ nân	ê- _____ yâhk
21	1st person plural '*we*' (incl.)	ki _____ naw	ê- _____ yahk
2P	2nd person plural '*you*'	ki _____ nâwâw	ê- _____ yêk
3P	3rd person plural '*they*'	_____ wak	ê- _____ cik
3'P	3rd person obviative plural '*their friend*'	_____ yiwa	ê- _____ yit

All tense indicators, preverbs, and verb stems can be placed in the blank spaces in the above paradigms. The standard verb structure for any verb follows the following pattern:

Person indicators "ni" and 'ki" OR "ê-" or "kâ-"	Tense Indicators kî-, wî-, ka-(ta-)	Preverbs	Verb stems	Verb endings

Verbs can be in the following tenses:

The present (tense indicator: none):	niwaniskân	– *I get up.*
The past (tense indicator: **kî-**):	ni**kî**-waniskân	– *I got up.*
The future intentional (tense indicator: **wî-**):	ni**wî**-waniskân	– *I am going to get up.*
The future definite (tense indicator: **ka-**):	ni**ka**-waniskân	– *I will get up.*

The future definite tense for 1st and 2nd person forms is "**ka-**" and "**ta-**" for third person forms. These future definite tenses are never used in the conjunct forms of verbs.

Another way of understanding the paradigm of verbs is to see the nature of the utterance as in who speaks, who is spoken to, and who is spoken about:

1ST PERSON SUBJECT: the speaker	2ND PERSON SUBJECT: the one/ones spoken to	3RD PERSON SUBJECT: the one/ones talked about
1 "ni_____n" The speaker talking about himself/herself: "I".	**2** "ki_____n" The addressee, i.e., the one spoken to: "you".	**3** "_____w" The topic, i.e., the one spoken about: "she/he/it".
1P "ni_____nân" The speaker talking about self and others but excluding the one spoken to: "we (excl.)".	**2P** "ki_____nâwâw" Two or more persons spoken to: "you (plural)".	**3P** "_____wak" Two or more persons spoken about: "they".
	21 "ki_____naw" The speaker talking about self and others and including the one spoken to: "we (incl.)"	**3'** "_____yiwa" The friend, relative or pet of a 3rd person: "his/her _____"
		3'P "_____yiwa" The friends, relatives or pets of 3rd persons: "their _____"

4.3.A INDICATIVE THIRD PERSON SUBJECT

THIRD PERSON SINGULAR (3): Statements with a third person singular subject (*he* or *she*) have a "**w**" at the end of verb stems:

EXAMPLES:

VERB STEM:	isiyihkâso – *be named/called*	itahtopiponê – *be of that age*	
3RD PERSON:	isiyihkâso**w** – *She/he is named*	itahtopiponê**w** – *She/he is of that age*	

VERB STEM:	wîki – *live/reside*	kiskinwahamâkosi – *be in school/class*
3RD PERSON:	wîki**w** – *She/he resides/lives*	kiskinwahamâkosi**w** – *She/he is in school/class*

VERB STEM:	ohpiki – *grow*	ohcî – *be from*
3RD PERSON:	ohpiki**w** – *She/he grows up*	ohcî**w** – *She/he is from*

Complete the following with singular third person subject (3) in the present tense, then translate:

nipâ – *sleep*
kâsîhkwê – *wash (your) face*
sîkaho – *comb (your) hair*
kîsitêpo – *cook*
kâkîsimo – *pray (traditionally)*
mîciso – *eat*

waniskâ – *wake up*
kistâpitêho – *brush (your) teeth*
pasikô – *stand up*
pimohtê – *walk*
api – *sit (be at home)*
minihkwê – *drink*

Third person plural (3P): To make the verb with a plural third person subject (*they*), add the "**wak**" to the verb stems:

EXAMPLES:

VERB STEM:	isiyihkâso – *be named/called*	itahtopiponê – *be of that age*
3P	isiyihkâso**wak** – *They are named*	itahtopiponê**wak** – *They are of that age*

VERB STEM:	wîki – *live/reside*	kiskinwahamâkosi – *be in school/class*
3P	wîki**wak** – *They reside/live*	kiskinwahamâkosi**wak** – *They are in school*

VERB STEM:	ohpiki – *grow*	ohcî – *be from*
3P	ohpiki**wak** – *They grow up*	ohcî**wak** – *They are from*

Complete the following with plural third person subject (3P) in the present tense, then translate:

nipâ – *sleep*
kâsîhkwê – *wash (your) face*
sîkaho – *comb (your) hair*
kîsitêpo – *cook*
kâkîsimo – *pray (traditionally)*
mîciso – *eat*

waniskâ – *wake up*
kistâpitêho – *brush (your) teeth*
pasikô – *stand up*
pimohtê – *walk*
api – *sit (be at home)*
minihkwê – *drink*

To make a past tense with a singular third person subject, add the "**kî**" in front of the verb:

EXAMPLES:

PRESENT:	isiyihkâsow – *She/he is named*	itahtopiponêw – *She/he is of that age*
PAST:	**kî**-isiyihkâsow – *She/he was named*	**kî**-itahtopiponêw – *She/he was of that age*

PRESENT:	wîkiw – *she/he lives*	kiskinwahamâkosiw – *She/he is in school/class*
PAST:	**kî**-wîkiw – *She/he lived*	**kî**-kiskinwahamâkosiw – *She/he was in school*

PRESENT:	ohpikiw – *She/he grows*	ohcîw – *She/he is from*
PAST:	**kî**-ohpikiw – *She/he grew up*	**kî**-ohcîw – *She/he was from (place)*

Complete the following with plural third person subject (3P) in the past tense, then translate:

nipâ – *sleep*

kâsîhkwê – *wash (your) face*

sîkaho – *comb (your) hair*

kîsitêpo – *cook*

kâkîsimo – *pray (traditionally)*

mîciso – *eat*

waniskâ – *wake up*

kistâpitêho – *brush (your) teeth*

pasikô – *stand up*

pimohtê – *walk*

api – *sit (be at home)*

minihkwê – *drink*

4.3.B INDICATIVE THIRD PERSON OBVIATIVE SUBJECT

The third person obviative form (3') of the verb is unique to the Algonquian family of languages. The ending for both the singular form and the plural form is the addition of "**yiwa**" to the verb stem. There is no easy way of determining if the subject is plural or singular unless the actor/agent is identified in the utterance as "*her/his friend* – otôtêma" for 3' and "*their friend* – otôtêmiwâwa" for 3'P.

EXAMPLES:

isiyihkâso**yiwa** – *His/her friend is named*

itahtopiponê**yiwa** – *Her/his friend is of that age*

wîki**yiwa** – *Her/his friend resides/lives*

kiskinwahamâkosi**yiwa** – *His/her friend goes to school*

nihtâwiki**yiwa** – *His/her friend is born*

Complete the following with 3' – third person singular obviative subject – in the present tense, then translate:

nipâ – *sleep*

kâsîhkwê – *wash (your) face*

sîkaho – *comb (your) hair*

kâskipâso – *shave*

waniskâ – *wake up*

kistâpitêho – *brush (your) teeth*

kisîpêkinastê – *bathe/shower*

tômihkwê – *put on make-up*

Complete the following with 3'P – third person plural obviative subject – in the past tense, then translate:

pasikô – *stand up*

kîsitêpo – *cook*

kâkîsimo – *pray (traditionally)*

mîciso – *eat*

kisîpêkiyâkanê – *wash dishes*

pihkahtêwâpôhkê – *make coffee*

pimohtê – *walk*

api – *sit (be at home)*

minihkwê – *drink*

kâsîyâkanê – *dry dishes*

4.3.C INDICATIVE FIRST PERSON SUBJECT

1ST PERSON SINGULAR:

The first person subject is identified in the conjugation charts by the number "1" notation. The first person subject of any verb is the speaker, and when a person talks about herself or himself the pronoun "*I*" is used. This "*I*" in Cree is included as part of the verb structure, signaled by the "**ni**" at the beginning and the "**n**" at the end of the verb structure: **ni_____n**.

To make a statement with a first person subject (*I*) with the above we must keep in mind two items that will affect the inflection. For all the verb stems that end in an "**ê**" we must change that "**ê**" to "**â**". If the verb stem, or preverb, begins with a vowel we must insert a connecting "**t**" between the person indicator "**ni**" and the verb stem or preverb. This "t-connection" rule only applies in the present tense. When we go into the various tenses, that "**t**" will no longer be needed. However, the "**ê**" will change for all tenses. With these rules in mind, then, we can make statements using the first person subject with the above verb stems by having the person indicator, followed by a "**t**" in the present tense or "**kî**" and hyphen in the past tense, followed by the verb stem and the "**n**" as an ending.

EXAMPLES:

PRESENT TENSE: The **t**-connection is used in some of the following verbs where needed and so is the **ê** to **â** rule in "itahtopiponê – *be of a certain age*":

VERB STEM:	isiyihkâso – *be named*	itahtopiponê – *be of a certain age*	
PRESENT TENSE:	ni**t**isiyihkâson – *I am named.*	ni**t**itahtopipon**â**n – *I am of that age.*	

VERB STEM:	wîki – *live/reside*	kiskinwahamâkosi – *be in school/class*	
PRESENT TENSE:	niwîkin – *I reside/live.*	nikiskinwahamâkosin – *I am in school/class.*	

VERB STEM:	ohpiki – *grow*	ohcî – *be from*	
PRESENT TENSE:	ni**t**ohpikin – *I grow up.*	ni**t**ohcîn – *I am from (someplace).*	

PAST TENSE: Note that the **t** is no longer used in these examples using the verbs from above, but the **ê** to **â** rule still applies for "*be of a certain age*":

nikî-isiyihkâson – *I was named.*   nikî-itahtopipon**â**n – *I was of that age.*
nikî-wîkin – *I resided/lived.*   nikî-kiskinwahamâkosin – *I was in school/class.*
nikî-ohpikin – *I grew up.*   nikî-ohcîn – *I was from (someplace).*

Complete the following with singular first person subject (1) in past tense and translate:

nipâ – *sleep*	waniskâ – *wake up*
kâsîhkwê – *wash (your) face*	kistâpitêho – *brush (your) teeth*
sîkaho – *comb (your) hair*	pasikô – *stand up*
kîsitêpo – *cook*	pimohtê – *walk*
kâkîsimo – *pray (traditionally)*	api – *sit (be at home)*
mîciso – *eat*	minihkwê – *drink*

1ST PERSON PLURALS:

There are two first person plural subject forms in Cree. The first, identified by the number/letter notation "1P" for "*we*", excludes the person or persons spoken to. The second, identified by the number notation "21" for "*we*", includes the person or persons spoken to.

EXAMPLES:

"**1P** - *we* (exclusive)" excludes the one spoken to:

niwîki**nân** – *We reside/live*   **ni**kiskinwahamâkosi**nân** – *We are in school/class.*
nitohpiki**nân** – *We grow up*   **nit**ohcî**nân** – *We are from (someplace).*

In full sentence the above can be arranged in this manner.

1) *Regina* niwîkinân. – *We live in Regina.*
2) *Regina* nikiskinwahamâkosinân. – *We are in school in Regina.*
3) *Regina* nikî-ohpikinân. – *We grew up in Regina.*
4) *Regina* nitohcînân. – *We are from Regina.*

"**21** - *we* (inclusive)" includes the one spoken to:

kiwîki**naw** – *We reside/live.*   **ki**kiskinwahamâkosi**naw** – *We are in school/class.*
kitohpiki**naw** – *We grow up.*   **kit**ohcî**naw** – *We are from (someplace).*

Complete the following with the first person plural exclusive subject (1P) in the future intentional (**wî**) tense, then translate:

nipâ – *sleep*   waniskâ – *wake up*
kâsîhkwê – *wash (your) face*   kistâpitêho – *brush (your) teeth*
sîkaho – *comb (your) hair*   pasikô – *stand up*

Complete the following with the first person plural inclusive (21) subject in the future definite (**ka**) tense, then translate:

kîsitêpo – *cook*   pimohtê – *walk*
kâkîsimo – *pray (traditionally)* api – *sit (be at home)*

4.3.D INDICATIVE SECOND PERSON SUBJECT

What goes for the first person subject inflections also applies for the second person except, of course, instead of "**ni**" we would use "**ki**" as the subject indicator. The second person singular ends in "**n**", while the second person plural ends in "**nâwâw**".

EXAMPLES:

2 - SECOND PERSON SINGULAR SUBJECT:

kitisiyihkâso**n** – *You are named*   **kit**itahtopipconâ**n** – *You are of that age*
kiwîki**n** – *You reside/live*   **ki**kiskinwahamâkosi**n** – *You go to school*

2P - SECOND PERSON PLURAL SUBJECT:

kiwîki**nâwâw** – *You reside/live*   **ki**kiskinwahamâkosi**nâwâw** – *You go to school*
kitohpiki**nâwâw** – *You grow up*   **kit**ohcî**nâwâw** – *You are from (someplace)*

Answer the following questions (verb stems are in bold type):

1. tânisi kit**isiyihkâs**on? _____

2. tân**itahtopiponê**yan? _____

3. tânitê ki**wîki**n mêkwâc? _____

4. tânitê kikî-pê-**kiskinwahamâkosi**n? _____

5. tânitê kayahtê kit**ohcî**n? _____

6. tânitê kikî-**nihtâwiki**n? _____

7. tânitê kikî-pê-**ohpik**in? _____

WORD LIST

tânisi – *how*

tânitahto – *how many*

mêkwâc – *now*

ohcî – *be from*

kiskinwahamâkosi – *be in school/class*

tânitahtopiponêyan – *How old are you?*

isiyihkâso – *be named*

tânitê – *where*

pê- – *come*

nihtâwiki – *be born*

itahtopiponê – *be of an age*

wîki – *live/reside*

ohpiki – *grow*

kayahtê – *originally*

Complete the following with second person singular (2) subject in the past tense (**kî**), then translate:

nipâ – *sleep*

kâsîhkwê – *wash (your) face*

sîkaho – *comb (your) hair*

kâskipâso – *shave*

waniskâ – *wake up*

kistâpitêho – *brush (your) teeth*

kisîpêkinastê – *bathe/shower*

tômihkwê – *put on make-up*

Complete the following with second person plural (2P) subject in the future intentional (**wî**) tense, then translate:

pasikô – *stand up*

kîsitêpo – *cook*

kâkîsimo – *pray (traditionally)*

mîciso – *eat*

kisîpêkiyâkanê – *wash dishes*

pihkahtêwâpôhkê – *make coffee*

pimohtê – *walk*

api – *sit (be at home)*

minihkwê – *drink*

kâsîyâkanê – *dry dishes*

EXERCISES

EXERCISE 1. The following sentences have deliberate errors designed to test your grammar knowledge. Find the errors and correct the sentences, using the English translations as cues:

1. wîpac kîkisêp ni**wî**-waniskân. (*I got up early this morning.*)

   _____

2. kîkisêpâki cî ki**kî**-pê-kiyokân? (*Are you going to come visit in the morning?*)

   _____

3. tipiskâyiki **wî**-pê-kiyokêw. (*She will come visit tonight.*)

   _____

4. otâkosîhk ni**ka**-itohtânân sâkahikanihk. (*We went to the lake yesterday.*)

   _____

5. anohc ki**kî**-nitawi-mîcisonaw KFCnâhk. (*Today we will go eat at KFC.*)

   _____

6. otâkosiki cî ki**ka**-nitawi-mîcisonâwâw mîcisowikamikohk? (*Are you (plural) going to go and eat at the café this evening (late afternoon)?*)

   _____

7. atâwêwikamikohk **ta**-itohtêwak nitôtêmak tipiskohk. (*My friends went to the store last night.*)

   _____

8. otôtêma **kî**-ati-nihtâ-nêhiyawêyiwa. (*Her/his friend is going to start speaking Cree well.*)

   _____

9. otôtêmiwâwa **wî**-nitawi-atoskêyiwa mônahisôniyâwânihk otâhk ispayiw. (*Their friend went to work at the mine last week.*)

   _____

EXERCISE 2. Know how to answer the following questions:

	QUESTIONS	ANSWERS
1.	tânisi kitisiyihkâson?	(*Your name*) nitisiyihkâson.
2.	tânitê ohci kiya kayahtê?	(*Place*) ohci niya kayahtê.
3.	tânitê kikî-nihtâwikin?	(*Place*) nikî-nihtâwikin.
4.	tânitê mêkwâc kiwîkin?	(*Place*) mêkwâc niwîkin.
5.	tânitahtopiponêyan?	(*Your age*) nititahtopiponân.
6.	tânispîhk kâ-tipiskaman?	(*Date*) ê-akimiht (*month*) nitipiskên.
7.	tânitahto kîsikâw mêkwâc?	(*Day of the week*) mêkwâc.
8.	kêko pîsim awa akimâw?	(*Month*) awa akimâw.
9.	tâniyikohk awa pîsim ê-akimiht?	(*Date*) awa pîsim akimâw.
10.	okiskinwahamâkan cî kiya?	âha, okiskinwahamâkan niya.

EXERCISE 3. Translate the story below, using the following list of words:

WORD LIST

tipiskohk – *last night*	itohtê – *go*	nîmihito – *dance*
kîkisêpâw – *It is morning*	misi- – *lots*	minihkwê – *drink*
kisîpêkinastê – *bath/shower*	kîwê – *go home*	asawâpi – *look about*
waniskâ – *get up*	tapasî – *flee*	papâsi- – *hurriedly*
namôya – *no/negator*	kîhtwâm – *again*	namôya kîhtwâm – *not again*
kapê-tipisk – *all night*	minihkwêwikamik – *bar*	ohci – *from*
êkota – *there*	nipêhtawâw – *I hear (someone)*	awiyak – *someone*
awîna êtikwê – *I wonder who?*	nititêyihtên – *I think*	sêmâk – *right away*
pêyâhtaki- – *carefully*	êsa – *evidently*	
matwê- – *hear of something happening in the distance*		
wahwâ! – *Holy Moly* (or any such exclamation)		

tipiskohk nikî-itohtân minihkwêwikamikohk. nikî-nîmihiton. nikî-misi-minihkwân kapê-tipisk.

_____

ê-kîkisêpâk nipêyâhtaki-waniskân. nipêhtawâw awiyak ê-matwê-kisîpêkinastêt.

_____

"awîna êtikwê awa kâ-matwê-kisîpêkinastêt," nititêyihtên. nitasawâpin. wahwâ!

_____

namôya êsa nikî-kîwân tipiskohk.   sêmâk êkota ohci nipapâsi-tapasîn.

_____

"namôya kîhtwâm nika-misi-minihkwân," nititêyihtên.

_____

EXERCISE 4. CONJUGATION OF ANIMATE INTRANSITIVE VERBS

IMPERATIVE

If "kîsitêpow = *s/he cooks*", how
would you say these commands:

2 _____

2P _____

21 _____

NEGATIVE IMPERATIVE

If "mâtow = *s/he cries*", how
would you say these commands:

2 _____

2P _____

21 _____

INDICATIVE MOOD

Indicative: Singular subject

If "atoskê = *work*", how
do we put the following in the past
tense with PV "nihtâ- – *ability to do*":

1 _____

2 _____

3 _____

3′ _____

Indicative: Plural subject:

If "masinahikê = *write*", how
do we do these in the future
definite with PV "kakwê- – *try to*":

1P _____

21 _____

2P _____

3P _____

3′P _____

Provide the following tense indicators:

Past tense indicator:

Future intentional tense indicator:

Future definite tense indicators:

_____ (already happened)

_____ (is going to happen)

_____ (will definitely happen)

Write out the following rules:

1) t-connection:
2) ê to â:
3) The verb-structure for all verbs follows the following pattern:

EXERCISE 5. On the next three pages, translate the sentences. Then find the verb stem and make sentences using the first person singular form. Put the first 12 pictures into the past tense, the next set of 12 into the future intentional tense, and the last set of 12 into the future definite tense.

nipâw awa.

waniskâw awa.

kâkîsimow awa.

kistâpitêhow awa.

sîkahow awa.

kâsîhkwêw awa.

postayiwinisêw awa.

kîsitêpow awa.

apiw awa.

mîcisow awa.

minihkwêw awa.

pasikôw awa.

wayawîw awa.

pimohtêw awa.

pôsiw awa sêhkêpayîsihk.

pimipayiw awa.

kapâw sêhkêpayîsihk.

atoskêw awa.

ayamihcikêw awa.

masinahikêw awa.

nikamow awa.

nîmihitow awa.

pâhpiw awa.

mâtow awa.

pimipahtâw awa.

sêsâwîw awa.

kîwêw awa.

pîhtokwêw awa.

nôhtêhkatêw awa.

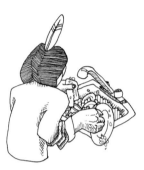

kisîpêkiyâkanêw awa.

kâsîyâkanêw awa.

nôhtêhkwasiw awa.

kêtayiwinisêw awa.

kisîpêkinastêw awa.

kawisimow awa.

matwêhkwâmiw awa.

EXERCISE 6. Complete the following conjugations and translate. In some cases, you will need to isolate the verb stem before proceeding with the exercises, as in the imperative below:

A. IMPERATIVE
If "nêhiyawêw = *s/he speaks Cree*",
how would you say these commands:

2 _____

2P _____

21 _____

B. NEGATIVE IMPERATIVE
If "âkayâsîmow = *s/he speaks English*",
how would you say these commands:

2 _____

2P _____

21 _____

C. INDICATIVE MOOD

INDICATIVE: SINGULAR SUBJECT
If "nikamo = *sing*", how
do we put the following in the past
tense with PV "nihtâ- – *ability to do*:"

1 _____

2 _____

3 _____

3' _____

INDICATIVE: PLURAL SUBJECT:
If "nîmihito = *dance*" how
do we say these in the future
definite with PV "kakwê- – *try to*:"

1P _____

21 _____

2P _____

3P _____

3'P _____

D. IMPERATIVE

If "waniskâw = *s/he awakes*", how
would you say these commands:

2 _____

_____

2P _____

_____

21 _____

_____

E. DELAYED IMPERATIVE

If "nipâwak = *they sleep*", how
would you say these commands:

2 _____

_____

2P _____

_____

21 _____

_____

F. CONJUNCT MOOD

CONJUNCT: SINGULAR SUBJECT

If "kîsitêpowak = *They cook*",
how do the following forms
go in the past tense with PV
"nôhtê- – *want to:*"

1 _____

_____

2 _____

_____

3 _____

_____

3' _____

_____

CONJUNCT: PLURAL SUBJECT

If "mîcisow = *She/he eats*", how
do we do these in the future
intentional with PV "kakwê- – *try to:*"

1P _____

_____

21 _____

_____

2P _____

_____

3P _____

_____

3'P _____

_____

G. Provide the following tense indicators:

Past tense indicator: _____ (already happened)

Future Intentional tense indicator: _____ (is going to happen)

Future definite tense indicator: _____ (will definitely happen
– 1st and 2nd persons)

_____ (will definitely happen
– 3rd persons)

EXERCISE 7. Read, then answer the following:

1. *Wally* isiyihkâsow awa wâpakosîs.
kiya mâka, tânisi kitisiyihkâson?

_____

2. kapê-tipisk kî-nipâw *Shaking-Spear*.
kiya mâka, kapê-tipisk cî kikî-nipân?

_____

3. wîpac kîkisêp kî-waniskâw.
kiya mâka, wîpac cî kikî-waniskân?

_____

4. kî-kistâpitêhow *Shaking-Spear*.
kiya mâka, kikî-kistâpitêhon cî?

_____

5. kî-papâsi-sîkahow.
kiya mâka, kikî-sîkahon cî?

6. kî-kâsîhkwêw *Shaking-Spear*.
kiya mâka, kikî-kâsîhkwân cî?

7. kapê-kîsik kiskinwahamâkosiwak.
kiya mâka, kapê-kîsik cî
kikî-kiskinwahamâkosin?

8. kî-minihkwêw sîwâpoy.
kiya mâka, sîwâpoy cî
kikî-minihkwân?

EXERCISE 8. Answer the questions about these daily activities:

waniskâw awa.
He wakes up.
nipâw cî awa?
Is he asleep?

_____

kiya mâka,
kinipân cî?
How about you,
are you sleeping?

_____

_____

kîsitêpow awa.
He cooks.
kîsitêpow cî awa?
Is he cooking?

_____

kiya mâka,
kikîsitêpon cî?
How about you,
are you cooking?

_____

_____

mîcisow awa.
He eats.
minihkwêw cî awa?
Is he drinking?

_____

kiya mâka,
kiminihkwân cî?
How about you,
are you drinking?

_____

_____

pimipayiw awa.
He is driving.
pimipayiw cî awa?
Is he driving?

_____

kiya mâka,
kipimipayin cî?
How about you,
are you driving?

_____

_____

kiskinwahamâkosiwak ôki.
They are in class.
kiskinwahamâkosiwak cî ôki?
Are they in class?

_____

kiya mâka,
kikiskinwahamâkosin cî?
How about you,
are you in class?

_____

_____

masinahikêw awa.
He is writing.
masinahikêw cî awa?
Is he writing?

_____

kiya mâka,
kimasinahikân cî?
How about you,
Are you writing?

_____

_____

minihkwêwak pihkahtêwâpoy.
They drink coffee.
minihkwêwak cî pihkahtêwâpoy.
Do they drink coffee?

_____

kiya mâka,
kiminihkwân cî
pihkahtêwâpoy?
Do you drink coffee?

_____

aywêpiwak ôki.
They rest.
aywêpiwak cî ôki?
Are they resting?

_____

kiya mâka,
kitaywêpin cî?
*How about you,
do you rest?*

_____

nôhtêhkwasiwak ôki.
They are sleepy.
nôhtêhkwasiwak cî ôki?
Are they sleepy?

_____

kiya mâka,
kinôhtêhkwasin cî?
*How about you,
are you sleepy?*

_____

ati-kîwêw awa.
He starts to go home.
ati-kîwêw cî awa?
Does he start for home?

_____

kiya mâka,
kitati-kîwân cî?
*How about you,
are you starting for home?*

_____

nôhtêhkwasiw awa.
He is sleepy.
nôhtêhkwasiw cî awa?
Is he sleepy?

_____

kiya mâka,
kinôhtêhkwasin cî?
*How about you,
are you sleepy?*

_____

ati-nipâw awa.
He starts to sleep.
ati-nipâw cî awa?
Does he start to sleep?

_____

kiya mâka,
kitati-nipân cî?
*How about you,
are you starting to sleep?*

_____

EXERCISE 9. TIMES OF DAY AND DAILY ACTIVITIES

Translate the following:

Time of Day/Activity	1st and 2nd person forms	3rd and 3' forms Note the difference in the time of day form.
This past morning: kîkisêp **Get up** – waniskâ	**A)** kîkisêp nikî-waniskân. **B)** kîkisêp kikî-waniskân.	**C)** kîkisêp kî-waniskâw. **D)** kîkisêp **o**tôtêm**a** kî-waniskâ**yiwa.**
Last night: tipiskohk **Sleep** – nipâ	**A)** tipiskohk nikî-nipân. **B)** tipiskohk kikî-nipân.	**C)** tipiskohk kî-nipâw. **D)** tipiskohk **o**tôtêm**a** kî-nipâ**yiwa.**
Drive – pimipayi	**A)** kîkisêp nikî-pimipayin. **B)** kîkisêp kikî-pimipayin.	**C)** kîkisêp kî-pimipayiw. **D)** kîkisêp **o**tôtêm**a** kî-pimipayi**yiwa.**
Noon: âpihtâ-kîsikâw **Eat** – mîciso	**A)** kâ-âpihtâ-kîsikâk nikî-mîcison. **B)** kâ-âpihtâ-kîsikâk kikî-mîcison.	**C)** kâ-âpihtâ-kîsikâ**yik** kî-mîcisow. **D)** kâ-âpihtâ-kîsikâyi**yik** **o**tôtêm**a** kî-mîciso**yiwa.**
Afternoon: pôni-âpihtâ-kîsikâw **Drink** – minihkwê	**A)** kâ-pôni-âpihtâ-kîsikâk nikî-minihkwân. **B)** kâ-pôni-âpihtâ-kîsikâk kikî-minihkwân.	**C)** kâ-pôni-âpihtâ-kîsikâ**yik** kî-minihkwêw. **D)** kâ-pôni-âpihtâ-kîsikâyi**yik** **o**tôtêm**a** kî-minihkwê**yiwa.**
Evening: otâkosin **Cook** – kîsitêpo	**A)** kâ-otâkosik nikî-papâsi-kîsitêpon. **B)** kâ-otâkosik kikî-papâsi-kîsitêpon.	**C)** kâ-otâkosi**niyik** kî-papâsi-kîsitêpow. **D)** kâ-otâkosi**niyik** **o**tôtêm**a** kî-papâsi-kîsitêpo**yiwa.**
Day: kîsikâw **Be in class/school** – kiskinwahamâkosi	**A)** kâ-kîsikâk nikî-kiskinwahamâkosin. **B)** kâ-kîsikâk kikî-kiskinwahamâkosin.	**C)** kâ-kîsikâ**yik** kî-kiskinwahamâkosiw. **D)** kâ-kîsikâyi**yik** **o**tôtêm**a** kî-kiskinwahamâkosi**yiwa.**
Night: tipiskâw **Write** – masinahikê	**A)** kâ-tipiskâk nikî-masinahikân. **B)** kâ-tipiskâk kikî-masinahikân.	**C)** kâ-tipiskâ**yik** kî-masinahikêw. **D)** kâ-tipiskâyi**yik** **o**tôtêm**a** kî-masinahikê**yiwa.**
Last night: tipiskohk **Rest** – aywêpi	**A)** tipiskohk nikî-aywêpin. **B)** tipiskohk kikî-aywêpin.	**C)** tipiskohk kî-aywêpiw. **D)** tipiskohk **o**tôtêm**a** kî-aywêpi**yiwa.**
Tonight: tipiskâki **Be sleepy** – nôhtêhkwasi	**A)** tipiskâki niwî-nôhtêhkwasin. **B)** tipiskâki kiwî-nôhtêhkwasin.	**C)** tipiskâ**yiki** wî-nôhtêhkwasiw. **D)** tipiskâ**yiki** **o**tôtêm**a** wî-nôhtêhkwasi**yiwa.**

EXERCISE 10. Working with a partner, read the text below the picture, then answer the questions.

1. ati-nôhtêhkwasiw.
Q1: nôhtêhkwasiw cî awa?
Q2: kiya mâka, kinôhtêkwasin cî?

2. pêyako-kawisimow.
Q1: kâkîsimow cî awa?
Q2: kiya mâka, kikawisimon cî?

3. mâci-matwêhkwâmiw
Q1: matwêhkwâmiw cî awa?
Q2: kiya mâka, kimatwêhkwâmin cî?

4. nisihkâci-waniskâw.
Q1: kawisimow cî awa?
Q2: kiya mâka, kikawisimon cî?

5. ati-kistâpitêhow.
Q1: kistâpitêhow cî awa?
Q2: kiya mâka, kikistâpitêhon cî?

6. pêyahtaki-sîkahow.
Q1: sîkahow cî awa?
Q2: kiya mâka, kisîkahon cî?

7. pêyâhtaki-kâsîhkwêw
Q1: kâsîhkwêw cî awa?
Q2: kiya mâka, kikâsîhkwân cî?

8. mâci-nôhtêhkatêw.
Q1: nôhtêhkwasiw cî awa?
Q2: kiya mâka, kinôhtêhkatân cî?

9. papâsi-kîsitêpow
Q1: kîsitêpow cî awa?
Q2: kiya mâka, kikîsitêpon cî?

10. ati-mîcisow
Q1: mîcisow cî awa?
Q2: kiya mâka, kimîcison cî?

EXERCISE 11. Working with a partner, practise the following questions and answers. **NOTE:** All the answers in these sections are possible.

Q. tânisi awa kâ-itahkamikisit?
What is he doing?
A. nipâw ana.

IF NO ANSWER TO THE QUESTION, ASK:

Q. waniskâw cî awa?
A. i) namôya, nipâw ana.
ii) namôya, namôya waniskâw.
iii) namôya, namôya waniskâw, nipâw ana.

Q. tânisi awa kâ-itahkamikisit?
What is he doing?
A. waniskâw ana.

IF NO ANSWER TO THE QUESTION, ASK:

Q. nipâw cî awa?
A. i) namôya, waniskâw ana.
ii) namôya, namôya nipâw.
iii) namôya, namôya nipâw, waniskâw ana.

Q. tânisi awa kâ-itahkamikisit?
A. kâkîsimow ana.

IF NO ANSWER TO THE QUESTION, ASK:

Q. kâkîsimow cî awa?
A. i) âha, kâkîsimow ana.

Q. tânisi awa kâ-itahkamikisit?
A. kistâpitêhow ana.

IF NO ANSWER TO THE QUESTION, ASK:

Q. kistâpitêhow cî awa?
A. i) âha, kistâpitêhow ana.

Q. tânisi awa kâ-itahkamikisit?
A. kâsîhkwêw ana.

IF NO ANSWER TO THE QUESTION, ASK:

Q. sîkahow cî awa?
A. i) namôya, kâsîhkwêw ana.
ii) namôya, namôya sîkahow.
iii) namôya, namôya sîkahow,
kâsîhkwêw ana.

Q. tânisi awa kâ-itahkamikisit?
A. sîkahow ana.

IF NO ANSWER TO THE QUESTION, ASK:

Q. kâsihkwêw cî awa?
A. i) namôya, sîkahow ana.
ii) namôya, namôya kâsîhkwêw.
iii) namôya, namôya kâsîhkwêw,
sîkahow ana.

Q. tânisi awa kâ-itahkamikisit?
A. postayiwinisêw ana.

IF NO ANSWER TO THE QUESTION, ASK:

Q. kîsitêpow cî awa?
A. i) namôya, postayiwinisêw ana.
ii) namôya, namôya kîsitêpow.
iii) namôya, namôya kîsitêpow,
postayiwinisêw ana.

Q. tânisi awa kâ-itahkamikisit?
A. kîsitêpow ana.

IF NO ANSWER TO THE QUESTION, ASK:

Q. postayiwinisêw cî awa?
A. i) namôya, kîsitêpow ana.
ii) namôya, namôya postayiwinisêw.
iii) namôya, namôya postayiwinisêw,
kîsitêpow ana.

Q. tânisi awa kâ-itahkamikisit?
A. apiw ana.

IF NO ANSWER TO THE QUESTION, ASK:

Q. apiw cî awa?
A. i) âha, apiw ana.

Q. tânisi awa kâ-itahkamikisit?
A. mîcisow ana.

IF NO ANSWER TO THE QUESTION, ASK:

Q. mîcisow cî awa?
A. i) âha, mîcisow ana.

Q. tânisi awa kâ-itahkamikisit?
A. minihkwêw ana.

IF NO ANSWER TO THE QUESTION, ASK:

Q. pasikôw cî awa?
A. i) namôya, minihkwêw ana.
ii) namôya, namôya pasikôw.
iii) namôya, namôya pasikôw,
minihkwêw ana.

Q. tânisi awa kâ-itahkamikisit?
A. pasikôw ana.

IF NO ANSWER TO THE QUESTION, ASK:

Q. minihkwêw cî awa?
A. i) namôya, pasikôw ana.
ii) namôya, namôya minihkwêw.
iii) namôya, namôya minihkwêw,
pasikôw ana.

Q. tânisi awa kâ-itahkamikisit?
A. wayawîw ana.

IF NO ANSWER TO THE QUESTION, ASK:

Q. pimohtêw cî awa?
A. i) namôya, wayawîw ana.
    ii) namôya, namôya pimohtêw.
    iii) namôya, namôya pimohtêw,
       wayawîw ana.

Q. tânisi awa kâ-itahkamikisit?
A. pimohtêw ana.

IF NO ANSWER TO THE QUESTION, ASK:

Q. wayawîw cî awa?
A. i) namôya, pimohtêw ana.
    ii) namôya, namôya wayawîw.
    iii) namôya, namôya wayawîw,
       pimohtêw ana.

Q. tânisi awa kâ-itahkamikisit?
A. pôsiw ana sêhkêpayîsihk.

IF NO ANSWER TO THE QUESTION, ASK:

Q. pôsiw cî awa sêhkêpayîsihk?
A. i) âha, pôsiw ana sêhkêpayîsihk.

Q. tânisi awa kâ-itahkamikisit?
A. pimipayiw ana.

IF NO ANSWER TO THE QUESTION, ASK:

Q. pimipayiw cî awa?
A. i) âha, pimipayiw ana.

Q. tânisi awa kâ-itahkamikisit?
A. kapâw ana sêhkêpayîsihk ohci.

IF NO ANSWER TO THE QUESTION, ASK:

Q. atoskêw cî awa?
A. i) namôya, kapâw ana.
   ii) namôya, namôya atoskêw.
   iii) namôya, namôya atoskêw,
     kapâw ana sêhkêpayîsihk ohci.

Q. tânisi awa kâ-itahkamikisit?
A. atoskêw ana.

IF NO ANSWER TO THE QUESTION, ASK:

Q. kapâw cî awa sêhkêpayîsihk ohci?
A. i) namôya, atoskêw ana.
   ii) namôya, namôya kapâw.
   iii) namôya, namôya kapâw,
     atoskêw ana.

Q. tânisi awa kâ-itahkamikisit.
A. masinahikêw ana.

IF NO ANSWER TO THE QUESTION, ASK:

Q. ayamihcikêw cî awa?
A. i) namôya, masinahikêw ana.
   ii) namôya, namôya ayamihcikêw.
   iii) namôya, namôya ayamihcikêw,
     masinahikêw ana.

Q. tânisi awa kâ-itahkamikisit.
A. ayamihcikêw ana.

IF NO ANSWER TO THE QUESTION, ASK:

Q. masinahikêw cî awa?
A. i) namôya, ayamihcikêw ana.
   ii) namôya, namôya masinahikêw.
   iii) namôya, namôya masinahikêw,
     ayamihcikêw ana.

Q. tânisi awa kâ-itahkamikisit?
A. nîmihitow ana.

IF NO ANSWER TO THE QUESTION, ASK:

Q. nîmihitow cî awa?
A. i) âha, nîmihitow ana.

Q. tânisi awa kâ-itahkamikisit?
A. nikamow ana.

IF NO ANSWER TO THE QUESTION, ASK:

Q. nikamow cî awa?
A. i) âha, nikamow ana.

Q. tânisi awa kâ-itahkamikisit?
A. mâtow ana.

IF NO ANSWER TO THE QUESTION, ASK:

Q. pâhpiw cî awa?
A. i) namôya, mâtow ana.
ii) namôya, namôya pâhpiw.
iii) namôya, namôya pâhpiw,
mâtow ana.

Q. tânisi awa kâ-itahkamikisit?
A. pâhpiw ana.

IF NO ANSWER TO THE QUESTION, ASK:

Q. mâtow cî awa?
A. i) namôya, pâhpiw ana.
ii) namôya, namôya mâtow.
iii) namôya, namôya mâtow,
pâhpiw ana.

Q. tânisi awa kâ-itahkamikisit?
A. sêsâwîw ana.

IF NO ANSWER TO THE QUESTION, ASK:

Q. pimipahtâw cî awa?
A. i) namôya, sêsâwîw ana.
ii) namôya, namôya pimipahtâw.
iii) namôya, namôya pimipahtâw,
sêsâwîw ana.

Q. tânisi awa kâ-itahkamikisit?
A. pimipahtâw ana.

IF NO ANSWER TO THE QUESTION, ASK:

Q. sêsâwîw cî awa?
A. i) namôya, pimipahtâw ana.
ii) namôya, namôya sêsâwîw.
iii) namôya, namôya sêsâwîw,
pimipahtâw ana.

Q. tânisi awa kâ-itahkamikisit?
A. kîwêw ana.

IF NO ANSWER TO THE QUESTION, ASK:

Q. kîwêw cî awa?
A. i) âha, kîwêw ana.

Q. tânisi awa kâ-itahkamikisit?
A. pîhtokwêw ana.

IF NO ANSWER TO THE QUESTION, ASK:

Q. pîhtokwêw cî awa?
A. i) âha, pîhtokwêw ana.

Q. tânisi awa kâ-itahkamikisit?
A. nôhtêhkatêw ana.

IF NO ANSWER TO THE QUESTION, ASK:

Q. kisîpêkiyâkanêw cî awa?
A. i) namôya, nôhtêhkatêw ana.
   ii) namôya, namôya kisîpêkiyâkanêw.
   iii) namôya, namôya kisîpêkiyâkanêw,
      nôhtêhkatêw ana.

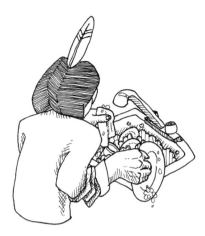

Q. tânisi awa kâ-itahkamikisit?
A. kisîpêkiyâkanêw ana.

IF NO ANSWER TO THE QUESTION, ASK:

Q. nôhtêhkatêw cî awa?
A. i) namôya, kisîpêkiyâkanêw ana.
   ii) namôya, namôya nôhtêhkatêw.
   iii) namôya, namôya nôhtêhkatêw,
      kisîpêkiyâkanêw ana.

Q. tânisi awa kâ-itahkamikisit?
A. kâsîyâkanêw ana.

IF NO ANSWER TO THE QUESTION, ASK:

Q. nôhtêhkwasiw cî awa?
A. i) namôya, kâsîyâkanêw ana.
   ii) namôya, namôya nôhtêhkwasiw.
   iii) namôya, namôya nôhtêhkwasiw,
      kâsîyâkanêw ana.

Q. tânisi awa kâ-itahkamikisit?
A. nôhtêhkwasiw ana.

IF NO ANSWER TO THE QUESTION, ASK:

Q. kâsîyâkanêw cî awa?
A. i) namôya, nôhtêhkwasiw ana.
   ii) namôya, namôya kâsîyâkanêw.
   iii) namôya, namôya kâsîyâkanêw,
      nôhtêhkwasiw ana.

Q. tânisi awa kâ-itahkamikisit?
A. kêtayiwinisêw ana.

IF NO ANSWER TO THE QUESTION, ASK:

Q. kêtayiwinisêw cî awa?
A. i) âha, kêtayiwinisêw ana.

Q. tânisi awa kâ-itahkamikisit?
A. kisîpêkinastêw ana.

IF NO ANSWER TO THE QUESTION, ASK:

Q. kisîpêkinastêw cî awa?
A. i) âha, kisîpêkinastêw ana.

Q. tânisi awa kâ-itahkamikisit?
A. kawisimow ana.

IF NO ANSWER TO THE QUESTION, ASK:

Q. matwêhkwâmiw cî awa?
A. i) namôya, kawisimow ana.
　 ii) namôya, namôya matwêhkwâmiw.
　 iii) namôya, namôya matwêhkwâmiw,
　　　 kawisimow ana.

Q. tânisi awa kâ-itahkamikisit?
A. matwêhkwâmiw ana.

IF NO ANSWER TO THE QUESTION, ASK:

Q. kawisimow cî awa?
A. i) namôya, matwêhkwâmiw ana.
　 ii) namôya, namôya kawisimow.
　 iii) namôya, namôya kawisimow,
　　　 matwêhkwâmiw ana.

4.4 CHAPTER FOUR REVIEW

VAI – IMPERATIVE

IMPERATIVE	NEGATIVE IMPERATIVE	DELAYED IMPERATIVE
2. _____	2. êkâwiya _____	2. _____ hkan
2P. _____ k	2P êkâwiya _____ k	2P. _____ hkêk
21. _____ tân	21. êkâwiya _____ tân	21. _____ hkahk

VAI – INDICATIVE, CONJUNCT, AND FUTURE CONDITIONAL FORMS

INDICATIVE	CONJUNCT	FUTURE CONDITIONAL
1. ni _____ n	1. ê- _____ yân	1. _____ yâni
2. ki _____ n	2. ê- _____ yan	2. _____ yani
3. _____ w	3. ê- _____ t	3. _____ ci
3' _____ yiwa	3'. ê- _____ yit	3'. _____ yici
1P. ni _____ nân	1P. ê- _____ yâhk	1P. _____ yâhki
21. ki _____ naw	21. ê- _____ yahk	21. _____ yahki
2P. ki _____ nâwâw	2P. ê- _____ yêk	2P. _____ yêko
3P _____ wak	3P. ê- _____ cik	3P. _____ twâwi
3'P _____ yiwa	3'P. ê- _____ yit	3'P. _____ yici

TENSE INDICATORS: these apply to all verbs for the Indicative and Conjunct forms, except for the future definite, which is not used in the Conjunct:

Past Tense:	kî-

Future Intentional: wî-

Future Definite: ka- for 1st and 2nd person actors
ta- for 3rd person actors

CHAPTER FIVE
INANIMATE INTRANSITIVE VERBS

5. INANIMATE INTRANSITIVE VERBS

Inanimate Intransitive verbs (VII) include weather terms, seasons, days of the week, and times of day. VIIs have an indefinite actor and this actor/subject is always the 3rd person "it".

VIIs do not undergo conjugation like the Animate Intransitive verbs (VAIs), but they can go into various tenses and appear in the Indicative Mood as well as in the Conjunct Mood.

5.1 WEATHER TERMS

The following are some of the more common Inanimate Intransitive Verbs (VII) that deal with weather set out in the Indicative, Conjunct, and Future Conditional:

INDICATIVE	ENGLISH	CONJUNCT	FUTURE CONDITIONAL
kimiwan	*It rains*	ê-kimiwahk	kimiwahki
yôtin	*It is windy*	ê-yôtihk	yôtihki
sîkipêstâw	*It is pouring*	ê-sîkipêstâk	sîkipêstâki
kimiwasin	*It is drizzling*	ê-kimiwasik	kimiwasiki
mispon	*It snows*	ê-mispok	mispoki
pîwan	*It drifts (blizzard)*	ê-pîwahk	pîwahki
sôhkiyowêw	*It is very windy*	ê-sôhkiyowêk	sôhkiyowêki
wâsêskwan	*It is clear/sunny*	ê-wâsêskwahk	wâsêskwahki
yîkwaskwan	*It is cloudy*	ê-yîkwaskwahk	yîkwaskwahki
âhkwatin	*It freezes*	ê-âhkwatihk	âhkwatihki
saskan	*It melts (chinook)*	ê-saskahk	saskahki
tihkitêw	*It melts*	ê-tihkitêk	tihkitêki
kisitêw	*It is hot*	ê-kisitêk	kisitêki
kisâstêw	*It is hot*	ê-kisâstêk	kisâstêki
kisinâw	*It is very cold*	ê-kisinâk	kisinâki
tahkâyâw	*It is cold*	ê-tahkâyâk	tahkâyâki
kîsapwêyâw	*It is warm*	ê-kîsapwêyâk	kîsapwêyâki

From the above we should be able to formulate rules on how to go from the **Indicative Mood** to the **Conjunct Mood** and from the **Conjunct** to the **Future Conditional.**

RULES: To go from the **Indicative Mood** to the **Conjunct Mood** of VIIs:
a) add "**ê-**" at the beginning;
b) drop last consonant of the Indicative mood, then:
  i) add "**k**" if the consonant dropped is "**w**"
  ii) add "**hk**" if the consonant dropped is "**n**" (there are a few exceptions to this rule)

To go from the **Conjunct Mood** to the **Future Conditional**:
a) Drop the "**ê-**" from the beginning
b) then add "**i**" at the end

Future conditionals refer to "if" or "when" events occur; if it is "when", then the word "ispîhk – *when*" precedes the future conditional form; otherwise, it is an "iffy" situation.

EXERCISES

EXERCISE 1.
1) Translate the following sentences;
2) use **cî** to ask questions of each other;
3) use the other question dealing with weather "tânisi kâ-isiwêpahk – *What's the weather like?*", using the following pictures (the first picture gives an example):

miyo-kîsikâw.

kisâstêw.

1) It's a nice day.
2) miyo-kîsikâw cî? – *Is it a nice day?*
3) tânisi kâ-isiwêpahk? – *What's the weather like?*

sîkipêstâw.

kîsapwêyâw.

kisitêw.

kimiwan.

wâsêskwan.

kisinâw.

tahkâyâw.

sôhkiyôwêw.

yôtin.

ati-yîkwaskwan.

EXERCISE 2. Provide what is required of these verbs:

1. "kimiwan = *It rains*"

If it rains _____

2. "kî-yôtin = *it was windy*"

Conjunct, future intentional: _____

3. "kî-wâsêskwan = *It was sunny*"

It will be sunny. _____

4. "ta-yîkwaskwan = *It will be cloudy*"

It was cloudy. _____

EXERCISE 3. Answer the following questions:

a. wâsêskwan cî ôta?

_____

b. kimiwan cî ôta?

_____

c. tânisi kâ-isiwêpahk ôta?

_____

d. yîkwaskwan cî ôta?

_____

e. tânisi kâ-isiwêpahk ôta?

_____

f. kimiwan cî ôta?

_____

5.2 FUTURE CONDITIONALS: VIIs

Future conditional forms refer to possible future happenings as in "if (something) happens". The easiest way of getting the future conditional form is to drop the "**ê**" from the beginning of the conjunct mood then add an "**i**" at the end as shown below:

ENGLISH	INDICATIVE	CONJUNCT	FUTURE CONDITIONAL
It is spring	sîkwan	ê-sîkwahk	sîkwahki
It is summer	nîpin	ê-nîpihk	nîpihki
It is fall	takwâkin	ê-takwâkik	takwâkiki
It is winter	pipon	ê-pipohk	pipohki

From the above data we can formulate the following chart:

INDICATIVE	CONJUNCT	FUTURE CONDITIONAL
VII ending in consonant preceded by a long vowel	Add **ê-** at the beginning, drop last consonant then add **k**: ê-_____ **k**	Drop **ê-** from the beginning of Conjunct, then add **i** at the end _____ **i**
VII ending in consonant preceded by a short vowel*	Add **ê-** at the beginning, drop last consonant then add **hk**: ê-_____ **hk**	Drop **ê-** from the beginning of Conjunct, then add **i** at the end _____ **i**

*There are three VIIs that do not follow this rule:
otâkosin – *It is late afternoon/early evening*; mispon – *It is snowing*; takwâkin – *It is fall*.

EXERCISES

EXERCISE 1. Translate the following sentences: the VAIs are in the future tense and the VIIs that follow are in the future conditional form:

1. *We will go inside if it rains.* _____

2. *I'm going outside if it is warm.* _____

3. *They are going to go skating if it is cold.* _____

4. *Are you going to go skiing if it snows?* _____

5. *She is not going to go canoeing if it is very windy.* _____

VAIS FOR THE ABOVE: wayawî – *go outside*; pîhtokwê – *go inside*; sôniskwâtahikê – *skate*; nîpawi-sôskwaciwêyâpoko – *ski (downhill)*; pôsi – *go boating/canoeing/get on board*.

Future conditionals indicate a possible happening in the future. Future conditionals occur in compound sentences made up of an independent clause (usually in the indicative but can include delayed imperatives) and a subordinate clause (which include the **ê-form**, the **kâ-form** [relative clause marker], the **ta-form** [infinitive clause marker] or the future conditional). Independent clauses can stand on their own to make complete sentences while subordinate clauses need the independent clause to be grammatically correct.

There are a number of subordinate clauses in Cree. Below are the more common types of subordinate clauses:

a)   The **ê-form**: this form of subordinate clause is often referred to as the conjunct mood. Use the ê-form after the following words:
    ayisk – *because*
    cikêmâ – *because*
    nama cî mâka – *isn't it so*

b)   The **kâ-form**: this form of subordinate clause occurs most often in content questions or in relative clauses that begin with "ispîhk – *when*."

c)   The **ta-form**: this form of subordinate clause often operates the same way as an infinite. Like the infinitive in English, this form is not marked for tense but unlike the English infinite which is not marked for person, the Cree 'infinitive' form is marked for person.

d)   The future conditional form.

Conditional clauses in English are marked with the presence of "if" in the clause; this is not the case in Cree. In Cree, the verb marking the conditional clause has the same structure as the verb marking a time clause. Consider the following:

1a.   ispîhk ati-kimiwahki kika-kîwânaw.
    When it begins to rain we will go home.

1b.   kîspin ati-kimiwahki kika-kîwânaw.
    If it begins to rain we will go home.

In comparing the sentence structure, one will note that the only difference is in the use of "ispîhk" in 1a and "kîspin" in 1b. 1a, marked by "ispîhk (*when*)", is the time clause: as such, it indicates that something is definitely going to happen. 1b, marked by "kîspin (*if*)", is the conditional clause: as such, there is a possibility of something happening, but only a possibility. When "ispîhk" and "kîspin" are used within a sentence structure, one can tell which is the time clause and which is the conditional clause. However, more often one would encounter a sentence such as:

1c.   kimiwahki kika-kîwânaw.

How would one know if this were a time clause or a conditional clause? In answering that question, consider some further examples:

2a. sôhki-atoskêyâni nika-ati-nihtâ-nêhiyawân.
2b. wîpac waniskâyâni nika-pê-itohtân kihci-kiskinwahamâtowikamikohk.
2c. mistahi mîcisoyani kika-kîspon.
2d. pwâtisimoci kika-mamihcihikonaw.

From 2a to 2d there are examples which can, at first glance, be taken as either a time clause with an "ispîhk (*when*)" understood to be there, or a conditional clause with a "kîspin (*if*)" understood to be there. This assumption, though perfectly logical given that the first verb form is in the same structure as in 1a and 1b above (i.e., all the first verbs end in an "i"), is erroneous. Consider yet another example:

2e. kîhtwâm kika-wâpamitonaw pa-pimâtisiyahki.

In this example the conditional verb form is in the last position. However, the ending "i" is the same as it is in all previous examples. Again there is an absence of both "ispîhk" and "kîspin", but to a fluent Cree speaker there is no question as to what is meant in this, and in the other examples. 2e essentially embodies the Cree philosophy of life which is to be lived "one day at a time". In other words, one does not assume that life continues further than that one day in which one is living; hence, the respect for life and the value it has is evident in conditional clauses. One need not say "kîspin" in conditional clauses, because "kîspin" is understood to be present in such clauses. If one meant "ispîhk" then one would say "ispîhk."

To sum up the difference between time clauses and conditional clauses, note that "kîspin" is optional and employed only for emphasis, while "ispîhk" is obligatory. The verb forms are nevertheless similar. With that in mind, here then are the translations of 2a-2e:

2a. *If I work hard* (conditional clause) – sôhki-atoskêyâni
     I will begin to be able to speak Cree (result clause) – nika-ati-nihtâ-nêhiyawân.

2b. *If I get up from bed early* (conditional clause) – wîpac waniskâyâni
     I will come (result clause) *to the university* – nika-pê-itohtân kihcikiskinwahamâtowikamikohk.

2c. *If you eat lots* (conditional clause) – mistahi mîcisoyani
     you will be full (result clause) – kika-kîspon.

2d. *If he dances pow-wow* (conditional clause) – pwâtisimoci
     he will make us proud (result clause) – kika-mamihcihikonaw.

2e. *We will see each other again* (result clause) – kîhtwâm kika-wâpamitonaw
     if we are alive and well (conditional clause). – pa-pimâtisiyahki.

It does not matter if the result clause (i.e., the event that could happen if a certain condition is met) precedes the conditional clause (i.e., the condition that must happen if the result clause is to come true) or vice versa, as is evident in example 2e. Incidentally, 2e is the standard parting phrase in Cree, similar to the "good-bye" in English.

RULES:

RESULT CLAUSE	CONDITIONAL CLAUSE
Must be in some **future tense** in either the **Indicative Mood** or **Conjunct Mood**. The **Delayed Imperative** form can also serve as a result clause.	The Cree word for "if" – "*kîspin*" – is optional, but can be included for emphasis.

MAKING FUTURE CONDITIONALS

1. INTRANSITIVE INANIMATE VERBS (VIIs):

a) start with Indicative Mood.

b) drop last consonant:

c) Add: i) "**ki**" at the end if last consonant dropped was a "**w**".

E.G.:   INDICATIVE: tipiskâw – *it is night/dark*.

         Drop w →   tipiskâ_

         Check vowel: **â** is long so add **ki**:

                        tipiskâ**ki** – *"if it is night/dark"* (literally)
                                         or *"tonight"* (common usage)

ii) add "**hki**" at the end if last consonant dropped was an "**n**".

E.G.:   INDICATIVE: kimiwan – *it rains*.

         Drop n →   kimiwa_

         Check vowel: **a** is short so add **hki**:

                        kimiwa**hki** – *if it rains*.

2. ANIMATE INTRANSITIVE VERBS (VAIs):

a) Use the Conjunct Mood;

     VERB STEM: atoskê – *work*

     CONJ. MD.:   ê-atoskêyân – *(As) I am working*.

b) Drop the ê from the Conjunct Mood form but retain the endings;
                  _atoskêyân

c) Add: i) "**i**" at the end of 1, 2, 1P and 21

           atoskêyân**i** – *If I am working*.

           atoskêyan**i** – *If you are working*.

           atoskêyâhk**i** – *If we (exclusive) are working*.

           atoskêyahk**i** – *If we (inclusive) are working*.

ii) "**o**" at the end of 2P

           atoskêyêk**o** – *If you (plural) are working*.

iii) "**i**" at the end of 3, 3' and 3'P but first change the last "**t**" to "**c**":

           atoskê**ci** – *If she/he/it is working*.

           atoskêyi**ci** – *If her/his___ is working*.

           atoskêyi**ci** – *If their ___ is working*.

d) For 3P only, start with the verb stem then add "**twâwi**" at the end:

           atoskê**twâwi** – *If they are working*.

5.3 SEASONS

Seasons, in Cree, are also VIIs. The chart below lists the seasons in various forms:

ENGLISH	PAST SEASON	PRESENT SEASON: Indicative	PRESENT SEASON: Conjunct	FUTURE CONDITIONAL
It is spring. (ice break-up)	sîkwanohk Last spring	sîkwan	ê-sîkwahk	sîkwahki If/When it is spring
It is late spring.	miyoskamik Last late spring	miyoskamin	ê-miyoskamik	miyoskamiki If/When it is late spring
It is summer.	nîpinohk Last summer	nîpin	ê-nîpihk	nîpihki If/When it is summer
It is fall.	takwâkohk Last fall	takwâkin	ê-takwâkik	takwâkiki If/When it is fall
It is early winter. (ice freeze-up)	mikiskohk. Last early winter.	mikiskon.	ê-mikiskohk	mikiskohki If/When it is early winter
It is winter.	piponohk Last winter	pipon	ê-pipohk	pipohki If/When it is winter

As you can see, seasons can be in both the Indicative and the Conjunct forms, including the Future Conditonal forms. Both the Indicative and Conjunct forms can use various preverbs, as well as go into various tenses. Both the past season forms above as well as the Future Conditional forms cannot go into various tenses since they already indicate a temporal reality; one deals with past seasons and the other deals with upcoming seasons. Below are some sentences to clarify how these differ from regular past tense forms and regular future tense forms of the seasons.

1) *Last fall the children started school early.*
   takwâkohk awâsisak kî-mâci-kiskinwahamâkosiwak wîpac.

2) *It was fall when the children came back to school.*
   kî-takwâkiniyiw* ispîhk awâsisak kâ-kî-pê-kiskinwahamâkosicik.**

3) *In the fall the children will start school early.*
   takwâkiniyiki awâsisak wîpac ta-mâci-kiskinwahamâkosiwak.

4) *It will be fall, anytime now the children will start school.*
   ta-takwâkin, pikwîspî êkwa awâsisak ta-mâci-kiskinwahamâkosiwak.

*This form here, and in number 3, is used when the subject of the main clause is 3rd person as is the case here; otherwise it would have been in the following forms: kî-takwâkin and takwâkiki.

** Any verb that follows "ispîhk – *when*" will use the conjunct mood/relative clause marker "kâ-" at the beginning with the regular conjunct mood endings, unless the verb is a future conditional.

5.3.A VITAL STATISTICS I

WORDS

niya – *I/me*   itahtopiponê – *be of a certain age* (VAI)
ohci – *from*   isiyihkâso – *be called/named* (VAI)
kiya – *you*   tânisi – *Greetings/Hello/how*
tânitê – *where*   tânitahto – *how many*

TEXT

Fill in the blanks below with your own information:

tânisi. – *Greetings!*

_____ nitisiyihkâson.   *My name is* _____.

_____ ohci niya kayahtê.   *I am from* _____ *originally.*

_____ nititahtopiponân.   *I am* _____ *years old.*

GRAMMAR

WORD ORDER: Pertinent information is given first, followed by the verb in its inflected form.

ANIMATE INTRANSITIVE VERBS:

- Animate Intransitive Verb (VAI - above) stems appear as orders given to one person (second person singular form of the Imperative);

- VAIs in the inflected form with a first person subject (*I/me*) begin with "**ni**" and end in "**n**" (ki____n – for second person), with the verb stem going in between;

- if a VAI stem begins with a vowel, then the person indicator (**ni**) is followed by a connecting "**t**": *Shaking-Spear* nitisiyihkâson. – *My name is Shaking-Spear.*

- if a VAI stem ends in "**ê**", then that "**ê**" must be changed to "**â**" in the inflected form when the subject is in the first person (singular and plural) or in the second person (singular and plural): nistomitanaw nikotwâs(ik)osâp nititahtopiponân. – *I am thirty-six years old.*

QUESTIONS

1. tânisi? – *Hello/How are you?* (ANS: namôya nânitaw ("*fine*") or repeat "tânisi.")
2. tânisi kitisiyihkâson? – *How are you called (what is your name)?*
3. tânitahtopiponêyan? – *How old are you?*
4. tânitê ohci kiya kayahtê? – *Where are you from originally?*

DO: Get students to write out a dialogue using 8" × 5" cards. Once the cards are prepared students can then pair up, doing the dialogue together. Each card has a section spoken by A and B and includes the following information:

CARD ONE:
> A. tânisi?
>
> B. namôya nânitaw, kiya mâka?

CARD TWO:
> A. pêyakwan. _____ nitisiyihkâson. kiya mâka, tânisi kitisiyihkâson?
>
> B. _____ nitisiyihkâson.

CARD THREE:
> A. _____ ohci niya kayahtê. kiya mâka, tânitê ohci kiya kayahtê?
>
> B. _____ ohci niya kayahtê.

CARD FOUR:
> A. _____ nititahtopiponân. kiya mâka, tânitahtopiponêyan?
>
> B. _____ nititahtopiponân.

CARD FIVE:
> A. okiskinwahamâkan niya. kiya mâka, okiskinwahamâkan cî kîsta?
> B. âha, okiskinwahamâkan nîsta.

After each of the pairs have done the above dialogue, ask the other students about the information given by the two who just finished:

1) tânisi awa isiyihkâsow? (point to one of the students).

2) tânitê awa (*student's name*) ohci kayahtê?

3) tânitahtopiponêt (*student's name*)?

4) okiskinwahamâkan cî awa (*student's name*)?

5.3.B VITAL STATISTICS II

WORDS

mêkwâc – *at this time*
wîki – *reside* (VAI)
pê- – *come* (PV)
ati- – *start* (PV)
sîkwan – *It is spring.* (VII)
nîpin – *It is summer.* (VII)

nihtâwiki – *be born* (VAI)
ohpiki – *grow* (VAI)
kiskinwahamâkosi – *be in school/class* (VAI)
pipon – *It is winter.* (VII)
takwâkin – *It is fall.* (VII)
kî- – *indicates past tense*

TEXT

Fill in the blanks below with appropriate information:

1. _____ nikî-nihtâwikin.   *I was born at* _____.

2. kî-ati-pipon.   *It was at the start of winter.*

3. _____ nikî-pê-ohpikin.   *I was raised in* _____.

4. _____ nikî-kiskinwahamâkosin.   *I went to school in* _____.

5. mêkwâc _____ niwîkin.   *I live in* _____ *at this time.*

GRAMMAR

PAST TENSE INDICATOR: The past tense indicator **"kî-"** comes after the person indicator and before a preverb. In the absence of a person indicator or preverb the past tense indicator is placed before the verb stem:

> **Present tense:** nikiskinwahamâkosin. – *I am in school/class.*
> **Past tense:** nikî-kiskinwahamâkosin. – *I was in school.*

PREVERBS: Preverbs are placed before the main verb (verb stem). Preverbs are like adverbs in English as they modify the meaning of the verb.

> **Present tense:** niwîkin ôta. – *I live/reside here.*
> **With preverb:** nipê-wîkin ôta. – *I come to live/reside here.*
> **Past tense:** nikî-wîkin ôta. – *I lived/resided here.*
> **With preverb:** nikî-pê-wîkin ôta. – *I came to live here.*

INANIMATE INTRANSITIVE VERBS: These verbs (VII) deal with seasons, times of day, days of the week, some colours and all weather terms. They cannot be conjugated like the VAIs, but they do take on all tenses and can use preverbs.

STANDARD VERB STRUCTURE: The following is the standard verb structure for any verb:

Person Indicator	Tense Indicator	Preverb	Verb stem	Ending

QUESTIONS AND ANSWERS

Students pair up to ask each other these questions. The person answering will then ask "kiya mâka? – *how about you?*" after answering.

QUESTIONS	ANSWERS
tânisi? *Hello, how are you?*	namôya nânitaw. kiya mâka? *Fine.*
tânisi kitisiyihkâson? *What is your name?*	_____ nitisiyihkâson. kiya mâka? *My name is* _____.
tânitahtopiponêyan? *How old are you?*	_____ nititahtopiponân. kiya mâka? *I am* _____ *years old.*
tânitê ohci kiya kayahtê ? *Where are you from originally?*	_____ ohci niya kayahtê. kiya mâka? *I am originally from* _____.
tânitê kikî-nihtâwikin? *Where were you born?*	_____ nikî-nihtâwikin. kiya mâka? *I was born in* _____.
tânisi kî-ihkin kâ-kî-nihtâwikiyan? *What season were you born in?*	(Any season in the past tense with or without a preverb.) kiya mâka?
tânitê kikî-pê-ohpikin? *Where were you raised?*	_____ nikî-pê-ohpikin. kiya mâka? *I came to be raised in* _____.
tânitê kikî-pê-kiskinwahamâkosin? *Where did you go to school?*	_____ nikî-pê-kiskinwahamâkosin. kiya mâka? *I went to school in* _____.
tânitê mêkwâc kiwîkin ? *Where do you live now?*	_____ mêkwâc niwîkin. kiya mâka? *I live in* _____ *now.*
nîpin cî mêkwâc? *Is it summer now?*	namôya, takwâkin. *No, it is fall.*

NOTE: if the above information exchanged is the same, answer "nîsta mîna – *me too!*"

EXERCISES

EXERCISE 1. Place the following into the past tense: The preverb "pê- – *come*" shows a process of time from the past to the present.

1. nîsitanaw nititahtopiponân. _____

2. *Saskatoon* ninihtâwikin. _____

3. *Regina* nipê-ohpikin. _____

4. *Regina* mîna nikiskinwahamâkosin. _____

5. *Saskatoon* niwîkin. _____

6. pipon. _____

7. sîkwan. _____

8. takwâkin. _____

9. nîpin. _____

10. namôya sîkwan, pipon. _____

5.3.C VITAL STATISTICS III

WORDS

ê-akimiht – *as it is counted*
kêko – *which*
akimâw – *it is counted*

pîsim – *month/sun*
tâniyikohk – *how much*
mâna – *usually*

TEXT

Fill in the blanks with your own information:

1. _____ akimâw awa pîsim. *It is the* _____ *of this month.*

2. _____ mâna ê-akimiht nitipiskên. *I have a birthday in* _____.

3. _____ ê-akimiht _____ mâna nitipiskên.

    I have a birthday on the _____ *of* _____.

QUESTIONS

Answer the following questions:

1) kêko pîsim awa akimâw mêkwâc? *Which month is counted now?*

_____

2) tâniyikohk awa pîsim akimâw mêkwâc? *What is the date now?*

_____

3) kêko pîsim mâna kitipiskên? *Which month is your birthday on?*

_____

4) tâniyikohk ê-akimiht êwako pîsim kitipiskên? *What date of that month is your birthday?*

_____

5) kêko pîsim mâna kimâci-kiskinwahamâkosin? *Which month do you usually start school?*

_____

6) tânispîhk mâna kâ-manitowi-kîsikâk? *When is it Christmas?*

_____

7) tânispîhk mâna kâ-ocêhtowi-kîsikâk? *When is New Year's Day?*

_____

8) tânispîhk kâ-okâwîmâwi-kîsikâk anohc kâ-askîwik? *When is Mother's Day this year?*

_____

9) tânispîhk kâ-ohtâwîmâwi-kîsikâk anohc kâ-askîwik? *When is Father's Day this year?*

_____

10) tânispîhk mâna kâ-cîpayi-tipiskâk? *When is Halloween night?*

_____

ADDITIONAL WORDS

tânispîhk – *when*
mâna – *usually*
cîpayi-tipiskâw – *Halloween*
anohc kâ-askîwik – *this year*

manitowi-kîsikâw – *Christmas*
ocêhtowi-kîsikâw – *New Year's Day*
okâwîmâwi-kîsikâw – *Mother's Day*
ohtâwîmâwi-kîsikâw – *Father's Day*

5.3.D DIALOGUE FIVE

A: tânisi* (name)
B: tânisi (name)

A: anohc tipiskam nitânis!**
B: kah, tânitahtopiponêt êkwa?

A: nîsitanaw pêyakosâp itahtopinonêw.
   kiya mâka, tânitahtopiponêyan?
B: kêkâ-nisto-mitanaw niya nititahtopiponân.

A: tânispîhk kâ-tipiskaman?
B: kêkâ-nîsitanaw ê-akimiht*** mikisiwi-pîsim.

A: *Hello* (name)
B: *Hello* (name)

A: *Today is my daughter's birthday!*
B: *Oh, so how old is she now?*

A: *She is twenty-one years old.*
   How about you, how old are you?
B: *I am twenty-nine years old.*

A: *When is your birthday?*
B: *On February 19th.*

VOCABULARY

anohc – *today*
kah – *oh*
êkwa – *now*
tânispîhk – *when*
kêkâ-nîsitanaw – *nineteen*
kêkâ-nistomitanaw – *twenty-nine*
mikisiwi-pîsim – *February*

tipiskam – *She/he has a birthday.*
tânitahtopiponêyan – *How old are you?*
nîsitanaw pêyakosâp – *twenty-one*
nititahtopiponân – *I am of that age.*
kâ-tipiskaman – *You have a birthday.*
ê-akimiht – *it is counted*
kititahtopiponân – *You are of that age.*

NOTES

*The greeting "tânisi" can be answered in a variety of ways: it can mean "*How are you?*" to which you can answer as "namôya nânitaw" meaning "*I am fine*". Or it can mean "*Hello*" to which you can answer as in the above dialogue "tânisi – *Hello.*"

**The phrase "tipiskam" meaning "*She/he has a birthday*" is the third person indicative mood form of the transitive inanimate verb – class 1 (VTI-1) "tipiska – *have a birthday*". The same verb appears on the second last line in the above dialogue in a relative clause (conjunct mood), second person form, as "kâ-tipiskaman". The last "a" in the verb stem "tipiska" changes to "ê" for the first and second person forms of the indicative mood. This rule applies to all VTI-1s in the indicative mood.

***The formula for saying the date is to say the date first, then the phrase meaning "ê-akimiht – *It is counted*", followed by the month, as in the above dialogue. "kêkâ-nistomitanaw ê-akimiht mikisiwi-pîsim."

DO the above dialogue with a classmate and substitute the phrase "kêkâ-nistomitanaw ê-akimiht mikisiwi-pîsim" with your own birthdate.

REVIEW: VITAL STATISTICS FOR 1ST , 2ND, AND 3RD PERSON FORMS

1st Person - talking about yourself	2nd person - talking to someone: usually used in questions	3rd person - talking about someone else	3rd person obviative - talking about someone else's someone/thing
1. tânisi kitisiyihkâson? _____ nitisiyihkâson.	 _____ kitisiyihkâson.	tânisi isiyihkâsow kitôtêm? _____ isiyihkâsow nitôtêm.	tânisi isiyihkâsoyiwa otôtêma? _____ isiyihkâsoyiwa.
2. tânitê kayahtê ohci kiya? _____ kayahtê ohci niya.	 _____ kayahtê ohci kiya.	tânitê kayahtê ohci wiya? _____ kayahtê ohci wiya.	 _____ kayahtê ohci.
3. tânitê mêkwâc kiwîkin? (Place) mêkwâc niwîkin.	 _____ mêkwâc kiwîkin.	tânitê mêkwâc wîkiw wiya? _____ mêkwâc wîkiw.	tânitê mêkwâc wîkiyiwa _____? _____ mêkwâc wîkiyiwa.
4. okiskinwahamâkan niya.	okiskinwahamâkan kiya.	okiskinwahamâkan wiya.	okiskinwahamâkan wiya.
5. tânitahtopiponêyan? _____ nititahtopiponân.	 _____ kititahtopiponân.	tânitahtopiponêt wiya? _____ itahtopiponêw.	tânitahtopiponêyit _____? _____ itahtopiponêyiwa.
6. kêko pîsim mâna kitipiskên? _____ mâna nitipiskên.	 _____ mâna kitipiskên.	kêko pîsimwa mâna tipiskam wiya? _____wa mâna tipiskam.	kêko pîsimwa mâna tipiskamiyiwa _____? _____wa mâna tipiskamiyiwa.
7. tâniyikohk ê-akimiht êwako pîsim mâna kitipiskên? _____ ê-akimiht _____ mâna nitipiskên.	 _____ ê-akimiht _____ mâna kitipiskên.	tâniyikohk ê-akimimiht êwakoni pîsimwa mâna tipiskam wiya? _____ ê-aki**mi**miht _____ mâna tipiskam.	tâniyikohk ê-akimimiht êwakoni pîsimwa mâna tipiskamiyiwa? _____ ê-aki**mi**miht _____ mâna tipiskamiyiwa.
8. tânisi kî-ihkin ispîhk kâ-kî-nihtâwikiyan? kî-(season) ispîhk kâ-kî-nihtâwikiyân..	kî-(season) ispîhk kâ-kî-nihtâwikiyan.	tânisi kî-ihkin ispîhk kâ-kî-nihtâwikit wiya? kî-(season)iyiw ispîhk kâ-kî-nihtâwikit.	tânisi kî-ihkiniyiw ispîhk kâ-kî-nihtâwikiyit ___? kî-(season)iyiw ispîhk kâ-kî-nihtâwikiyit.

9. tânitê kikî-nihtâwikin? (*Place*) nikî-nihtâwikin.	_____ kikî-nihtâwikin.	tânitê kî-nihtâwikiw wiya? _____ kî-nihtâwikiw.	tânitê kî-nihtâwikiyiwa _____? _____ kî-nihtâwikiyiwa.
10. tânitê kikî-pê-ohpikin? (*Place*) nikî-pê-ohpikin.	(*Place*) kikî-pê-ohpikin.	tânitê kî-pê-ohpikiw wiya? (*Place*) kî-pê-ohpikiw.	tânitê kî-pê-ohpikiyiwa _____? (*Place*) kî-pê-ohpikiyiwa.
11. tânitê kikî-pê-kiskinwahamâkosin? (*Place*) nikî-pê-kiskinwahamâkosin.	_____ kikî-pê-kiskinwahamâkosin.	tânitê kî-pê-kiskinwahamâkosiw wiya? _____ kî-pê-kiskinwahamâkosiw.	tânitê kî-pê-kiskinwahamâkosiyiwa? kî-pê-kiskinwahamâkosiyiwa.
12. tânitê mêkwâc kikiskinwahamâkosin? mêkwâc *Regina* nikiskinwahamâkosin.	mêkwâc *Regina* kikiskinwahamâkosin.	tânitê mêkwâc kiskinwahamâkosiw wiya? mêkwâc *Regina* kiskinwahamâkosiw.	tânitê mêkwâc kiskinwahamâkosiyiwa? mêkwâc *Regina* kiskinwahamâkosiyiwa. _____

EXERCISES

EXERCISE 1. Translate the following English sentences into Cree:

VOCABULARY

niska – *goose* (NA)
kôna – *snow* (NA)
namôya – *no/negator*
kaskatin – *ice freezes* (VII)
namôya osâm – *not very*
oskana kâ-asastêki – *Regina*
sîkwan – *It is spring.*
nîpin – *It is summer.*
takwâkin – *It is fall.*
pipon – *It is winter.*
miyoskamin – *It is late spring.*
mikiskâw – *It is early winter.*

wâstêpakâw – *leaves change colour* (VII)
tihkiso – *melt* (VAI)
nîpiy – *leaf* (NI)
pimihamo – *migrate* (VAI)
pê-itohtê – *come* (VAI)
iyikohk – *until*
sîkwanohk – *last spring*
nîpinohk – *last summer*
takwâkohk – *last fall*
piponohk – *last winter*
miyoskamik. – *last late spring*
mikiskohk. – *last early winter*

kwâskwêpicikê – *fish* (VAI)
pâtimâ – *later*
kakwâtaki – *very*
ispîhk – *when*
wîpac – *soon/early*

1. *Last late spring I came to Regina.*

    _____

2. *It was late spring when I came to Regina.*

    _____

3. *Last spring the snow melted early.*

    _____

4. *It was spring but the snow didn't melt early.*

    _____

5. *Last summer we went fishing.*

    _____

6. *It was summer when we went fishing.*

    _____

7. *Last fall the leaves turned colour early.*

    _____

8. *It was fall but the geese didn't migrate until early winter.*

    _____

9. *Last early winter the ice didn't freeze until much later.*

    _____

10. *It was early winter when he came to town.*

    _____

11. *Last winter was very cold!*

    _____

12. *It was winter but it wasn't very cold.*

    _____

EXERCISE 2. Talking about seasonal activities: students will pair up to read, translate, then ask each other questions on seasons and seasonal activities, found on the following seven pages:

SPRING – sîkwan

1. ispîhk mâna kâ-sîkwahk ôki pîsimwak akimâwak: niski-pîsim, ayîki-pîsim, êkwa sâkipakâwi-pîsim.
   Q. kêko pîsimwak akimâwak ispîhk kâ-sîkwahk?

   _____

2. ispîhk mâna kâ-sîkwahk tâh-tihkitêw, sâh-sâkipakâw êkwa wâpikwaniya ohpikinwa.
   Q. tânisi mâna kâ-isiwêpahk ispîhk kâ-sîkwahk?

   _____

3. ispîhk mâna kâ-sîkwahk nitipiskên nîsosâp ê-akimiht* sâkipakâwi-pîsim.
   Q. kiya mâka, tânispîhk mâna kâ-tipiskaman ispîhk kâ-sîkwahk?

   _____

4. ispîhk mâna kâ-sîkwahk nicîhkêyihtên ta-tihtipêpiskamân** cihcipayapisikanis.
   Q. kiya mâka, kicîhkêyihtên cî ta-tihtipêpiskaman cihcipayapisikanis ispîhk kâ-sîkwahk?

   _____

5. ispîhk mâna kâ-sîkwaniyik*** tipiskam nisîmis nisto ê-akimimiht ayîki-pîsimwa.****
   Q. tânispîhk mâna kâ-tipiskahk nisîmis ispîhk kâ-sîkwaniyik?

   _____

6. ispîhk mâna kâ-sîkwaniyik cihkêyihtam nisîmis ta-pahkahtowêt.
   Q. cihkêyihtam cî nisîmis ta-pahkahtowêt ispîhk kâ-sîkwaniyik?

   _____

NOTES:

* ê-akimiht – *It is counted.* This form changes to ê-akimimiht when the topic of discussion is someone else other than the speaker or the one spoken to.

** ta-tihtipêpiskamân is a Transitive Inanimate Verb-class 1 (VTI-1). There are two other VTI-1 verbs here: tipiska – *have a birthday*; cîhkêyihta – *like something*. The **ta-** that begins the verb here is an infinite clause marker, a form of conjunct, so it uses the conjunct mood endings of verbs.

*** kâ-sîkwaniyik is the form used to write "*spring*" when the topic of discussion is someone other than the speaker or the one spoken to. kâ-sîkwahk is the form used when the subject of the verb in the main clause is 1st or 2nd person.

**** ayîki-pîsimwa is the form used to write "*month*" when the topic of discussion is someone other than the speaker or the one spoken to. The **wa** that ends the month here is not used when the subject of the verb in the main clause is 1st or 2nd person.

SUMMER – nîpin

1. ispîhk mâna kâ-nîpihk ôki pîsimwak akimâwak: pâskâwihowi-pîsim, paskowi-pîsim, êkwa ohpahowi-pîsim.
   Q. kêko pîsimwak akimâwak ispîhk kâ-nîpihk?

   _____

2. ispîhk mâna kâ-nîpihk kâh-kitowak* piyêsiwak, kâh-kisâstêw êkwa kâh-kimiwan.
   Q. tânisi mâna kâ-isiwêpahk ispîhk kâ-nîpihk?

   _____

3. ispîhk mâna kâ-nîpihk nitipiskên nistosâp ê-akimiht ohpahowi-pîsim.
   Q. kiya mâka, tânispîhk mâna kâ-tipiskaman ispîhk kâ-nîpihk?

   _____

4. ispîhk mâna kâ-nîpihk nicîhkêyihtên ta-kwâskwêpicikêyân.
   Q. kiya mâka, kicîhkêyihtên cî ta-kwâskwêpicikêyan ispîhk kâ-nîpihk?

   _____

5. ispîhk mâna kâ-nîpiniyik tipiskam nimis nîsitanaw ê-akimimiht paskowi-pîsimwa.
   Q. tânispîhk mâna kâ-tipiskahk nimis ispîhk kâ-nîpiniyik?

   _____

6. ispîhk mâna kâ-nîpiniyik cîhkêyihtam nimis ta-papâmiskât.
   Q. cîhkêyihtam cî nimis ta-papâmiskât ispîhk kâ-nîpiniyik?

   _____

NOTE: ON REDUPLICATION

The weather conditions in these entries are marked with reduplications: reduplicating the first syllable of the word to mark recurrent events or events that are in process at the time of speaking. Reduplication in Cree comes in two forms depending on the situation:

1) Reduplicate the consonant of the first syllable along with a long "**â**" and an "**h**" when the action is one that is known to occur on a regular basis: hence "kâh-kitowak – *there is thunder*", an event that is known to happen in the summer. If the first syllable of the word begins with a vowel then "**âh-**" comes before the first syllable: e.g., regular form: "âcimow – *he tells a story*" and with reduplication: âh-âcimow – *he tells a story* (on a regular basis)

2) Reduplicate the consonant of the first syllable along with a short vowel when the action is one that is in process of occurring, intermittently: hence "**ka**-kitowak – *there is thunder*" shows that the event is occurring at the time of speaking. If the first syllable begins with a vowel then "**ay-**" precedes the first syllable. Technically, though, the situation marking these actions with words that begin with a vowel is not reduplication since no letter is repeated, but the meaning it reflects in the words is the same as those where reduplication occurs, so this is included here.

AUTUMN – takwâkin

1. ispîhk mâna kâ-takwâkik ôki pîsimwak akimâwak: takwâki-pîsim, pinâskowi-pîsim, êkwa ihkopîwi-pîsim.
   Q. kêko pîsimwak akimâwak ispîhk kâ-takwâkik?

2. ispîhk mâna kâ-takwâkik nîpiya pâh-pahkihtinwa, ati-tâh-tahkâyâw êkwa wîpac ta-pipon.
   Q. tânisi mâna kâ-isiwêpahk ispîhk kâ-takwâkik?

3. ispîhk mâna kâ-takwâkik nitipiskên nîsitanaw nêwosâp ê-akimiht ihkopîwi-pîsim.
   Q. kiya mâka, tânispîhk mâna kâ-tipiskaman ispîhk kâ-takwâkik?

4. ispîhk mâna kâ-takwâkik nicîhkêyihtên ta-mâcîyân.
   Q. kiya-mâka, kicîhkêyihtên cî ta-mâcîyan ispîhk kâ-takwâkik?

5. ispîhk mâna kâ-takwâkiniyik tipiskam nistês nistomitanaw pêyakosâp ê-akimimiht pinâskowi-pîsimwa.
   Q. tânispîhk mâna kâ-tipiskahk nistês ispîhk kâ-takwâkiniyik?

6. ispîhk mâna kâ-takwâkiniyik cîhkêyihtam nistês ta-sêsâwipahtât.
   Q. cîhkêyihtam cî nistês ta-sêsâwipahtât ispîhk kâ-takwâkiniyik?

WINTER – pipon

1. ispîhk mâna kâ-pipohk ôki pîsimwak akimâwak: pawâcakinasîsi-pîsim, kisê-pîsim, êkwa mikisiwi-pîsim.
   Q. kêko pîsimwak akimâwak ispîhk kâ-pipohk?

2. ispîhk mâna kâ-pipohk kâh-kisinâw, pâh-pîwan êkwa mâh-mispon.
   Q. tânisi mâna kâ-isiwêpahk ispîhk kâ-pipohk?

3. ispîhk mâna kâ-pipohk nitipiskên nêwosâp ê-akimiht mikisiwi-pîsim.
   Q. kiya mâka, tânispîhk mâna kâ-tipiskaman?

4. ispîhk mâna kâ-pipohk nicîhkêyihtên ta-yahki-sôskoyâpawiyân.
   Q. kiya mâka, kicîhkêyihtên cî ta-yahki-sôskoyâpawiyan ispîhk kâ-pipohk?

5. ispîhk mâna kâ-piponiyik tipiskam niciwâm niyânan ê-akimimiht kisê-pîsimwa.
   Q. tânispîhk mâna kâ-tipiskahk niciwâm ispîhk kâ-piponiyik?

6. ispîhk mâna kâ-piponiyik cîhkêyihtam niciwâm ta-sôniskwâtahikêt.
   Q. cîhkêyihtam cî niciwâm ta-sôniskwâtahikêt ispîhk kâ-piponiyik?

See section 1.4 on page 14 for a list of numbers and months to help with the above exercise.

NOTE:
Saying the date follows these formulae:
Date in present statements as an independent clause: (date) akimâw (month)
Date in present statement as part of a subordinate clause: (date) ê-akimiht (month)

Relative clause with 1st and 2nd person subject in independent clause followed by infinitive:

WINTER
ispîhk mâna kâ-pipohk nicîhkêyihtên ta-yahki-sôskoyâpawiyân.
   Whenever it is winter I like to go cross-country skiing.

Q1. kiya mâka, kicîhkêyihtên cî ta-yahki-sôskoyâpawiyan ispîhk mâna kâ-pipohk?
   How about you, do you like to go cross-country skiing whenever it is winter?
PA (POSSIBLE ANSWERS):
   a) namôya, namôya nicîhkêyihtên ta-yahki-sôskoyâpawiyân ispîhk mâna kâ-pipohk.
   b) âha, nîsta nicîhkêyihtên ta-yahki-sôskoyâpawiyân ispîhk mâna kâ-pipohk.

Q2. kîkwây mîna kicîhkêyihtên ta-itôtaman ispîhk mâna kâ-pipohk?
   What else do you like to do when it is winter?
PA: nicîhkêyihtên mîna ta-sôniskwâtahikêyân ispîhk mâna kâ-pipohk.
   I also like to skate when it is winter.

Possible winter activities in VS form which can replace the underlined infinite forms above:
   pîcicî – *dance round-dance*   nîpawi-sôskwaciwêyâpoko – *ski (downhill)*
   nîpawi-napakihtaki-sôskwaciwêyâpoko – *snow-board* sôniskwâtahikê-mêtawê – *play hockey*

SPRING

ispîhk mâna kâ-sîkwahk nicîhkêyihtên ta-sêsâwipahtâyân.
> *Whenever it is spring I like to go jogging.*

Q1. kiya mâka, kicîhkêyihtên cî ta-<u>sêsâwipahtâ</u>yan ispîhk mâna kâ-sîkwahk?
> *How about you, do you like to go jogging whenever it is spring?*

PA: a) namôya, namôya nicîhkêyihtên ta-<u>sêsâwipahtâ</u>yân ispîhk mâna kâ-sîkwahk.
b) âha, nîsta nicîhkêyihtên ta-<u>sêsâwipahtâ</u>yân ispîhk mâna kâ-sîkwahk.

Q2. kîkwây mîna kicîhkêyihtên ta-itôtaman ispîhk mâna kâ-sîkwahk?
> *What else do you like to do when it is spring?*

PA: nicîhkêyihtên mîna ta-<u>pâkâhtowê</u>yân ispîhk mâna kâ-sîkwahk.
> *I also like to play soccer when it is spring.*

Possible spring activities in VR form which can replace the underlined infinitive forms above:

cihcipayîsi-sôniskwâtahikê – *roller-blade*   kwâskohti – *jump*
sêsâwohtê – *walk for exercise*   pakâsimo – *swim*

SUMMER

ispîhk mâna kâ-nîpihk nicîhkêyihtên ta-<u>kwâskwêpicikê</u>yân.
> *Whenever it is summer I like to go fishing.*

Q1. kiya mâka, kicîhkêyihtên cî ta-<u>kwâskwêpicikê</u>yan ispîhk mâna kâ-nîpihk?
> *How about you, do you like to go fishing whenever it is summer?*

PA: a) namôya, namôya nicîhkêyihtên ta-<u>kwâskwêpicikê</u>yân ispîhk mâna kâ-nîpihk.
b) âha, nîsta nicîhkêyihtên ta-<u>kwâskwêpicikê</u>yân ispîhk mâna kâ-nîpihk.

Q2. kîkwây mîna kicîhkêyihtên ta-itôtaman ispîhk mâna kâ-nîpihk?
> *What else do you like to do when it is summer?*

PA: nicîhkêyihtên mîna ta-<u>papâmi-pwâtisimo</u>yân ispîhk mâna kâ-nîpihk.
> *I also like to go about powwow dancing when it is summer.*

Possible summer activities in VR form which can replace the underlined infinitive forms above:

pôsi – *go boating/canoeing*   papâmiskâ – *go paddling (canoeing)*
papâmi-mânokê – *go camping*   maskatêpwê – *barbecue*

AUTUMN

ispîhk mâna kâ-takwâkik nicîhkêyihtên ta-<u>papâmi-mâcî</u>yân.
> *Whenever it is autumn I like to go about hunting.*

Q1. kiya mâka, kicîhkêyihtên cî ta-<u>papâmi-mâcî</u>yan ispîhk mâna kâ-takwâkik?
> *How about you, do you like to go about hunting whenever it is autumn?*

PA: a) namôya, namôya nicîhkêyihtên ta-<u>papâmi-mâcî</u>yân ispîhk mâna kâ-takwâkik.
b) âha, nîsta nicîhkêyihtên ta-<u>papâmi-mâcî</u>yân ispîhk mâna kâ-takwâkik.

Q2. kîkwây mîna kicîhkêyihtên ta-itôtaman ispîhk mâna kâ-takwâkik?
What else do you like to do when it is autumn?

PA: nicîhkêyihtên mîna ta-<u>kostâci-mamâhtâwisîho</u>yân ispîhk mâna kâ-takwâkik, ispîhk kâ-cîpayi-tipiskâk.
I also like to dress-up in a scary costume when it is autumn, when it's Halloween.

Possible autumn activities in the VR form which can replace the underlined infinitive forms above:

papâmi-atâwê – *go about shopping*   têhamâ – *play cards*
kiyokê – *visit*   mêtawê – *play*

Relative clause with 3rd person subject in independent clause followed by infinitive: Note the difference in the ending of the season when there is a 3rd person subject in the independent clause.

WINTER

ispîhk mâna kâ-piponiyik cîhkêyihtam awa ta-<u>yahki-sôskoyâpawi</u>t.
Whenever it is winter she/he likes to go cross-country skiing.

Q1. cîhkêyihtam cî awa ta-yahki-sôskoyâpawit ispîhk kâ-piponiyik?
PA: âha, cîhkêyihtam awa ta-yahki-sôskoyâpawit ispîhk kâ-piponiyik.

Q2. kiya mâka, kicîhkêyihtên cî ta-<u>yahki-sôskoyâpawi</u>yan ispîhk mâna kâ-pipohk?
How about you, do you like to go cross-country skiing whenever it is winter?
PA: a) namôya, namôya nicîhkêyihtên ta-<u>yahki-sôskoyâpawi</u>yân ispîhk mâna kâ-pipohk.
  b) âha, nîsta nicîhkêyihtên ta-<u>yahki-sôskoyâpawi</u>yân ispîhk mâna kâ-pipohk.

Possible winter activities in VR form which can replace the underlined infinite forms above:

pîcicî – *dance round-dance*   nîpawi-sôskwaciwêyâpoko – *ski (down-hill)*
nîpawi-napakihtaki-sôskwaciwêyâpoko – *snow-board* sôniskwâtahikê-mêtawê – *play hockey*

SPRING

ispîhk mâna kâ-sîkwaniyik cîhkêyihtam awa ta-sêsâwipahtât.
Whenever it is spring she/he likes to go jogging.

Q1. cîhkêyihtam cî awa ta-sêsâwipahtât ispîhk kâ-sîkwaniyik?
PA: âha, cîhkêyihtam awa ta-sêsâwipahtât ispîhk kâ-sîkwaniyik.

Q2. kiya mâka, kicîhkêyihtên cî ta-<u>sêsâwipahtâ</u>yan ispîhk mâna kâ-sîkwahk?
How about you, do you like to go jogging whenever it is spring?
PA: a) namôya, namôya nicîhkêyihtên ta-<u>sêsâwipahtâ</u>yân ispîhk mâna kâ-sîkwahk.
  b) âha, nîsta nicîhkêyihtên ta-<u>sêsâwipahtâ</u>yân ispîhk mâna kâ-sîkwahk.

Possible spring activities in VR form which can replace the underlined infinitive forms above:

cihcipayîsi-sôniskwâtahikê – *roller-blade*   kwâskohti – *jump*
sêsâwohtê – *walk for exercise*   pakâsimo – *swim*

SUMMER

ispîhk mâna kâ-nîpiniyik cîhkêyihtam awa ta-<u>kwâskwêpicikê</u>t.
Whenever it is summer she/he likes to go fishing.

Q1. cîhkêyihtam cî awa ta-<u>kwâskwêpicikê</u>t ispîhk mâna kâ-nîpiniyik?

PA: âha, cîhkêyihtam awa ta-<u>kwâskwêpicikê</u>t ispîhk mâna kâ-nîpiniyik.

Q2. kiya mâka, kicîhkêyihtên cî ta-<u>kwâskwêpicikê</u>yan ispîhk mâna kâ-nîpihk?
How about you, do you like to go fishing whenever it is summer?

PA: a) namôya, namôya nicîhkêyihtên ta-<u>kwâskwêpicikê</u>yân ispîhk mâna kâ-nîpihk.

b) âha, nîsta nicîhkêyihtên ta-<u>kwâskwêpicikê</u>yân ispîhk mâna kâ-nîpihk.

Possible summer activities in VR form which can replace the underlined infinitive forms above:

pôsi – *go boating/canoeing* papâmiskâ – *go paddling (canoeing)*
papâmi-mânokê – *go camping* maskatêpwê – *barbecue*

AUTUMN

ispîhk mâna kâ-takwâkiniyik cîhkêyihtam awa ta-<u>papâmi-mâcî</u>t.
Whenever it is autumn she/he likes to go about hunting.

Q1. cîhkêyihtam cî awa ta-<u>papâmi-mâcî</u>t ispîhk mâna kâ-takwâkiniyik

PA: âha, cîhkêyihtam awa ta-<u>papâmi-mâcî</u>t ispîhk mâna kâ-takwâkiniyik

Q2. kiya mâka, kicîhkêyihtên cî ta-<u>papâmi-mâcî</u>yan ispîhk mâna kâ-takwâkik?
How about you, do you like to go about hunting whenever it is autumn?

PA: a) namôya, namôya nicîhkêyihtên ta-<u>papâmi-mâcî</u>yân ispîhk mâna kâ-takwâkik.

b) âha, nîsta nicîhkêyihtên ta-<u>papâmi-mâcî</u>yân ispîhk mâna kâ-takwâkik.

Q2. kîkwây mîna kicîhkêyihtên ta-itôtaman ispîhk mâna kâ-takwâkik?
What else do you like to do when it is autumn?

PA: nicîhkêyihtên mîna ta-<u>kostâci-mamâhtâwisîho</u>yân ispîhk mâna kâ-takwâkik,
ispîhk kâ-cîpayi-tipiskâk.
I also like to dress-up in a scary costume when it is autumn, when it's Halloween.

Possible autumn activities in the VR form which can replace the underlined infinitive forms above:

papâmi-atâwê – *go about shopping* têhamâ – *play cards*
kiyokê – *visit* mêtawê – *play*

BONUS: A SAMPLE CALENDAR FOR THE MONTH OF OCTOBER

pinâskowi-pîsim

ayamihêwi-kîsikâw	pêyako-kîsikâw	nîso-kîsikâw	nisto-kîsikâw	nêwo-kîsikâw	niyânano-kîsikâw	nikotwâso-kîsikâw
	1 pêyak akimâw	**2** nîso akimâw	**3** nisto akimâw	**4** nêwo akimâw	**5** niyânan akimâw	**6** nikotwâsik akimâw
	miyo-kîsikâw	**tahkâyâw**			**tipiskam nitôtêm.**	
7 têpakohp akimâw	**8** ayênânêw akimâw **nanâskomowi-kîsikâw**	**9** kêkâ-mitâtaht akimâw	**10** mitâtaht akimâw	**11** pêyakosâp akimâw	**12** nîsosâp akimâw	**13** nistosâp akimâw
14 nêwosâp akimâw **ati-yîkwaskwan**	**15** niyânanosâp akimâw	**16** nikotwâsosâp akimâw	**17** têpakohposâp akimâw	**18** ayênânêwosâp akimâw	**19** kêkâ-mitâtahtosâp akimâw	**20** nîsitanaw akimâw **yôtin**
21 nîsitanaw pêyakosâp akimâw	**22** nîsitanaw nîsosâp akimâw	**23** nîsitanaw nistosâp akimâw	**24** nîsitanaw nêwosâp akimâw	**25** nîsitanaw niyânanosâp akimâw	**26** nîsitanaw nikotwâsosâp akimâw	**27** nîsitanaw têpakohposâp akimâw **mispon**
28 nîsitanaw ayênânêwosâp akimâw	**29** nîsitanaw kêkâ-mitâtahtosâp akimâw **wâwiyêsiw tipiskâwi-pîsim**	**30** nistomitanaw akimâw	**31** nistomitanaw pêyakosâp akimâw **cîpayi-tipiskâw**			

EXERCISE 3.

DO: After the students do the foregoing exercise have them prepare similar dialogues using information from their own lives, including their interests. Each student works on the season in which they have a birthday. The following section lists a choice of the more common activities from which the students can get their information for what they like to do. Their projects can include pictures and must have the following topics, with text and questions similar to the units listed in Exercise 2. Students prepare their projects for class presentation, where they will ask classmates the questions they have prepared.

Class presentation must include the following:

a) season with months;
b) weather activities during that season;
c) student's own birthday;
d) what a student likes to do – this can include three activities;
e) a relative's birthday during that season (Exercise 4, p. 21, lists relatives);
f) what that relative likes to do during that season.

EXERCISE 4. LIKES

The forms below are ways people express what they like to do in the infinitive form, a type of conjunct that begins with a **ta-** followed by conjunct mood endings of verbs. VAI roots can go in the blanks below:

Put the verb stems of VAI in the following blank for 1st person: ta-_____yân.

Put the verb stems of VAI in the following blank for 2nd person: ta-_____an.

Put the verb stems of VAI in the following blank for 3rd person: ta-_____t.

DO: first say what you like to do, then ask someone if they like to do that too:

SPEAKER A:
nicîhkêyihtên **ta-**pakâsimo**yân**. – *I like to swim.*
kiya mâka, kicîhkêyihtên cî kîsta **ta-**pakâsimo**yan**? – *How about you, do you like to swim too?*

SPEAKER B:
POSSIBLE ANSWERS:
a) namôya, namôya nicîhkêyihtên ta-pakâsimoyân. – *No, I do not like to swim.*
b) âha, nîsta nicîhkêyhtên ta-pakâsimoyân. – *Yes, I like to swim too.*

5.4 LIKES AND DISLIKES

A. LIKES:

ANIMATE
Fill the spaces below with
Animate nouns (singular):

nimiywêyimâw _____

(*I like* _____)

nicîhkêyimâw _____

(*I like* _____)

INANIMATE
Fill the spaces below with
Inanimate nouns (or verbs*):

nimiywêyihtên _____

(*I like* _____)

nicîhkêyihtên _____

(*I like* _____)

Fill the spaces below with
Animate nouns (foods):

niwîhkipwâw _____

(*I like the taste of* _____)

Fill the spaces below with
Inanimate nouns (foods):

niwîhkistên _____

(*I like the taste of* _____)

B. DISLIKES

ANIMATE

nipakwâtâw _____

(*I dislike* _____)

niwînêyimâw _____

(*I detest* _____)

INANIMATE

nipakwâtên _____

(*I dislike* _____)

niwînêyihtên _____

(*I detest* _____)

*the verb-forms following on the next page can be used in the blanks above.

LIKES:
The following is a list of things people like to do. The forms are this way when the person expressing what she/he likes to do is the speaker (1st person) and is in the infinitive form, a type of conjunct that begins with a **ta-** followed by conjunct mood endings of verbs. We will begin with a list of activities using VAIs:

Put the verb stems of VAI in the following blank for 1st person: ta-_____yân.

Put the verb stems of VAI in the following blank for 2nd person: ta-_____yan.

Put the verb stems of VAI in the following blank for 3rd person: ta-_____t.

nicîhkêyihtên – *I like:*

ta-pimohtêyân – *to walk*

ta-sêsâwîyân – *to exercise*

ta-nikamoyân – *to sing*

ta-nîmihitoyân – *to dance*

ta-pîcicîyân – *to dance round dance*

ta-kiskinwahamâkêyân – *to teach*

ta-kîwêyân – *to go home*

ta-kiyokêyân – *to visit*

ta-kiyôtêyân – *to visit (far away)*

ta-pôsiyân – *to go boating/canoeing*

ta-papâmiskâyân – *to paddle about*

ta-pakâsimoyân – *to swim*

ta-maskatêpwêyân – *to barbecue*

ta-mêtawêyân – *to play*

ta-pâhkâhtowêyân – *to play soccer*

ta-kwâskwêtahikêyân – *to play golf*

ta-sôniskwâtahikêyân – *to skate*

ta-pahkopêyân – *to wade*

ta-nîpawi-sôskwaciwêyâpokoyân – *to ski*

ta-nîpawi-sôskwaciwêyâpokoyân nipîhk – *to water ski*

ta-papâmi-atâwêyân – *to go shopping*

ta-nîpawi-napakihtaki-sôskwaciwêyân – *to snowboard*

ta-sôniskwâtahikê-mêtawêyân – *to play hockey*

ta-cihcipayîsi-sôniskwâtahikêyân – *to rollerblade*

ta-sêsâwohtêyân – *to walk for exercise*

ta-sêsâwipahtâyân – *to jog*

ta-nêhiyawêyân – *to speak Cree*

ta-pwâtisimoyân – *to dance Pow-wow*

ta-mâcîyân – *to hunt*

ta-kiskinwahamâkosiyân – *to be in class/school*

ta-kîwêpayiyân – *drive home*

ta-kaskikwâsoyân – *to sew*

ta-mîkisîhkâcikêyân – *to bead*

ta-mîkisistahikêyân – *to bead*

ta-papâmi-mânokêyân – *to go camping*

ta-kwâskwêpicikêyân – *to go fishing*

ta-kotawêyân – *to make a campfire*

ta-têhamâyân – *to play cards*

ta-masinahikêyân – *to write*

ta-ayamihcikêyân – *to read*

ta-sôskwaciwêyân – *to slide (go sledding)*

ta-yâh-yahki-sôskoyâpawiyân – *to ski cross-country*

ta-kwâskohtiyân – *to jump*

The following is a list of few things people like to do that requires **transitive verbs**:

ta-tihtipêpiskamân cihcipayapisikanis – *to ride a bike*

ta-têhtapiyân mistatim – *to ride a horse*

ta-kanawâpahtamân cikâstêpayihcikan – *to watch a movie*

ta-kanawâpahtamân cikâstêpayihcikanis – *to watch television*

DO: first, say what you like to do, then ask someone if they like to do that too:

SPEAKER A:

nicîhkêyihtên **ta**-têhtapi**yân** mistatimwak. – *I like to ride horses.*

kiya mâka, kicîhkêyihtên cî kîsta **ta**-têhtapi**yan** mistatimwak?

   – *How about you, do you like to ride horses too?*

SPEAKER B:
POSSIBLE ANSWERS:

   a) namôya, namôya nicîhkêyihtên ta-têhtapiyân mistatimwak. – *No, I do not like to ride horses.*

   b) âha, nîsta nicîhkêyihtên ta-têhtapiyân mistatimwak. – *Yes, I like to ride horses too.*

C. TEXT: LETTERS TO A FRIEND

The following is an introductory letter to a possible pen pal:

LETTER ONE

mikisiwi-pîsim, *(February,,)*
nîsitanaw ayênânêwosâp ê-akimiht *(28th)*

hâw, nitôtêm, *(Okay, my friend,)*
apisîs ka-masinahamâtin. *Joseph Wacaskos* nitisiyihkâson. ayênânêwosâp nititahtopiponân.
(I will write you a little. My name is Joseph Wacaskos. I am 18 years old.)
âmaciwîspimowinihk ohci niya mâka mêkwâc oskana kâ-asastêki niwîkin. namôya osâm
(I am from Stanley Mission but now live in Regina. I don't much)
nicîhkêyihtên ôta ta-wîkiyân mâka ohcitaw piko ôta ta-ayâyân ayisk ê-kiskinwahamâkosiyân.
(like living here but I have to be here because I am going to school.)
êkwâni nîso askîwina ôta kihci-kiskinwahamâtowikamikohk ê-pê-kiskinwahamâkosiyân.
(It's been two years since I've come to the University for school.)
mistahi mâna nikaskêyihtên âmaciwîspimowin. *(I get so lonesome for Stanley Mission.)*
hâw, êkosi pitamâ, *(Okay, that's it for now,)*

> niya kitôtêm, *(I am your friend,)*
> *Joseph Wacaskos.*

QUESTIONS:

1. tâniyikohk akimâw mikisiwi-pîsim ispîhk awa kâ-masinahikêt?

   _____

2. tânisi awa kâ-isiyihkâsot?

   _____

3. tânitê awa ohci?

   _____

4. tânitê awa mêkwâc kâ-wîkit?

   _____

5. tânêhki awa êkotê kâ-wîkit?

   _____

ASSIGNMENT: Have students write letters similar to the one above. Have them include all the information contained above.

LETTER TWO: Translate the following letter, then answer the questions.

niski-pîsim,
niyânanosâp ê-akimiht.

hâw, nitôtêm,

kwayask nicîhkêyihtên ê-pê-masinahamawiyan. mahti nika-kakwê-naskwêwasihtân kahkiyaw kikakwêcihkêmowina. tâpwê ot âni okiskinwahamâkan niya mâka mistahi kotak kîkwây ta-itôtamân nicîhkêyihtên. nicîhkêyihtên ta-papâmohtêyân êkwa mîna ta-sâh-sêsâwipahtâyân wayawîtimihk. namôya osâm nicîhkêyihtên ta-sêsâwipahtâyân pîhcâyihk mêtawêwikamikohk. nicîhkêyihtên mîna ta-pakâsimoyân sâkahikanihk ispîhk kâ-nîpihk. namôya osâm nicîhkêyihtên ta-pakâsimoyân pîhcâyihk kâ-pipohk. ispîhk kâ-pipohk nicîhkêyihtên ta-yahki-sôskoyâpawiyân mîna ta-sôniskwâtahikêyân mîna ta-nâh-nîmihitoyân.

kiya mâka, kîkwây kicîhkêyihtên ta-itôtaman ispîhk kâ-nîpihk êkwa ispîhk kâ-pipohk.

êkosi pitamâ, niya kitôtêm,
Joseph Wacaskos

WORDS

kwayask – *very much*	kahkiyaw – *all*	naskwêwasihtâ – *answer* (VTI-2)
tâpwê ot âni – *it is so true*	kotak – *another*	wayawîtimihk – *outside*
namôya osâm – *not really*	pîhcâyihk – *inside*	mêtawêwikamik – *gym*
sâkahikan – *lake*	êkosi pitamâ – *that's it for now*	kîkwây asici – *what else?*
cîhkêyihta – *like it* (VTI-1)	sêsâwipahtâ – *jog* (VAI)	pakâsimo – *swim* (VAI)
nîmihito – *dance* (VAI)	sôniskwâtahikê – *skate* (VAI)	itôta – *do* (VTI-1)
mistahi – *lots*	papâmohtê – *walk about* (VAI)	okiskinwahamâkan – *student* (NA)
yahki-sôskoyâpawi – *ski cross-country* (VAI)		
masinahamaw – *write to someone* (VTA)		
kikakwêcihkêmowina – *your questions* (NI)		

QUESTIONS:

1. cîhkêyihtam cî awa ta-sâh-sêsâwipahtât mêtawêwikamikohk?

_____

2. cîhkêyihtam cî awa ta-pakâsimot sâkahikanihk?

_____

3. cîhkêyihtam cî ta-pakâsimot pîhcâyihk kâ-piponiyik?

_____

4. cîhkêyihtam cî ta-sôniskwâtahikêt kâ-piponiyik?

_____

5. kîkwây asici cîhkêyihtam ta-itôtahk ispîhk kâ-piponiyik?

_____

5.5 DAYS OF THE WEEK

Days of the week are also Inanimate Intransitive verbs (VII). Below is a list of the days of the week in various forms.

ENGLISH	INDICATIVE	CONJUNCT	FUTURE CONDITIONAL
Sunday	ayamihêwi-kîsikâw *It is Sunday*	ê-ayamihêwi-kîsikâk *It is Sunday*	ayamihêwi-kîsikâki *It is Sunday* *(If Sunday comes / On Sunday)*
Monday	pêyako-kîsikâw *It is Monday*	ê-pêyako-kîsikâk *It is Monday*	pêyako-kîsikâki *It is Monday* *(If Monday comes / On Monday)*
Tuesday	nîso-kîsikâw *It is Tuesday*	ê-nîso-kîsikâk *It is Tuesday*	nîso-kîsikâki *It is Tuesday* *(If Tuesday comes / On Tuesday)*
Wednesday	nisto-kîsikâw *It is Wednesday*	ê-nisto-kîsikâk *It is Wednesday*	nisto-kîsikâki *It is Wednesday* *(If Wednesday comes / On Wednesday*
Thursday	nêwo-kîsikâw *It is Thursday*	ê-nêwo-kîsikâk *It is Thursday*	nêwo-kîsikâki *It is Thursday* *(If Thursday comes / On Thursday)*
Friday	niyânano-kîsikâw *It is Friday*	ê-niyânano-kîsikâk *It is Friday*	niyânano-kîsikâki *It is Friday* *(If Friday comes / On Friday)*
Saturday	nikotwâso-kîsikâw *It is Saturday*	ê-nikotwâso-kîsikâk *It is Saturday*	nikotwâso-kîsikâki *It is Saturday* *(If Saturday comes / On Saturday)*

QUESTIONS ABOUT DAYS OF THE WEEK:

1. tânitahto kîsikâw anohc? – *What day is today?*

2. tânitahto kîsikâw mâna kâ-mâci-kiskinwahamâkosiyan? – *What day do you start school?*

3. tânitahto kîsikâw mâna kâ-kîsi-kiskinwahamâkosiyan? – *What day do you finish school?*

4. tânitahto kîsikâw kâ-wî-pê-kiyokêyan? – *What day are you coming to visit?*

EXERCISES

EXERCISE 1. Complete the following chart. Note the difference in the form of the days of the week when the subjects of the main clause is 1st and 2nd persons in comparision to the forms when the subjects of the main clause is in the 3rd person:

DAY OF THE WEEK: INDICATIVE	CONJUNCT	FUTURE CONDITIONAL
pêyako-kîsikâw *It is Monday* (Use when subject of main clause is 1st and 2nd person) pêyako-kîsikâ**yiw** *It is Monday* (Use when subject of main clause is 3rd person)	ê-pêyako-kîsikâk ê-pêyako-kîsikâ**yik**	pêyako-kîsikâki pêyako-kîsikâ**yiki**
nîso-kîsikâw		
nisto-kîsikâw		
nêwo-kîsikâw		
niyânano-kîsikâw		
nikotwâso-kîsikâw		
ayamihêwi-kîsikâw		

EXERCISE 2. Choose the correct form of the day of the week in the following:

1. *On Monday my friend is going to go to work.*

   pêkayo-kîsikâyiki

   pêyako-kîsikâki   wî-nitawi-atoskêw nitôtêm.

2. *On Tuesday I will go and work.*

   nîso-kîsikâki

   nîso-kîsikâyiki   nika-nitawi-atoskân.

3. *On Wednesday, his/her friend is going to go to work.*

   nisto-kîsikâyiki

   nisto-kîsikâki   wî-nitawi-atoskêyiwa otôtêma.

4. *On Thursday, my friend will try to play.*

   nêwo-kîsikâki

   nêwo-kîsikâyiki   ta-kakwê-mêtawêw nitôtêm.

5. *On Friday, his/her friend is going to finish classes.*

   niyânano-kîsikâyiki

   niyânano-kîsikâki   wî-kîsi-kiskinwahamâkosiyiwa otôtêma.

6. *On Saturday, my friend is going to dance.*

   nikotwâso-kîsikâki

   nikotwâso-kîsikâyiki   wî-nîmihitow nitôtêm.

7. *On Sunday, I'm going to go to the lake.*

   ayamihêwi-kîsikâyiki

   ayamihêwi-kîsikâki   niwî-itohtân sâkahikanihk.

EXERCISE 3. Translate the following:

The days of the week in the following are in two forms: past tense and future conditional form. Go back to 5.3 and 5.5 for the future conditional forms; for the days of the week in the past tense in the following sentences use the relative clause forms: **kâ-** with past tense marker **kî-** and the conjunct endings. The first two are done for you:

1. *I went fishing on Saturday.* nikî-nitawi-kwâskwêpicikân kâ-kî-nikotwâso-kîsikâk

2. *Do you want to go fishing on Saturday?* kinôhtê-nitawi-kwâskwêpicikân cî nikotwâso-kîsikâki?

3. *He had a barbecue on Sunday.*

   _____

4. *Is he going to barbecue on Sunday?*

   _____

5. *I went to work on Monday.*

   _____

6. *Are you going to work on Monday?*

   _____

7. *We* (exclusive) *went shopping on Tuesday.*

   _____

8. *Are you* (plural) *going to go shopping on Tuesday?*

   _____

9. *She went camping on Wednesday.*

   _____

10. *Are you going camping on Wednesday?*

    _____

VAIS FOR THE ABOVE:

maskatêpwê – *have a barbecue*   atoskê – *work*
papâmi-atâwê – *go shopping*   papâmi-mânokê – *go camping*

5.6 TEMPORAL UNITS

Temporal units refer to times of day including the terms for weeks. Here are the more common temporal units which we will encounter during conversations.

If these occur in compound sentences and the subject of one of the clauses is 1st or 2nd person, then these are the forms used:

ENGLISH	INDICATIVE	CONJUNCT	FUTURE CONDITIONAL
It is dawn.	wâpan	ê-wâpahk	wâpahki
It is morning.	kîkisêpâw	ê-kîkisêpâk	kîkisêpâki
It is day.	kîsikâw	ê-kîsikâk	kîsikâki
It is noon.	âpihtâ-kîsikâw	ê-âpihtâ-kîsikâk	âpihtâ-kîsikâki
It is afternoon.	pôni-âpihtâ-kîsikâw	ê-pôni-âpihtâ-kîsikâk	pôni-âpihtâ-kîsikâki
It is evening.	otâkosin	ê-otâkosik	otâkosiki
It is night.	tipiskâw	ê-tipiskâk	tipiskâki
It is midnight.	âpihtâ-tipiskâw	ê-âpihtâ-tipiskâk	âpihtâ-tipiskâki
It is twilight.	wawâninâkwan	ê-wawâninâkwahk	wawâninâkwahki

If these occur in compound sentences and the subject of the main clause is a 3rd person, then these are the forms used:

ENGLISH	INDICATIVE	CONJUNCT	FUTURE CONDITIONAL
It is dawn.	wâpaniyiw	ê-wâpaniyik	wâpaniyiki
It is morning.	kîkisêpâyiw	ê-kîkisêpâyik	kîkisêpâyiki
It is day.	kîsikâyiw	ê-kîsikâyik	kîsikâyiki
It is noon.	âpihtâ-kîsikâyiw	ê-âpihtâ-kîsikâyik	âpihtâ-kîsikâyiki
It is afternoon.	pôni-âpihtâ-kîsikâyiw	ê-pôni-âpihtâ-kîsikâyik	pôni-âpihtâ-kîsikâyiki
It is evening.	otâkosiniyiw	ê-otâkosiniyik	otâkosiniyiki
It is night.	tipiskâyiw	ê-tipiskâyik	tipiskâyiki
It is mid-night.	âpihtâ-tipiskâyiw	ê-âpihtâ-tipiskâyik	âpihtâ-tipiskâyiki
It is twilight.	wawâninâkwaniyiw	ê-wawâninâkwaniyik	wawâninâkwaniyiki

EXAMPLES OF COMPOUND SENTENCES:

1. *He's going to arrive at dawn.* wî-takosin wâpaniyiki.
   Independent clause with 3rd person subject: wî-takosin. – *He's going to arrive.*
   Subordinate clause agrees with subject: wâpaniyiki. – *If it is dawn.*

2. *I'm going to arrive at dawn (tomorrow).* niwî-takosinin wâpahki.
   Independent clause with 1st person subject: niwî-takosinin. – *I'm going to arrive.*
   Subordinate clause agrees with subject: wâpahki. – *If it is dawn (tomorrow).*

last week	– otâhk ispayiw
next week	– kotak ispayiki
one week	– pêyak ispayiw
this week	– anohc kâ-ispayik
tomorrow	– wâpahki
day after tomorrow	– awasi-wâpahki
yesterday	– otâkosîhk
day before yesterday	– awasitâkosîhk
last night	– tipiskohk
night before last night	– awasi-tipiskohk
tonight	– tipiskâki
year	– askîwin
this year	– anohc kâ-askîwik
last year	– otâhk askîwin
next year	– kotak askîwiki

TRANSLATE:

1. *This year we* (incl.) *will go to the lake early.*

2. *Last year they came early.*

3. *Let's go to town this evening.*

TEMPORAL UNITS IN VARIOUS FORMS:

INDICATIVE:

PRESENT TENSE:	*It is morning.*	– kîkisêpâw
PAST TENSE:	*It was morning.*	– kî-kîkisêpâw
FUTURE INTENTIONAL:	*It's going to be morning.*	– wî-kîkisêpâw
FUTURE DEFINITE:	*It will be morning.*	– ta-kîkisêpâw
PRESENT WITH PREVERB:	*Morning's coming.*	– pê-kîkisêpâw

CONJUNCT: Add **ê** at the beginning of the Indicative, replace last consonant with **k** if the last vowel is long, but if the last vowel is short, then use **hk**:

PRESENT TENSE:	*It is morning.*	– ê-kîkisêpâk
PAST TENSE:	*It was morning.*	– ê-kî-kîkisêpâk
FUTURE INTENTIONAL:	*It's going to be morning.*	– ê-wî-kîkisêpâk
FUTURE DEFINITE:	(Not possible in Conjunct mood.)	
PRESENT WITH PREVERB:	*Morning's coming.*	– ê-pê-kîkisêpâk
FUTURE CONDITIONAL:	*If it is morning.*	– kîkisêpâki

5.6.A DIALOGUE SIX

A: *Shaking-Spear!*
B: kîkwây!
A: tânitahto tipahikan ôma mêkwâc?*
B: kêkâc nisto tipahikan.
A: kinôhtê-nitawi-minihkwân cî
   pihkahtêwâpoy?
B: âhâw, pâcimâsîs ici. pitamâ
   niwî-kîsihtân ôma.
A: tânispîhk mâka?
B: pâtimâ ici nisto tipahikan
   mîna âpihtaw ispayiki.
A: ahâw, pê-nâsihkan ici.

A: *Shaking-Spear!*
B: *What!*
A: *What time is it now?*
B: *It's almost three o'clock.*
A: *Do you want to go and drink
   coffee?*
B: *Okay, in a little while. For now
   I want to finish this.*
A: *When then?*
B: *Later at three thirty
   (if/when it comes about).*
A: *Okay, come get me then.*

VOCABULARY

kîkwây – *What!*
ôma – *this*
pihkatêwâpoy – *coffee*
ici – *at that time*
pâtimâ – *later*
nâs – *get him/her (VTA)*
miyâskam – *it goes past*

tânitahto – *how many*
kêkâc – *almost*
ahâw – *okay*
pitamâ – *for now*
mîna – *also*
ispayiki – *if/when it comes*
pâmwayês – *before*

tipahikan – *time*
nisto – *three*
pâcimâsîs – *in a little while*
kîsihtâ – *finish it (VTA-2)*
âpihtaw – *half*
cipahikanis – *minutes*

NOTES

*On asking about time in Cree the usual question is:
   tânitahto tipahikan ôma? – *What time is it?*

In answering the question you can use the following formulas:

   ON THE HOUR: (number) tipahikan ôma mêkwâc. – *It is* (number) *right now.*

   AT HALF PAST: (number) tipahikan mîna âpihtaw. – *It is half past* (number).

   PAST THE HOUR: (number) cipahikanis miyâskam (number) tipahikan. – *It is* (number) *minutes
      past* (number) *o'clock.*

   BEFORE THE HOUR: (number) cipahikanis pâmwayês (number) tipahikan. – *It is* (number)
      minutes before (number) *o'clock.*

Of course there are other options to the above: the most common of these options is the use of
"kêkâc – *almost*" placed before any of the above formulas.

DO the above dialogue with your partner.

5.6.B DIALOGUE SEVEN

A: tânitahto tipahikan kâ-wî-kîwêyan ?

B: nânitaw êtikwê niyânan tipahikan ispayiki. tânêhki?

A: ê-pakosêyimoyân ta-pôsihiyan.*

B: âhâw, tânitê mâka ê-wî-itohtêyan?

A: awâsis-nâkatawêyimâwasowinihk ê-wî-môsahkinak nikosis.

B: âhâw, êkota ici ka-pêhitin...

A: namôya katâc, namôya wahyaw êkota ohci niwîkinân.

B: âhâw.

A: hâw, kinanâskomitin.

B: pikw îspî, pikw îspî…

A: *What time are you going home?*

B: *Perhaps around five o'clock, if/when it comes. Why?*

A: *I am hoping for a ride.*

B: *Okay, but where is it you're going?*

A: *At the child-care center, as I am picking up my son.*

B: *Okay, I'll wait for you there…*

A: *That's not necessary, we don't live far from there.*

B: *Okay.*

A: *'kay, thanks so much.*

B: *Anytime, anytime…*

VOCABULARY

êtikwê – *about*

êkota – *there*

namôya katâc – *not necessary*

ka-pêhitin – *I will wait for you*

kinanâskomitin – *I thank you*

awâsis-nâkatawêyimâwasowinihk – *at the Day Care*

pakosêyimo – *hope, wish, desire* (VAI)

pôsihin – *give me a ride* (VTA)

môsahkin – *pick someone up* (VTA)

namôya wahyaw – *not far*

pikw îspî – *anytime*

NOTES

*The Transitive Animate verb forms (VTA) above are merely an introduction to these verbs. We'll cover them more extensively later in this book. Note, at this point, the following ways of saying common utterances like "*I will wait for you*" and "*I thank you.*" The clause "*ta-pôsihiyan*" means literally "*for you to give me a ride*" and is another VTA form: more on the "ta-" with conjunct mood ending later.

DO: After you've finished the dialogue, practise asking about the time of daily activities using the following question:

tânitahto tipahikan mâna kâ-<u>waniskâ</u>yan – *What time do you usually get up?*

Replace the underlined Animate Intransitive verb stem with any other verb stem that deals with daily activities. The answer to the above question will use the Indicative form of the verb as in

têpakohp tipahikan mâna ni<u>waniskâ</u>n – *I usually get up at seven o'clock.*

You could also ask about some future intended activity with the use of the future intentional "**wî-**" following the relative clause marker "**kâ-**". Verbs that use this "**kâ-**" marker are in the subordinate clause, and their endings will be the same as the "**ê-**" conjunct/conjunct marker. So, here is the question that would ask about some future intended activity:

tânitahto tipahikan kâ-wî-<u>kîwê</u>yan – *What time do you intend to go home?*

5.6.C TIME PHRASES

Common Expressions: ...place time here in blanks.

1. *I'll meet you at* (time) *tomorrow.*   kika-nakiskâtin <u>(time)</u> wâpahki.
   - *... in the morning*   ... kîkisêpâyâki
   - *... at noon*   ... âpihtâ-kîsikâki
   - *... in the afternoon*   ... pôni-âpihtâ-kîsikâki
   - *... late afternoon/early evening*   ... otâkosiki
   - *... at night*   ... tipiskâki

2. *I'll see you at* _____TIME_____ *tomorrow.*

   kika-wâpamitin _____TIME_____ wâpahki.

3. *I want to see you at* _____TIME_____ *tomorrow.*

   kinôhtê-wâpamitin _____TIME_____ wâpahki.

4. *Come see me tomorrow at* _____TIME_____ .

   pê-wâpamihkan _____TIME_____ wâpahki.

5. *Come visit me tomorrow at* _____TIME_____ .

   pê-kiyokawihkan _____TIME_____ wâpahki.

6. *Can you come see me at* _____TIME_____ *tomorrow?*

   ka-kî-pê-wâpamin cî _____TIME_____ wâpahki?

7. *What time does the store, etc., close?*

   tânitahto tipahikan kâ-kipahikâtêk _____ ?

BUILDINGS

atâwêwikamik – *store*   âhkosîwikamik (maskihkîwikamik) – *hospital*
kiskinwahamâtowikamik – *school*   maskihkîwikamikos – *clinic*
simâkanisîwikamik – *police station*   kipahotowikamik – *jail*
oyasiwêwikamik – *courthouse*   oyasiwêwiyiniwikamik (pântwâhpis) – *Band Office*

To use the above in a sentence asking or talking about location, you need to add the proper locative endings (see section 2.3 on page 51).

Place the "building" nouns (from the previous page) in the blanks below:

8. *What time is* _____ *open?*   tânitahto tipahikan kâ-yôhtênikâtêk _____ ?

9. *When is the meeting?*   tânispîhk kâ-mâmawipihk?
When is the dance?   tânispîhk kâ-nîmihitohk? or tânispîhk kâ-nîmihk?
When is the movie?   tânispîhk kâ-cikâstêpayihcikêhk?
When are we going fishing?   tânispîhk kâ-wî-nitawi-kwâskwêpicikêyahk?

10. *When is the* _____ *open?*   tânispîhk kâ-yôhtênikâtêk _____ ?

Possible answers to the above questions:

after _____ .   pôni- _____ /*after* _____ .

e.g.: *after the meeting*   pôni-mâmawapihki
after the wedding   pôni-wîkihtohki
after the feast   pôni-wîhkôhtohki
after the games   pôni-mêtawêhki
after church service   pôni-ayamihâhki

before _____ . (The above forms minus the pôni-(PV) can be placed in the blank.)

mwayî- _____   (PV) . _____ *before* .

early   wîpac
yesterday   otâkosîhk
day before yesterday   awasitâkosîhk
already   âsay
not yet   namôya cêskwa
later   mwêstas
later on   pâtimâ
not for now   namôya pitamâ
in a little while   wîpacîs
a little while later   pâcimâsîs
never   namôya wîhkâc
every now and then   âyâskaw
sometimes   âskaw
every   tahto- (PV)
all the time   kapê
forever and ever   kâkikê mîna kâkikê

5.6.D REVIEW OF TEMPORAL UNITS

1. **DAYS OF THE WEEK**

Sunday (it is)	ayamihêwi-kîsikâw
Monday (it is)	pêyako-kîsikâw
Tuesday (it is)	nîso-kîsikâw
Wednesday (it is)	nisto-kîsikâw
Thursday (it is)	nêwo-kîsikâw
Friday (it is)	niyânano-kîsikâw
Saturday (it is)	nikotwâso-kîsikâw *or* mâtinawê-kîsikâw

2. **FUTURE**

When Sunday comes	ayamihêwi-kîsikâki = *When it is Sunday*

   For these future conditions of events, simply drop the "**w**" from the above days and add "**-ki**".

3. **PAST**

When it was Sunday	kâ-kî-ayamihêwi-kîsikâk

   For these past events, add "**kâ-kî-**" to the above days of the week at the beginning, then add "**k**" at the end after the "**w**" has been dropped.

4. **OTHER TEMPORAL WORDS**

all night	kapê-tipisk
all day	kapê-kîsik
this week	anohc kâ-ispayik
next week	kotak ispayiki
last week	otâhk ispayiw
tomorrow	wâpahki
the day after tomorrow	awasi-wâpahki
yesterday	otâkosîhk
the day before yesterday	awasitâkosîhk
last night	tipiskohk
the night before last	awasi-tipiskohk
as it comes about	ê-ispayik
it comes/happens	ispayin

Days of the week with activity (in 1st person singular) and time when the activity is done.

MONDAY

Day of the week	Activity	Time of activity
ispîhk mâna kâ-pêyako-kîsikâk *When it is Monday*	niwaniskân *I get up/wake up*	têpakohp tipahikan mîna âpihtaw kâ-ispayik. *at 7:30.*
	nikisîpêkinastân *I bathe/shower*	niyânanosâp cipahikanis pâmwayês ayênânêw tipahikan kâ-ispayik. *at 7:45.*
	nisîkahon *I comb my hair*	ayênânêw tipahikan kâ-ispayik. *at 8:00.*
	nikîkisêpâ-mîcison *I eat breakfast*	niyânan cipahikanis miyâskam ayênânêw tipahikan kâ-ispayik. *at 8:05.*

Replace the underlined verb stem below with the above verbs:

QUESTION:

kiya mâka, tânitahto tipahikan mâna k<u>iwaniskâ</u>n ispîhk kâ-pêyako-kîsikâk?
How about you, what time do you get up when it is Monday?

TUESDAY

Day of the week	Activity	Time of activity
ispîhk mâna kâ-nîso-kîsikâk *When it is Tuesday*	ninitawi-kiskinwahamâkosin *I go to school/class*	ayênânêw tipahikan mîna âpihtaw kâ-ispayik. *at 8:30.*
	nikîsi-kiskinwahamâkosin *I finish class/school*	niyânanosâp cipahikanis miyâskam pêyakosâp tipahikan kâ-ispayik. *at 11:15.*
	nitâpihtâ-kîsikani-mîcison *I eat lunch*	nîsosâp tipahikan kâ-ispayik. *at 12:00.*
	nitati-kîwân *I begin to go home*	nîsitanaw cipahikanis pâmwayês niyânan tipahikan kâ-ispayik. *at 4:40.*

Replace the underlined verb stem below with the above verbs:

QUESTION:

kiya mâka, tânitahto tipahikan mâna k<u>initawi-kiskinwahamâkosin</u> ispîhk kâ-nîso-kîsikâk?
How about you, what time do you go to class on Tuesday?

WEDNESDAY

Day of the week	Activity	Time of activity
ispîhk mâna kâ-nisto-kîsikâk *On Wednesday*	nisêsâwîn *I exercise*	niyânan tipahikan mîna âpihtaw kâ-ispayik. *at 5:30.*
	nitayamihcikân *I read*	niyânanosâp cipahikanis pâmwayês kêkâ-mitâtaht tipahikan kâ-ispayik. *at 8:45.*
	nimasinahikân *I write*	mitâtaht tipahikan kâ-ispayik. *at 10:00.*
	nitati-kawisimon *I begin to lay down to sleep*	mitâtaht cipahikanis miyâskam pêyakosâp tipahikan kâ-ispayik. *at 11:10.*

Replace the underlined verb stem below with the above verbs:

QUESTION:

kiya mâka, tânitahto tipahikan mâna ki<u>sêsâwîn</u> ispîhk kâ-nisto-kîsikâk?
How about you, what time do you exercise when it is Wednesday?

THURSDAY

Day of the week	Activity	Time of activity
ispîhk mâna kâ-nêwo-kîsikâk *On Thursday*	ninitawi-atoskân *I go to work*	têpakohp tipahikan mîna âpihtaw kâ-ispayik. *at 7:30.*
	nikîsi-atoskân *I finish work*	nikotwâsik tipahikan kâ-ispayik. *at 6:00.*
	nitati-kîwêpayin *I drive home*	nîsosâp cipahikanis miyâskam nikotwâsik tipahikan kâ-ispayik. *at 6:12.*
	nitati-piminawason *I begin to cook*	nîsitanaw cipahikanis pâmwayês ayênânêw tipahikan kâ-ispayik. *at 7:40.*

Replace the underlined verb stem below with the above verbs:

QUESTION:

kiya mâka, tânitahto tipahikan mâna ki<u>nitawi-atoskân</u> ispîhk kâ-nêwo-kîsikâk?
How about you, what time do you go to work when it is Thursday?

FRIDAY

Day of the week	Activity	Time of activity
ispîhk mâna kâ-niyânano-kîsikâk *When it is Friday*	nisêsâwipâhtân *I jog*	nikotwâsik tipahikan mîna âpihtaw kâ-ispayik. *at 6:30.*
	nikisîpêkiyâkanân *I wash dishes*	niyânanosâp cipahikanis pâmwayês têpakohp tipahikan kâ-ispayik. *at 6:45.*
	niminihkwân pihkahtêwâpoy *I drink coffee*	nisto tipahikan kâ-ispayik. *at 3:00.*
	nitotâkwani-mîcison *I eat supper*	niyânanosâp cipahikanis miyâskam nikotwâsik tipahikan kâ-ispayik. *at 6:15.*

Replace the underlined verb stem below with the above verbs:

QUESTION:

kiya mâka, tânitahto tipahikan mâna ki<u>sêsâwipâht</u>ân ispîhk kâ-niyânano-kîsikâk?
How about you, what time do you jog on Fridays?

SATURDAY

Day of the week	Activity	Time of activity
ispîhk mâna kâ-nikotwâso-kîsikâk *When it is Saturday*	ninitawi-papâmi-atâwân *I go shopping*	kêkâ-mitâtaht tipahikan mîna âpihtaw kâ-ispayik. *at 9:30.*
	nipapâmitâpâson *I ride around*	niyânanosâp cipahikanis miyâskam nîso tipahikan kâ-ispayik. *at 2:15.*
	ninitawi-nîmihiton *I go dancing*	mitâtaht tipahikan kâ-ispayik. *at 10:00.*
	nikîsi-nîmihiton *I finish dancing*	nîsitanaw cipahikanis pâmwayês nîso tipahikan kâ-ispayik. *at 1:40.*

Replace the underlined verb stem below with the above verbs:

QUESTION:

kiya mâka, tânitahto tipahikan mâna ki<u>nitawi-papâmi-atâwâ</u>n ispîhk kâ-nikotwâso-kîsikâk?
How about you, what time do you go shopping on Saturdays?

Day of the week	Activity	Time of activity
ispîhk mâna kâ-ayamihêwi-kîsikâk *When it is Sunday*	nikakwê-waniskân *I try to get up*	têpakohp tipahikan mîna âpihtaw kâ-ispayik. *at 7:30.*
	ninitawi-ayamihân *I go to church*	niyânanosâp cipahikanis pâmwayês pêyakosâp tipahikan kâ-ispayik. *at 10:45.*
	nipapâmi-kiyokân *I go about visiting*	nêwo tipahikan kâ-ispayik. *at 4:00.*
	nikakwê-maskatêpwân *I try to barbecue*	niyânan cipahikanis miyâskam nikotwâsik tipahikan kâ-ispayik. *at 6:05.*

Replace the underlined verb stem below with the above verbs:

QUESTION:

> kiya mâka, tânitahto tipahikan mâna k<u>ikakwê-waniskâ</u>n ispîhk kâ-ayamihêwi-kîsikâk?
> *How about you, what time do you try to get up on Sundays?*

RELATED QUESTIONS ABOUT ACTIVITIES DURING THE DAYS OF THE WEEK.

1. tânitahto kîsikâw anohc? – *What day is it today?*
   POSSIBLE ANSWERS:
   a. pêyako-kîsikâw anohc – *It is Monday today.*
   b. nîso-kîsikâw anohc. – *It is Tuesday today.*
   c. nisto-kîsikâw anohc – *It is Wednesday today.*
   d. nêwo-kîsikâw anohc. – *It is Thursday today.*
   e. niyânano-kîsikâw anohc. – *It is Friday today.*
   f. nikotwâso-kîsikâw anohc. – *It is Saturday today.*
   g. ayamihêwi-kîsikâw anohc. – *It is Sunday today.*

2. tânispîhk mâna kiya kâ-papâmi-atâwêyan? – *When do you go shopping?*
   (The verb can be replaced with whatever activity you are asking about.)
   ANSWER: kâ-nikotwâso-kîsikâk mâna nipapâmi-atâwân.

3. kinitawi-ayamihân cî mâna ispîhk kâ-ayamihêwi-kîsikâk?
   Do you go to church whenever it is Sunday (or 'on Sunday')?
   ANSWER: âha, ninitawi-ayamihân mâna ispîhk kâ-ayamihêwi-kîsikâk.

4. tânisi mâna kâ-itahkamikisiyan ispîhk kâ-nikotwâso-kîsikâk?
   What do you do when it is Saturday (replace with any day of the week)?
   ANSWER: nipapâmi-atâwân mâna ispîhk kâ-nikotwâso-kîsikâk?

Read the text, then answer the questions:

6:00

kapê-tipisk nikî-nipân.

wîpac kîkisêp nikî-waniskân,
nânitaw êtikwê nikotwâsik
tipahikan ê-ispayik.

QUESTIONS:

1. kapê-tipisk cî awa kî-nipâw?

    _____

2. kiya mâka, kapê-tipisk cî kikî-nipân tipiskohk?

    _____

3. wîpac cî awa kî-waniskâw?

    _____

4. kiya mâka, wîpac cî kikî-waniskân kîkisêp?

    _____

5. tânitahto tipahikan mâna kâ-waniskâyan kâ-kîkisêpâk?

    _____

6:30

nikî-kîsitêpon nikotwâsik tipahikan
mîna âpihtaw ê-ispayik.

6:50

nikî-mâci-kîkisêpâ-mîcison mitâtaht
cipahikanis pâmwayês têpakohp
tipahikan ê-ispayik.

QUESTIONS:

1. tânitahto tipahikan mâna kâ-kîsitêpot awa nâpêw?

    _____

2. kiya mâka, tânitahto tipahikan mâna kâ-kîsitêpoyan?

    _____

3. tânitahto tipahikan mâna kâ-kîkisêpâ-mîcisot awa nâpêw?

    _____

4. kiya mâka, tânitahto tipahikan mâna kâ-kîkisêpâ-mîcisoyan?

    _____

5. tahto-kîkisêpâw cî mâna kikîkisêpâ-mîcison?

    _____

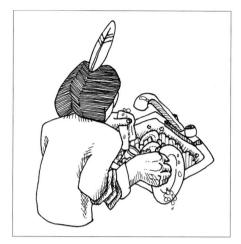

nitati-kisîpêkiyâkanân nânitaw
nîsitanaw cipahikanis ê-miyâskahk
têpakohp tipahikan ê-ispayik.

nikîsi-kâsîyâkanân nîsitanaw cipahikanis
pâmwayês ayênânêw tipahikan ê-ispayik.
nipakwâtên ta-kisîpêkiyâkanêyân.

QUESTIONS:

1. tânitahto tipahikan mâna kâ-ati-kisîpêkiyâkanêt awa nâpêw?

   _____

2. kiya mâka, tânitahto tipahikan mâna kâ-kisîpêkiyâkanêyan?

   _____

3. pakwâtam cî ta-kisîpêkiyâkanêt awa awêkâ cî cîhkêyihtam?

   _____

4. kiya mâka, kicîhkêyihtên cî ta-kisîpêkiyâkanêyan awêkâ cî kipakwâtên?

   _____

5. tânitahto tipahikan mâna kîsi-kâsîyâkanêw awa nâpêw?

   _____

ayênânêw tipahikan ê-ispayik nipimohtân
kihci-kiskinwahamâtowikamikohk isi
ê-nitawi-kiskinwahamâkosiyân.

iyaw! nimwêstasisinin! âsay niyânanosâp
cipahikanis miyâskam kêkâ-mitâtaht tipahikan
ê-ispayik. kwayask nitati-sôhki-pimipahtân.

QUESTIONS:

1. tânitahto tipahikan ê-ispayiyik kâ-pimohtêt kihci-kiskinwahamâtowikamikohk isi?

   _____

2. kiya mâka, tânitahto tipahikan mâna kâ-itohtêyan kihci-kiskinwahamâtowikamikohk?

   _____

3. mwêstasisin cî awa nâpêw?

   _____

4. kiya mâka, kinihtâ-mwêstasisinin cî mâna?

   _____

5. tânitahto tipahikan ê-ispayiyik awa kâ-mâci-sôhki-pimipahtât?

   _____

kêkâ-mitâtaht tipahikan mîna âpihtaw ê-kîkisêpâk nitakohtân mâka âsay kîsi-kiskinwahamâkosiwak niwîcêwâkanak.

nipôni-kiskinwahamâkosin nêwo tipahikan mîna âpihtaw ê-ispayik kâ-pôni-âpihtâ-kîsikâk. nicîhkêyihtên ayisk ê-wî-nîmihitoyân tipiskâki.

QUESTIONS:

1. tânitahto tipahikan ê-kîkisêpâyik takohtêw kihci-kiskinwahamâtowikamikohk?

_____

2. âsay cî kîsi-kiskinwahamâkosiyiwa owîcêwâkana?

_____

3. kiya mâka, tânitahto tipahikan mâna kitakohtân kihci-kiskinwahamâtowikamikohk?

_____

4. tânitahto tipahikan mâna kâ-pôni-kiskinwahamâkosicik *Shaking-Spear* êkwa *Monique*?

_____

5. tânêhki awa *Shaking-Spear* kâ-cîhkêyihtahk?

_____

2:00

4:00

wahwâ! kwayask nimôcikihtân. osâm piko kapê-tipisk ê-nîmihitoyân. nîso tipahikan ê-kîkisêpâk isko ninîmihiton.

nêwo tipahikan ê-kîkisêpâk nitati-kawisimon. ahpô êtikwê kîkisêpâki mâka mîna wîpac nika-waniskân. ta-kî-ihkin mâni-mâka.

QUESTIONS:

1. kî-môcikihtâw cî *Shaking-Spear*?

2. tânitahto tipahikan isko kî-nîmihitow?

3. kiya mâka, kinîmihiton cî mâna isko nîso tipahikan ê-kîkisêpâk?

4. tânitahto tipahikan kâ-ati-kawisimot?

5. kiya mâka, tânitahto tipahikan mâna kâ-kawisimoyan?

EXERCISES

EXERCISE 1. In the sentences below, keep the times of day (VII) as they are, but change the following action verbs (VAI) to correspond in tense to the VII:

1. tipiskohk wîpac ni**ka**-kawisimon. (*Last night I went to bed early.*)

    _____

2. tipiskâki ni**kî**-nitawi-nîmihitonân. (*We (excl.) will go dance tonight.*)

    _____

3. wîpac kîkisêp ki**wî**-kakwê-waniskânaw (We (incl.) *tried to get up early this morning.*)

    _____

4. âpihtâ-kîsikâyiki **kî**-pê-mîcisowak. (*They will come to eat at noon.*)

    _____

5. otâkosiniyiki **ta**-kîwêw. (*He is going to go home this evening.*)

    _____

6. wîpac kîkisêp **ta**-papâsi-waniskâw. (*Early this morning she/he got up in a hurry.*)

    _____

7. kîkisêpâyiki **kî**-kiskinwahamâkosiw. (*In the morning he/she will go to class.*)

    _____

8. ispîhk kâ-kîkisêpâk ni**wî**-kistâpitêhon. (*When it is morning I brush my teeth.*)

    _____

9. âpihtâ-kîsikâyiki **wî**-ayamihcikêw. (*She/he will read at noon.*)

    _____

10. pôni-âpihtâ-kîsikâki ni**kî**-masinahikân. (*I'm going to write this afternoon.*)

    _____

11. ispîhk kâ-âpihtâ-kîsikâk ki**ka**-mâci-kiskinwahamâkosin. (*When it is noon you start class.*)

    _____

12. otâkosiki ni**ka**-kakwê-kîsitêpon. (*I'm going to try to cook this evening.*)

    _____

13. tipiskohk **wî**-sôhki-nîmihitow. (*She/he danced hard last night.*)

    _____

14. tipiskâki ki**kî**-nitawi-nikamon. (*You will go and sing tonight.*)

    _____

EXERCISE 2. Read the text below the picture, then answer the questions:

Words needed: âha – *yes*; and namôya – *no*.

Highlighting the difference of time of day forms when the subject of the independent clause verb is 3rd person as is the text under the picture as well as the Q1 in each and when the subject is 2nd and 1st person as in Q2.

1. ispîhk kâ-tipiskâyik ati-nôhtêhkwasiw.
Q1: nôhtêhkwasiw cî awa ispîhk kâ-tipiskâyik?

_____

_____

Q2: kiya mâka, kitati-nôhtêhkwasin cî ispîhk kâ-tipiskâk?

_____

_____

2. ispîhk kâ-tipiskâyik pêyako-kawisimow.
Q1: kâkîsimow cî awa ispîhk kâ-tipiskâyik?

_____

_____

Q2: kiya mâka, kikawisimon cî ispîhk kâ-tipiskâk?

_____

_____

3. ispîhk kâ-tipiskâyik matwêhkwâmiw.
Q1: matwêhkwâmiw cî awa ispîhk kâ-tipiskâyik?

_____

_____

Q2: kiya mâka, kimatwêhkwâmin cî ispîhk kâ-tipiskâk?

_____

_____

4. nisihkâci-waniskâw ispîhk kâ-kîkisêpâyik.
Q1: nisihkâci-kawisimow cî awa ispîhk kâ-kîkisêpâyik?

_____

_____

Q2: kiya mâka, kikawisimon cî ispîhk kâ-kîkisêpâk?

_____

_____

5. ispîhk kâ-kîkisêpâyik ati-kistâpitêhow.

Q1: ati-kistâpitêhow cî awa ispîhk kâ-kîkisêpâyik.

_____

_____

Q2: kiya mâka, kikistâpitêhon cî ispîhk kâ-kîkisêpâk?

_____

6. ispîhk kâ-kîkisêpâyik pêyâhtaki-sîkahow.

Q1: pêyâhtaki-sîkahow cî awa ispîhk kâ-kîkisêpâyik?

_____

_____

Q2: kiya mâka, kisîkahon cî ispîhk kâ-kîkisêpâk?

_____

7. ispîhk kâ-kîkisêpâyik kâsîhkwêw.

Q1: kâsîhkwêw cî awa ispîhk kâ-kîkisêpâyik?

_____

_____

Q2: kiya mâka, kikâsîhkwân cî ispîhk kâ-kîkisêpâk?

_____

8. ispîhk kâ-âpihtâ-kîsikâyik mâci-nôhtêhkatêw.

Q1: mâci-nôhtêhkwasiw cî awa ispîhk kâ-âpihtâ-kîsikâyik?

_____

_____

Q2: kiya mâka, kinôhtêhkatân cî ispîhk kâ-âpihtâ-kîsikâk?

_____

9. ispîhk kâ-âpihtâ-kîsikâyik minihkwêw.

Q1: minihkwêw cî awa ispîhk
kâ-âpihtâ-kîsikâyik?

_____

_____

Q2: kiya mâka, kiminihkwân cî
ispîhk kâ-âpihtâ-kîsikâk?

_____

_____

10. ispîhk kâ-otâkosiniyik ayamihcikêw.

Q1: ayamihcikêw cî awa ispîhk
kâ-otâkosiniyik?

_____

_____

Q2: kiya mâka, kitayamihcikân cî
ispîhk kâ-otâkosik?

_____

_____

11. ispîhk kâ-tipiskâyik nikamow.

Q1: nikamow cî awa ispîhk
kâ-tipiskâyik?

_____

_____

Q2: kiya mâka, kinikamon cî ispîhk
kâ-tipiskâk?

_____

_____

12. ispîhk kâ-âpihtâ-tipiskâyik nîmihitow.

Q1: nîmihitow cî awa ispîhk
kâ-âpihtâ-tipiskâyik?

_____

_____

Q2: kiya mâka, kinîmihiton cî
ispîhk kâ-âpihtâ-tipiskâk?

_____

_____

EXERCISE 3. Pair up to do the following:

Q: tânisi kâ-isiwêpahk ôta?
What's the weather like here?
A: mispon êkota.
It snows there.

Q: kimiwan cî ôta?
Does it rain here?
A: i) namôya, mispon êkota.
ii) namôya, namôya kimiwan êkota.
iii) namôya, namôya kimiwan êkota,
mispon anima.

Q: tânisi kâ-isiwêpahk ôta?
What's the weather like here?
A: miyo-kîsikâw êkota.
It's a nice day there.

Q: miyo-kîsikâw cî ôta?
Is it a nice day here?
A: i) âha, miyo-kîsikâw êkota.

Q: tânisi kâ-isiwêpahk ôta?
What's the weather like here?
A: kîsapwêyâw êkota.
It is warm there.

Q: kîsapwêyâw cî ôta?
Is it warm here?
A: âha, kîsapwêyâw êkota.

Q: tânisi kâ-isiwêpahk ôta?
What's the weather like here?
A: ati-kimiwan êkota.
It begins to rain there.

Q: ati-kimiwan cî ôta?
Does it begin to rain here?
A: âha, ati-kimiwan êkota.

Q: tânisi kâ-isiwêpahk ôta?
What's the weather like here?

A: kimiwan êkota.
It rains there.

Q: mispon cî ôta?
Does it snow here?

A: i) namôya, kimiwan êkota.
ii) namôya, namôya mispon êkota.
iii) namôya, namôya mispon êkota,
kimiwan anima.

Q: tânisi kâ-isiwêpahk ôta?
What's the weather like here?

A: kisâstêw êkota.
It's a hot day there.

Q: tahkâyâw cî ôta?
Is it a cold day here?

A: i) namôya, kisâstêw êkota.
ii) namôya, namôya tahkâyâw.
iii) namôya, namôya tahkâyâw,
kisâstêw anima êkota.

Q: tânisi kâ-isiwêpahk ôta?
What's the weather like here?

A: kisinâw êkota.
It is very cold there.

Q: yôtin cî ôta?
Is it windy here?

A: i) namôya, kisinâw êkota.
ii) namôya, namôya yôtin êkota.
iii) namôya, namôya yôtin êkota,
kisinâw anima.

Q: tânisi kâ-isiwêpahk ôta?
What's the weather like here?

A: wâsêskwan êkota.
It's a clear sunny day there.

Q: miyo-kîsikâw cî ôta?
Is it a nice day here?

A: i) âha, miyo-kîsikâw êkota.
wâsêskwan anima!

Q: tânisi kâ-isiwêpahk ôta?
What's the weather like here?
A: sôhkiyowêw êkota.
It is very windy there

Q: sôhkiyowêw cî ôta?
Is it very windy here?
A: âha, sôhkiyowêw êkota.

Q: tânisi kâ-isiwêpahk ôta?
What's the weather like here?
A: tahkâyâw êkota.
It is a cold day there.

Q: tahkâyâw cî ôta?
Is it a cold day here?
A: âha, tahkâyâw êkota.

Q: tânisi kâ-isiwêpahk ôta?
What's the weather like here?
A: ati-yîkwaskwan êkota.
It begins to be cloudy there.

Q: yôtin cî ôta?
Is it windy here?
A: i) namôya, ati-yîkwaskwan êkota.
ii) namôya, namôya yôtin êkota.
iii) namôya, namôya yôtin êkota,
yîkwaskwan êkota.

Q: tânisi kâ-isiwêpahk ôta?
What's the weather like here?
A: yôtin êkota.
It's windy there.

Q: ati-yîkwaskwan cî ôta?
Is it getting cloudy here?
A: i) namôya, yôtin êkota.
ii) namôya, namôya ati-yîkwaskwan.
iii) namôya, namôya ati-yîkwaskwan,
yôtin êkota.

5.7 REVIEW: INANIMATE INTRANSITIVE VERBS

DAYS OF THE WEEK

INDICATIVE	CONJUNCT: Put ê at the beginning, replace the last w with k	FUTURE CONDITIONAL: Drop ê from conjunct forms then add i
pêyako-kîsikâw	ê-pêyako-kîsikâk	pêyako-kîsikâki
nîso-kîsikâw	ê-nîso-kîsikâk	nîso-kîsikâki
nisto-kîsikâw	ê-nisto-kîsikâk	nisto-kîsikâki
nêwo-kîsikâw	ê-nêwo-kîsikâk	nêwo-kîsikâki
niyânano-kîsikâw	ê-niyânano-kîsikâk	niyânano-kîsikâki
nikotwâso-kîsikâw	ê-nikotwâso-kîsikâk	nikotwâso-kîsikâki
ayamihêwi-kîsikâw	ê-ayamihêwi-kîsikâk	ayamihêwi-kîsikâki

WEATHER CONDITIONS

INDICATIVE	CONJUNCT:	FUTURE CONDITIONAL:
kimiwan – *It rains.*	ê-kimiwahk	kimiwahki
kimiwasin – *It drizzles.*	ê-kimiwasik	kimiwasiki
pahkipêstâw – *It rains heavy.*	ê-pahkipêstâk	pahkipêstâki
sîkipêstâw – *It pours.*	ê-sîkipêstâk	sîkipêstâki
yîkowan – *It is foggy.*	ê-yîkowahk	yîkowahki
mispon – *It snows.*	ê-mispok	mispoki
pîwan – *It is drifting snow.*	ê-pîwahk	pîwahki
yôtin – *It is windy.*	ê-yôtihk	yôtihki
wâsêskwan – *It is sunny.*	ê-wâsêskwahk	wâsêskwahki
yîkwaskwan – *It is cloudy.*	ê-yîkwaskwahk	yîkwaskwahki
âhkwatin – *It freezes.*	ê-âhkwatihk	âhkwatihki
tihkitêw – *It melts.*	ê-tihkitêk	tihkitêki
kisâstêw – *It is hot.*	ê-kisâstêk	kisâstêki
kîsapwêyâw – *It is warmish.*	ê-kîsapwêyâk	kîsapwêyâki
kîsapwêw – *It is warm.*	ê-kîsapwêk	kîsapwêki
tahkâyâw – *It is cold.*	ê-tahkâyâk	tahkâyâki
kisinâw – *It is very cold.*	ê-kisinâk	kisinâki
miyo-kîsikâw – *It is a nice day.*	ê-miyo-kîsikâk	miyo-kîsikâki
maci-kîsikâw – *It is a miserable day.*	ê-maci-kîsikâk	maci-kîsikâki
wîpâci-kîsikâw – *It is a nasty day.*	ê-wîpâci-kîsikâk	wîpâci-kîsikâki

TIMES OF DAY

INDICATIVE	CONJUNCT: Put ê at the beginning, replace the last w or n with k or hk	FUTURE CONDITIONAL: Drop ê from conjunct forms then add i
wâpan – *It is dawn/day.*	ê-wâpahk	wâpahki
kîkisêpâw – *It is morning.*	ê-kîkisêpâk	kîkisêpâki
kîsikâw – *It is day.*	ê-kîsikâk	kîsikâki
âpihtâ-kîsikâw – *It is noon.*	ê-âpihtâ-kîsikâk	âpihtâ-kîsikâki
pôni-âpihtâ-kîsikâw – *It is afternoon.*	ê-pôni-âpihtâ-kîsikâk	pôni-âpihtâ-kîsikâki
otâkosin – *It is evening.*	ê-otâkosik	otâkosiki
tipiskâw – *It is night.*	ê-tipiskâk	tipiskâki
âpihtâ-tipiskâw – *It is midnight.*	ê-âpihtâ-tipiskâk	âpihtâ-tipiskâki
wawâninâkwan – *It is twilight.*	ê-wawâninâkwahk	wawâninâkwahki

SEASONS

INDICATIVE	CONJUNCT	FUTURE CONDITIONAL
sîkwan – *It is sping.*	ê-sîkwahk	sîkwahki
nîpin – *It is summer.*	ê-nîpihk	nîpihki
takwâkin – *It is fall.*	ê-takwâkik	takwâkiki
pipon – *It is winter.*	ê-pipohk	pipohki

5.8 CHAPTER FIVE EXERCISES WITH VAIs AND VIIs

EXERCISE 1. Change the following VAIs into their conjunct forms, then translate:

1. nikî-nipân otâkosîhk.

    _____

2. âsay cî kikî-mîcison?

    _____

3. kî-mâtow.

    _____

4. kî-nîpâyâstêw.

    _____

5. nikî-otâkwani-mîcison.

    _____

6. masinahikêyiwa.

    _____

7. wî-mêtawêwak wayawîtimihk.

    _____

8. kitâkayâsîmonâwâw cî.

    _____

9. kikî-ayamihcikânaw âsay.

    _____

10. kî-sôhki-atoskêw.

    _____

EXERCISE 2. Complete the following:

1. If "mîciso" is the AI verb stem of "*eat*" and "nôhtê-" is the preverb for "*to want to*", how would you write the following in Cree?

   a) *Do you want to eat?* _____

   b) *Let's eat.* _____

   c) *He wanted to eat.* _____

   d) *They want to eat.* _____

   e) *We* (incl.) *will want to eat.* _____

   f) *We* (excl.) *are going to want to eat later.* _____

   g) *Did you* (pl.) *want to eat?* _____

   h) *Eat* (you-pl.) *later.* _____

2. Put the II verb "miyo-kîsikâw – *it is a nice day*" into the following forms and translate each form:

   a) Conjunct Mood, past tense: _____

   b) Indicative Mood, future definite tense: _____

   c) Indicative Mood, Past tense: _____

   d) Indicative Mood with preverb "ati-",
      future intentional tense: _____

   e) Future Conditional form: _____

3. Put the II verb "yôtin – *it is windy*" into the following forms and translate:

   a) Conjunct Mood, past tense: _____

   b) Indicative Mood, future definite tense: _____

   c) Indicative Mood, Past tense: _____

   d) Indicative Mood, future intentional tense: _____

   e) Future Conditional form: _____

EXERCISE 3. Answer the following questions in Cree.

1. tânisi?_____

2. tânisi kitisiyihkâson?_____

3. tânitê ohci kiya kayahtê?_____

4. tânisi kâ-isiwêpahk mêkwâc?_____

5. âsay cî kikî-mîcison?_____

EXERCISE 4. Complete the following (the personal pronouns are used only to identify the actor of the sentences – the verbs are in their verb stem forms; they need to be placed in their correct forms). Times of day will dictate the tenses of the VAIs:

1. nâpêsisak (nôhtê-nitawi-mêtawê) wayawîtimihk mwêstas.
   (*The boys will want to go and play outside later.*)

   _____

2. ana iskwêw (nihtâ-âkayâsîmo). (*That woman knows how to speak English.*)

   _____

3. niya (sôhki-atoskê) tipiskohk. (*I worked hard last night.*)

   _____

4. âsay cî kiyawâw (mîciso)? (*Did you (pl.) eat already?*)

   _____

5. (nêhiyawê) cî kiya? (*Do you speak Cree!*)

   _____

6. (sipwêhtê) kiyânaw. (IMP. Md.) (*Let's leave.*)

   _____

7. wîpac (kîwê) niyanân (Fut. Int. tense). (*We intend to go home soon.*)

   _____

8. *John* otôtêma (nihtâ-pwâtisimo). (*John's friend knows how to dance pow-wow.*)

_____

9. êkâwiya (nipâ) kiyawâw (IMP. Md.) (*Don't sleep!*)

_____

10. mahti (kakwê-nêhiyawê) kiyawâw. (*Please try to speak Cree*)

_____

EXERCISE 5. Using the times of day as reference, put the following verbs (in brackets) into their correct tenses as well as in their correct person (the future tense could be in either the future intentional tense "**wî**" or the future definite "**ka**" [for 1st and 2nd persons] or "**ta**" [for 3rd persons]):

1. otâkosîhk (miyo-mêtawê) awâsisak. (*Yesterday the children played well.*)

_____

2. otâkosiki (nitawi-atoskê) niya. (*I intend to go to work this evening.*)

_____

3. tipiskohk cî (pê-itohtê) wiya? (*Did she/he come last night?*)

_____

4. tipiskâyiki (kakwê-masinahikê) otôtêma. (*Her/his friend is going to write tonight.*)

_____

5. âpihtâ-kîsikâki cî (nitawi-mêtawê) kiyawâw? (*Are you going to go and play at noon?*)

_____

EXERCISE 6. Correct the tense in the following VAI forms using the times of day as your cue for the tenses needed in the VAI forms (take the English translation as your cue):

1. tipiskâki nikî-sôhki-atoskân. (*Tonight I will work hard.*)

_____

2. kîkisêp wî-kakwê-sipwêhtêwak wîpac. (*This past morning they tried to leave early.*)

_____

3. tipiskohk ta-nitawi-mêcawêsiyiwa otôtêma pinkô. (*Last night his friend went to play a little bingo.*)

_____

4. wâpahki cî ê-kî-nôhtê-nitawi-pwâtisimoyêk?
   (*Tomorrow are you going to want to go and dance pow-wow?*)

_____

5. mispon êkâwiya nipâhkan wayawîtimihk. (*If it snows, don't sleep outside.*)

_____

6. kimiwahki ati-kîwêtân. (*If it rains, let's go home.*)

_____

7. âpihtâ-kîsikâki cî kikî-nitawi-mîcisonâwâw? (*If/when it is noon, are you going to go and eat?*)

_____

8. ati-pipohki kî-ati-nihtâ-nêhiyawêw ana iskwêsis.
   (*If/when winter comes, that girl will start speaking Cree well.*)

_____

9. otâkosîhk nika-pôni-âkayâsîmonân. (*Yesterday we stopped speaking English.*)

_____

10. ati-tahkâyâki êkâwiya nipâ wayawîtimihk. (*If/when it gets cold, don't sleep outside*).

_____

CHAPTER SIX
• • • • • • • • • • • • • •

POSSESSIVES: KINSHIP TERMS

6. THE NATURE OF POSSESSIVES IN CREE

Possessives can be either alienable or inalienable. Alienable possessive forms are those that can undergo a transfer of ownership. Inalienable possessive forms cannot undergo a transfer of ownership. Examples of alienable possessive nouns are objects like hat and shoe (conjugated below), while inalienable nouns include body parts and kinship terms.

Like the verbs, nouns in possessive forms can be conjugated as in the following alienable nouns (the noun is underlined below):

	astotin – *hat*		**maskisin** – *shoe*
1	nitastotin – *my hat*	**1**	nimaskisin – *my shoe*
2	kitastotin – *your hat*	**2**	kimaskisin – *your shoe*
3	otastotin – *her/his hat*	**3**	omaskisin – *her/his shoe*
3'	otastotiniyiw – *her/his friend's hat*	**3'**	omaskisiniyiw – *his/her friend's shoe*
1P	nitastotininân – *our hat*	**1P**	nimaskisininân – *our shoe*
21	kitastotininaw – *our hat*	**21**	kimaskisininaw – *our shoe*
2P	kitastotiniwâw – *your hat*	**2P**	kimaskisiniwâw – *your shoe*
3P	otastotiniwâw – *their hat*	**3P**	omaskisiniwâw – *Their shoe*
3'P	otastotiniyiwa – *Their friend's hats*	**3'P**	omaskisiniyiwa – *Their friend's shoes*

The underlined parts above show the noun stem before taking on the possessive form.

RULE: Use a connective "**t**" for nouns that begin with a vowel for 1st, 2nd and 3rd person forms.

Nouns that begin with "**m(i)**" have different forms depending on whether the noun is alienable or inalienable. Let's look at those nouns that begin with "**m(i)**":

INALIENABLE NOUN		**ALIENABLE NOUN**
micihciy – *hand*		**mistikowat** – *box*
1 nicihciy – *my hand*	**1**	nimistikowat – *my box*
2 kicihciy – *your hand*	**2**	kimistikowat – *your box*
3 ocihciy – *her/his hand*	**3**	omistikowat – *her/his box*
3' ocihciyiw – *her/his friend's hand*	**3'**	omistikowatiyiw – *her/his friend's box*

1P	nicihcînân – *our hand*		**1P**	nimistikowatinân – *our box*
21	kicihcînaw – *our hand*		**21**	kimistikowatinaw – *our box*
2P	kicihcîwâw – *your hand*		**2P**	kimistikowatiwâw – *your box*
3P	ocihcîwâw – *their hand*		**3P**	omistikowatiwâw – *their box*
3'P	ocihcîyiwa – *their friend's hands*		**3'P**	omistikowatiyiwa – *their friend's boxes*

RULE: For inalienable nouns that begin with "**m(i)**" – drop the "**m(i)**", then add the appropriate person indicators "**n(i)**," "**k(i)**" or "**o**" (or "**w**"). All alienable nouns, including those that begin with "**mi**", take on the "**ni**," "**ki**" and "**o**" possessive markers.

6.1 KINSHIP TERMS

In conversations about yourself you will often want to tell people about your family: how many brothers and sisters you have, or if you are a parent yourself, how many children you have. There are two ways of giving this type of information: in one way you would use the Transitive Animate verb "ayâw – *have him/her*", as in the following:

nitayâwâwak nisto nistêsak. – I have three older brothers.

However, there are two serious problems with that particular way of talking: 1) this form, though grammatical, is never used because 2) it indicates that you possess, as in owning, other human beings. Clearly problem number two is the more serious problem since no other human should have possession of another.

Although the above phrase is syntactically correct, semantically it gives rise to a serious problem that people would not accept. Therefore, the acceptable way of expressing the idea that you have relatives does not include the VTA "ayâw"; rather, the idea of possession is included within the kinship term in its animate intransitive verb form (e.g., "ostêsi – *have an older brother*"). Thus, "nisto nitostêsin = *I have three older brothers*". Here, then, is a list of kinship terms; one column shows "*my, your,* and *her/his*" (but keep in mind that these can be inflected for all the forms in the conjugation patterns) and the other shows the animate intransitive verb forms "*I have, you have,* and *she/he has (kin).*"

NOUNS

OLDER BROTHER
nistês – *my older brother*
kistês – *your older brother*
ostêsa – *Her/his older brother*

OLDER SISTER
nimis – *my older sister*
kimis – *your older sister*
omisa – *Her/his older sister*

VERBS

nitostêsin – *I have an older brother(s)*
kitostêsin – *You have an older brother(s)*
ostêsiw – *She/he has an older brother(s)*

nitomisin – *I have an older sister(s)*
kitomisin – *You have an older sister(s)*
omisiw – *She/he has an older sister(s)*

6.1.A KINSHIP TERMS: VERBS AND NOUNS

Kinship terms can be in a verb form but they can also be in the noun form. In fact, talking about kin in the noun form is more common than talking about them in the verb form. While English has the generic terms brother, sister, mother, father, and so on, Cree does not have those terms as such; instead, one must use the possessive forms in talking about these family members. Compare the following list of verbs and their noun counterparts:

VAI – FORMS	NOUNS
osîmisi – *have a younger sibling*	nisîmis – *my younger sibling*
ostêsi – *have an older brother*	nistês – *my older brother*
omisi – *have an older sister*	nimis – *my older sister*
okosisi – *have a son*	nikosis – *my son*
otânisi – *have a daughter*	nitânis – *my daughter*
ôsisimi – *have a grandchild*	nôsisim – *my grandchild*
owîkimâkani – *have a spouse*	niwîkimâkan – *my spouse*
otawâsimisi – *have a child*	nitawâsimis – *my child*
wîtisâni – *have a sibling*	nîtisân – *my sibling*
ohtâwî – *have a father*	nohtâwiy – *my father*
okâwî – *have a mother*	nikâwiy – *my mother*
ohkomi – *be a grandmother*	nohkom – *my grandmother*
omosômi – *be a grandfather*	nimosôm – *my grandfather*

Like the verb forms the noun forms can be put in the paradigm indicating whose kin is being discussed. Let's take a look at "nikosis – *my son*" put in the following paradigm:

1	nikosis – *my son*	**1P**	nikosisinân – *our son*	
2	kikosis – *your son*	**21**	kikosisinaw – *our son*	
3	okosisa – *her/his son*	**2P**	kikosisiwâw – *your son*	
3'	okosisiyiwa – *her/his ____ son*	**3P**	okosisiwâwa – *their son*	
3'P	okosisiyiwa – *their ____ son*			

Most of the kinship terms will follow the above paradigm. Compare those above with the two which have long vowels toward the beginning:

	GRANDCHILD	SIBLING
1	nôsisim – _____	nîtisân – _____
2	kôsisim – _____	kîtisân – _____
3	ôsisima – _____	wîtisâna – _____
3'	ôsisimiyiwa – _____	wîtisâniyiwa – _____
1P	nôsisiminân – _____	nîtisâninân – _____

21	kôsisiminaw – _____	kîtisâninaw – _____
2P	kôsisimiwâw – _____	kîtisâniwâw – _____
3P	ôsisimiwâwa – _____	wîtisâniwâwa – _____
3'P	ôsisimiyiwa – _____	wîtisâniyiwa – _____

EXERCISES

EXERCISE 1. Translate the following (nouns are on the left and verbs on the right):

YOUNGER BROTHER OR SISTER

nisîmis – _____   nitosîmisin – _____

kisîmis – _____   kitosîmisin – _____

osîmisa – _____   osîmisiw – _____

SIBLING: BROTHERS AND/OR SISTERS

nîtisân – _____   niwîtisânin – _____

kîtisân – _____   kiwîtisânin – _____

wîtisâna – _____   wîtisâniw – _____

CHILD – awâsis

nitawâsimis – _____   nitotawâsimisin – _____

kitawâsimis – _____   kitotawâsimisin – _____

otawâsimisa – _____   otawâsimisiw – _____

NOTE: The connective "**t**" in the above used with "_child_" becomes a "**c**" in some communities to show endearment.

Another interesting aspect of this particular kinship term for "*child*" is that it differs from other kinship terms (excepting "*my man*" and "*my woman*" listed below) in that it seems to be similar to alienable nouns with the use of the distinct possessive markers "**ni**," "**ki**" and "**o**." However the inflection toward the end of these nouns will indicate that they are nevertheless inalienable nouns. The possessive indicators "**ni**," "**ki**" and "**o**" used in these three terms shows an aspect of Cree culture that many people have forgotten — namely that should the child's main caretakers, or the man or woman's significant other, leave for the spirit world, then they can be taken care of by someone else.

SON

nikosis – _____   nitokosisin – _____

kikosis – _____   kitokisisin – _____

okosisa – _____   okosisiw – _____

DAUGHTER

nitânis – _____   nitotânisin – _____

kitânis – _____   kitotânisin – _____

otânisa – _____   otânisiw – _____

GRANDCHILD

nôsisim – _____   nitôsisimin – _____

kôsisim – _____   kitôsisimin – _____

ôsisima – _____   ôsisimiw – _____

WOMAN - iskwêw

nitiskwêm – _____   nitotiskwêmin – _____

kitiskwêm – _____   kitotiskwêmin – _____

otiskwêma – _____   otiskwêmiw – _____

MAN - nâpêw

ninâpêm – _____   nitonâpêmin – _____

kinâpêm – _____   kitonâpêmin – _____

onâpêma – _____   onâpêmiw – _____

EXERCISE 2. Translate the following, keeping in mind that your personal information about your family can follow the same format, with you replacing the numbers or deleting the irrelevant information and adding your relevant information:

Solomon nitisiyihkâson. âmaciwîspimowinihk ohci niya.

_____

okiskinwahamâkêw niya. nikotwâsik mâmawi nitowîtisânin;

_____

pêyak nitostêsin, nîso nitomisin, êkwa nisto nitosîmisin.

_____

nîso nitocawâsimisin: pêyak nitokosisin êkwa pêyak nitotânisin.

_____

âsay kîsi-ohpikiwak nitawâsimisak. nêwo mîna nitôsisimin.

_____

EXERCISE 3. Write a paragraph about your own immediate family:

_____

_____

_____

_____

_____

_____

_____

_____

6.1.B KINSHIP TERMS: NOUNS (Fill in the blanks)

SPOUSE – wîkimâkan

niwîkimâkan – *my spouse*

_____ – *your spouse*

_____ – *her/his spouse*

MOTHER

nikâwiy – *my mother*

_____ – *your mother*

_____ – *his/her mother*

YOUNGER BROTHER/SISTER

_____ – *my younger brother/sister*

_____ – *your younger brother/sister*

osîmisa – *his/his younger brother/sister*

OLDER SISTER

_____ – *my sister*

kimis – *your sister*

_____ – *his/her sister*

*NOTE: The term for paternal uncle is the one used for step-father.

UNCLE (MATERNAL)**

nisis – *my uncle*

_____ – *your uncle*

_____ – *his/her uncle*

**NOTE: The term for maternal uncle is also the term for father-in-law.

GRANDMOTHER

_____ – *my grandmother*

_____ – *your grandmother*

ohkoma – *his/her grandmother*

PARENTS

_____ – *my parents*

_____ – *your parents*

onîkihikwa – *his/her parents*

FATHER

_____ – *my father*

kohtâwiy – *your father*

_____ – *his/her father*

OLDER BROTHER

nistês – *my older brother*

_____ – *your older brother*

_____ – *his/her older brother*

UNCLE (PATERNAL)*

_____ – *my uncle*   **ALSO:** nohcâwîs

_____ – *your uncle*   kohcâwîs

ohkomisa – *his/her uncle*   ohcâwîsa

GRANDFATHER

_____ – *my grandfather*

kimosôm – *your grandfather*

_____ – *his/her grandfather*

AUNT (PATERNAL)***

nisikos – *my aunt*

_____ – *your aunt*

_____ – *her/her aunt*

***NOTE: The term for the paternal aunt is also the term for mother-in-law.

AUNT (MATERNAL)****

_____ – *my aunt*   ALSO: _____

kitôsis – *your aunt*   _____

_____ – *his/her aunt*   okâwîsa

****NOTE: The term for maternal aunt is the one used for step-mother.

MALE COUSIN – USED BY MALE-MALE (SON OF PATERNAL UNCLE OR MATERNAL AUNT)

This term is also used for step-brother by males.

niciwâm – *my cousin*

kiciwâm – _____

ociwâma – _____

NOTE: In addressing each other most people usually address each other as younger brother or older brother. The above terms would be used in talking about these cousins.

MALE COUSIN - USED BY MALE-MALE (SON OF MATERNAL UNCLE OR PATERNAL AUNT)

This term can be used by males in referring to brothers-in-law.

nîstâw – _____

kîstâw – *your cousin*

wîstâwa – _____

COUSIN OF THE OPPOSITE SEX

This term can also be used for sister-in-law or for brother-in-law if these in-laws referring to each other are of the opposite sex.

nîtim – _____

kîtim – _____

wîtimwa – *his/her cousin*

NOTE: Males: use in reference to paternal aunt's daughter or maternal uncle's daughter.

Females: use in reference to son of paternal aunt or son of maternal uncle.

FEMALE COUSIN - USED BY FEMALE-FEMALE
(DAUGHTER OF PATERNAL AUNT OR THE MATERNAL UNCLE)

This term can also be used by females in referring to sisters-in-law.

nicâhkos – *my cousin*

kicâhkos – _____

ocâhkosa – _____

FEMALE COUSIN - USED BY FEMALE-FEMALE
(DAUGHTER OF PATERNAL UNCLE OR MATERNAL AUNT)

Most people usually address each other as older sister or young sister in this situation. This is also the term used for step-sister by females.

niciwâmiskwêm – _____

kiciwâmiskwêm – *your cousin*

ociwâmiskwêma – _____

NOTE: Both the mother's sister's siblings and father's brother's siblings can be addressed as younger or older brother and sister. However the next terms are used for male-female cousins who are the children from these lines.

COUSIN - USED BY MALE-FEMALE; FEMALE-MALE
(OFFSPRING OF FATHER'S BROTHER OR MOTHER'S SISTER)

nitawêmâw – _____

kitawêmâw – _____

otawêmâwa – *his/her cousin*

SON

nikosis – *my son*

kikosis – _____

okosisa – _____

DAUGHTER

nitânis – _____

kitânis – *your daughter*

otânisa – _____

NOTE: These terms can also be used in referring to a brother's children if you are male or a sister's children if you are female.

NIECE (MALE'S SISTER'S CHILDREN OR FEMALE'S BROTHER'S CHILDREN)

nistim – _____

kistim – _____

ostima – *his/her niece*

NOTE: This term can also be used for daughter-in-law.

NEPHEW (MALE'S SISTER'S CHILDREN OR FEMALE'S BROTHER'S CHILDREN)

nitihkwatim – _____

kitihkwatim – *your nephew*

otihkwatima – _____

NOTE: This term can also be used for son-in-law

NIECE (MALE'S BROTHER'S DAUGHTER OR FEMALE'S SISTER'S DAUGHTER)

nitôsimiskwêm – *my niece*

kitôsimiskwêm – _____

otôsimiskwêma – _____

NOTE: This term can also be used for step-daughter.

NEPHEW (MALE'S BROTHER'S SON OR FEMALE'S SISTER'S SON)

nitôsim – _____   ALSO: nikosim

kitôsim – _____   kikosim

otôsima – *his/her nephew*   okosima

NOTE: These terms can also be used for step-son.

RELATIVES/KINFOLK

niwâhkômâkan – *my relative*

_____ – *your relative*

_____ – *his/her relatives*

FRIEND/TRIBESMAN

_____ – *my friend/tribesman*

kitôtêm – *your friend/tribesman*

_____ – *her/his friend/tribesman*

SON-IN-LAW

_____ – *my son-in-law*

_____ – *your son-in-law*

onahâhkisîma – *her/his son-in-law*

DAUGHTER-IN-LAW

_____ – *my daughter-in-law*

kinahâhkaniskwêm – *your daughter-in-law*

_____ – *her/his daughter-in-law*

THE PARENTS OF MY SON-IN-LAW OR DAUGHTER-IN-LAW

nitihtâwâw – *my co-parent-in-law*

_____ – *your co-parent-in-law*

_____ – *her/his co-parent-in-law*

6.2 CREE KINSHIP

6.2.A COUSINS AND SIBLINGS

Compare the following columns:

SOURCE/ GOAL:	Children of: Father's brother OR Mother's sister	Children of: Father's sister OR Mother's brother	Siblings:
Female to female	niciwâmiskwêm	nicâhkos	nîtisân
Female to younger female	nisîmis	nicâhkos	nisîmis
Female to older female	nimis	nicâhkos	nimis
Female to male / male to female	nitawêmâw	nîtim	nîtisân
Female to older male	nistês	nîtim	nistês
Female to younger male	nisîmis	nîtim	nisîmis
Male to male	niciwâm	nîstâw	nîtisân
Male to older male	nistês	nîstâw	nistês
Male to younger male	nisîmis	nîstâw	nisîmis
Male to older female	nimis	nîtim	nimis
Male to younger female	nisîmis	nîtim	nisîmis

6.2.B CREE KINSHIP SYSTEM: SEVEN GENERATIONS

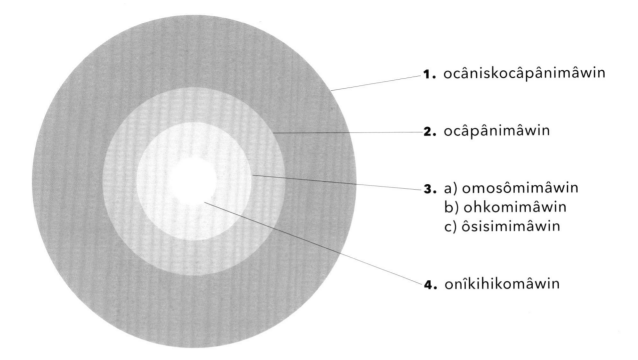

1. ocâniskocâpânimâwin

2. ocâpânimâwin

3. a) omosômimâwin
b) ohkomimâwin
c) ôsisimimâwin

4. onîkihikomâwin

KINSHIP WITHIN THE CIRCLE:

1. The term for great-great grandparents "ocâniskocâpânimâwin" is also the same for great-great grandchildren;

2. The term for great-grandparents "ocâpânimâwin" is also the same for great-grandchildren;

3. a) The term for grandfather "omosômimâwin" applies to all males of that generation;
    b) The term for grandmother "ohkomimâwin" applies to all females of that generation;
    c) The term for grandchild "ôsisimimâwin" applies to all children of that generation;

4. The term for parenthood "onîkihikomâwin" indicates the responsibility parents have for the care of their children, especially when we consider the meaning of the underlined "nîki" which means "*my home*". With this consideration, then, the meaning of parents in Cree can be viewed as "*those who provide a home*". Since a home is supposed to be a safe haven for people to learn and grow then the responsibility of parenthood as indicated in the Cree word is clear.

6.3 VITAL STATISTICS

WORDS

osîmisi – *have a younger sibling* (VAI)
otawâsimisi – *have a child* (VAI)
osîmimâw – *youngest sibling*
omisimâw – *oldest sister*
nimis – *my older sister*
ostêsi – *have an older brother* (VAI)
omisi – *have an older sister* (VAI)
kîsi- – *finish* (PV)

nisîmis – *my younger sibling*
nitawâsimis – *my child*
ostêsimâw – *oldest brother*
nistês – *my older brother*
wîkihto – *be married* (VAI)
kahkiyaw – *all*
iskonikan – *reserve*
êkota – *there*

TEXT. The speaker in the following text is not married and has no children, so he'll talk about his siblings.

tânisi, *Shaking-Spear* nitisiyihkâson.
– *Hello, my name is Shaking-Spear.*

nistomitanaw nikotwâs(ik)osâp nititahtopiponân.
– *I am thirty-six years old.*

iskonikanihk nikî-nihtâwikin. niyânanosâp mâna ê-akimiht ayîki-pîsim nitipiskên.
– *I was born on the reserve. My birthday is on April 15th.*

ôtênâhk nikî-pê-ohpikin, êkota mîna nikî-pê-kiskinwahamâkosin.
– *I was raised in the city, and it was there also that I went to school.*

namôya niwîkihton. nikotwâsik niwîtisânin.
– *I am not married. I have six siblings.*

pêyak nitostêsin êkwa nîso nitomisin. nisto nitosîmisin.
– *I have one older brother and two older sisters. I have three younger siblings.*

kahkiyaw kîsi-ohpikiwak nîtisânak.
– *All my siblings are grown.*

nêmitanaw niyânanosâp itahtopiponêw omisimâw, *Maggie* isiyihkâsow.
– *The oldest sister is 45 years old, her name is Maggie.*

nistomitanaw kêkâ-mitâtahtosâp itahtopiponêw ostêsimâw, *George* isiyihkâsow.
– *The oldest brother is 39 years old, his name is George.*

nîsitanaw kêkâ-mitâtahtosâp itahtopiponêw osîmimâw, *Judy* isiyihkâsow.
– *The youngest sibling is 29 years old, her name is Judy.*

kahkiyaw nîtisânak iskonikanihk wîkiwak.
– *All my siblings live on the reserve.*

QUESTIONS. The preceding text is in the 1st person. The following questions are in the 3rd person. Go back to the preceding text to answer these questions:

1. tânisi isiyihkâsow awa nâpêw?

2. tânitahtopiponêt awa nâpêw?

3. tânispîhk mâna kâ-tipiskahk awa?

4. tânitê kî-pê-ohpikiw awa?

5. ôtênâhk cî mîna kî-pê-kiskinwahamâkosiw?

6. wîkihtow cî awa?

7. tânitahto ocawâsimisiw awa?

8. tânitahto wîtisâniw awa?

9. tânitahto ostêsiw awa?

10. tânitahto osîmisiw awa?

11. tânisi isiyihkâsow osîmimâw?

12. tânitahtopiponêt osîmimâw?

13. tânisi isiyihkâsow ostêsimâw?

14. tânitahtopiponêt ostêsimâw?

VITAL STATISTICS (continued...)

WORDS

okosisi – *have a son* (VAI)
otânisi – *have a daughter* (VAI)
ohtâwîmâwi – *be a father* (VAI)
okâwîmâwi – *be a mother* (VAI)
owîkimâkani – *be a spouse* (VAI)
ninâpêm – *my husband*
iskwêsis – *a girl*
êwako – *that one*

nikosis – *my son*
nitânis – *my daughter*
nohtâwiy – *my father*
nikâwiy – *my mother*
niwîkimâkan – *my spouse*
nitiskwêm – *my wife*
nâpêsis – *a boy*
kayâs – *a long time ago*

TEXT. Translate the following text:

Megan nitisiyihkâson. kayâs nikî-wîkihton.

_____

George isiyihkâsow ninâpêm.

_____

nîso nitotawâsimisinân: pêyak iskwêsis êkwa pêyak nâpêsis.

_____

Mandy isiyihkâsow nitânis, omisimâw êwako.

_____

mitâtaht itahtopiponêw nitânis.

_____

Georgie isiyihkâsow nikosis, osîmimâw êwako.

_____

ayênânêw itahtopiponêw nikosis.

_____

GRAMMAR: NEGATION

Negation of the Indicative Mood involves the insertion of "namôya" before the affirmative statement in the Indicative mood. Place "namôya" to make negative statements below:

AFFIRMATIVE	NEGATIVE
niwîkihton	_____ niwîkihton.
nitotawâsimisin.	_____ nitotawâsimisin.
nitokâwîmâwin.	_____ nitokâwîmâwin.
nitohtâwîmâwin.	_____ nitohtâwîmâwin.

Read the text below the picture, then answer the questions.

"tânisi. *Shaking-Spear*
nitisiyihkâson," itwêw awa
nâpêw. "awîna kiya?"
"*Darren* niya," itwêw ana
kotak nâpêw.

Q. tânisi isiyihkâsow awa pêyak nâpêw?

_____

Shaking-Spear itohtêw
kihci-kiskinwahamâtowikamikohk.
mostohtêw êkotê isi.
ati-wâpamêw wâposwa.
mêtoni miyo-kîsikâw!

Q. tânitê awa nâpêw ê-itohtêt?

_____

"tânisi, wâpakosîs niya,"
itwêw awa. "kiya mâka,
awîna ôma kiya?"

Q. wâpakosîs cî awa?

_____

wâpos awa.
miyonâkosiw awa wâpos.
wâpiskisiw awa wâpos.

Q. awîna awa?

_____

6.4 KINSHIP TERMS: NOUNS AND VERBS OVERVIEW

NOUNS	VERB: *BE*	NOUNS	VERB: *HAVE*
ohkomimâw *- a grandmother*	ohkomimâwi *- be a grandmother*	nohkom *- my grandmother*	ohkomi *- have a grandmother*
omosômimâw *- a grandfather*	omosômimâwi *- be a grandfather*	nimosôm *- my grandfather*	omosômi *- have a grandfather*
okâwîmâw *- a mother*	okâwîmâwi *- be a mother*	nikâwiy *- my mother*	okâwîwi *- have a mother*
ohtâwîmâw *- a father*	ohtâwîmâwi *- be a father*	nohtâwiy *- my father*	ohtâwîwi *- have a father*
ostêsimâw *- the eldest brother*	ostêsimâwi *- be an elder brother*	nistês *- my older brother*	ostêsi *- have an older brother*
omisimâw *- the eldest sister*	omisimâwi *- be an older sister*	nimis *- my older sister*	omisi *- have an older sister*
osîmimâw *- the youngest sibling*	osîmimâwi *- be a younger sibling*	nisîmis *- my younger sibling*	osîmisi *- have a younger sibling*
awâsis *- a child*	awâsisiwi *- be a child*	nitawâsimis *- my child*	otawâsimisi *- have a child*
okosisimâw *- a son*	okosisimâwi *- be a son*	nikosis *- my son*	okosisi *- have a son*
otânisimâw *- a daughter*	otânisimâwi *- be a daughter*	nitânis *- my daughter*	otânisi *- have a daughter*

QUESTIONS. Answer the following questions in Cree.

1. okâwîmâw cî kiya? _____

2. ohtâwîmâw cî kiya? _____

3. ostêsimâw cî kiya? _____

4. osîmimâw cî kiya? _____

5. kitostêsin cî? _____

6. kitomisin cî? _____

7. kitosîmisin cî? _____

8. kitotawâsimisin cî? _____

CHAPTER SEVEN

TRANSITIVE INANIMATE VERBS

7. TRANSITIVE INANIMATE VERBS

Transitive Inanimate Verbs (VTIs) are the verbs which require an inanimate noun as the object in the sentence structure. For Animate Intransitive Verbs (VAIs) one does not need an object to have a complete sentence in the Imperative Moods, the Indicative Mood, or the Conjunct Mood. Intransitive verbs need no object; Transitive verbs need objects. In giving orders (i.e., Imperatives), one cannot get away with simply saying "nâta – *get it*" without the person being spoken to asking: "kîkwây? – *What?*"

In giving orders using the transitive verbs, it is not enough to say just the verb; one must specify what is being requested. Consider the following:

nâta kimasinahikan. – *Get your book.*

This order is clear and does not prompt the one being spoken to to ask, "What?" Compare the Imperative Moods of a VAI and a VTI-1.

VAI atoskê – *work*

2   atoskê – *Work* (you-sg.)
2P   atoskêk – *Work* (you-pl.)
21   atoskêtân – *Let's work.* (you and me)

VTI-1 atoskâta – *work at/on* (*something*)

2   atoskâta kinêhiyawêwin   – *Work at your Cree.* (you-sg.)
2P   atoskâtamok kinêhiyawêwiniwâw – *Work at your Cree.* (you-pl.)
21   atoskâtêtân kinêhiyawêwininaw – *Let's work at our Cree.* (you and me)

NOTE: The verb stem again is taken from the 2 of the Imperative Mood. Note also that the "**a**" in 21 has been changed to "**ê**" in this mood; the "**a**" in the verb stem changes to "**ê**" for 21 of the Imperative Mood and for 1, 2, 1P, 21, and 2P of the Indicative Mood.

The chart for the Imperative Mood of VTI-1:

IMPERATIVE MOOD

2	_____*
2P	_____mok
21	_____tân

NEGATIVE IMPERATIVE

2	êkâwiya _____
2P	êkâwiya _____mok
21	êkâwiya _____tân

*The blank represents where the verb stem is placed.

Imperatives are commands telling one or more people to do something while the negative Imperatives are commands telling one or more people **not** to do something. Other forms of Imperatives are the delayed Imperatives, commands given that are to be carried out at a later time.

DELAYED IMPERATIVE OF VTI-1

2	_____mohkan
2P	_____mohkêk
21	_____mohkahk

The standard verb structure applies to all verbs including the VTIs:

Person Indicator	Tense Indicator	Preverb	Verb stem	Ending

The two other TRANSITIVE INANIMATE VERBS, class 2 and class 3, follow the VAI conjugation patterns. These different classes can be identified by their endings:

VTI-1 roots all end in "**a**":
kanawâpahta – *look at it*

VTI-2 roots all end in "**â**". Some VAIs end in "**â**"; however, those verbs do not take an object as VTIs do:
osîhtâ – *make it.*
nâcipahtâ – *run for/toward it*
pêtâ – *bring it*
ayamihtâ – *read it*

VTI-3 roots all end with "**i**".
mîci – *eat it*

This chapter will concentrate on the VTI-1 forms.

As with the VAI, the VTI-1 verbs in the Indicative and Conjunct forms can have nine possible agents/subjects carrying out the action identified in the conjugation pattern:

NO.	SUBJECT/AGENT	INDICATIVE MOOD	CONJUNCT
1	1st person singular 'I'	ni_____n	ê-_____mân
2	2nd person singular 'you'	ki_____n	ê-_____man
3	3rd person singular 's/he/it'	_____m	ê-_____hk
3'	3rd person obviative 'her friend'	_____miyiw	ê-_____miyit
1P	1st person plural 'we' (excl.)	ni_____nân	ê-_____mâhk
21	1st person plural 'we' (incl.)	ki_____naw	ê-_____mahk
2P	2nd person plural 'you'	ki_____nâwâw	ê-_____mêk
3P	3rd person plural 'they'	_____mwak	ê-_____hkik
3'P	3rd person obviative plural 'their friend'	_____miyiwa	ê-_____miyit

All tense indicators, preverbs, and verb stems can be placed in the blank spaces in the above paradigms. The standard verb structure for any verb follows the pattern below:

Person Indicators "ni" and "ki"	Tense Indicators kî-, wî-, ka-(ta-)	Preverbs	Verb stems	Verb Endings

Verbs can be in the following tenses:

      The present (tense indicator: none): ninâtên – *I get (fetch) it.*
      The past (tense indicator: **kî-**): ni**kî**-nâtên – *I got (fetched) it.*
      The future intentional (tense indicator: **wî-**): ni**wî**-nâtên – *I am going to get it.*
      The future definite (tense indicator: **ka-**): ni**ka**-nâtên – *I will get it.*

The future definite tense for 1st and 2nd person forms is "ka-" and "ta-" for third person forms. The future definite tenses are never used in the Conjunct forms of verbs.

Another way of understanding the paradigm of verbs is to see the nature of the utterance, as in who speaks, who is spoken to, and who is spoken about:

1st person subject: the speaker	2nd person subject: the one/ones spoken to	3rd person subject: the one/ones talked about
1 - "ni_____n" The speaker talking about himself/herself: "I".	**2** - "ki_____n" The addressee, i.e., the one spoken to: "You" singular.	**3** - "_____m" The topic, i.e., the one spoken about: "She/he/it."
1P - "ni_____nân" The speaker talking about self and others but excludes the one spoken to: "We (excl.)".	**2P** - "ki_____nâwâw" Two or more persons spoken to: "You" plural.	**3P** - "_____mwak" Two or more persons spoken about: "They."
21 - "ki_____naw" The speaker talking about self and others and includes the one spoken to: "We (incl.)"		**3'** - "_____miyiw" The friend, relative or pet of a 3rd person: "His/her _____"
		3'P - "_____miyiwa" The friends, relatives or pets of 3rd persons: "Their _____"

7.1 TRANSITIVE INANIMATE VERBS – CLASS 1 (VTI-1)

Connect any of these units from left to right to make a sentence:

PERSON INDICATORS	TENSE	PREVERB	VERB STEM VTI-CLASS 1	ENDINGS
INDICATIVE: ni (1, 1P) ki (2, 21, 2P)	**kî-** past **wî-** future intent **ka-** future definite (1, 2) **ta-** future definite (3 person) **ka-kî-** modal indicator Present tense has no tense indicator.	kakwê- *(try)* nitawi- *(go and/to)* nôhtê- *(want)* nihtâ- *(can do well)* mâci- *(begin)* pêyako- *(alone)* pôni- *(stop)* ati- *(start)* pê- *(come)* pêci- *(come)* sâpo- *(through)* papâsi- *(hurriedly)* nisihkâci- *(slowly)*	otina *(take it)* nâta *(fetch it)* sâmina *(touch it)* mîskona *(feel it)* pêhta *(hear it)* natohta *(listen to it)* nitawêyihta *(want it)* natona *(search for it)* miska *(find it)* wâpahta *(see it)* kanawâpahta *(look at it)* kocispita *(taste it)* paswâta *(sniff it))*	**INDICATIVE:** n (1, 2) m (3) miyiw (3') nân (1P) naw (21) nâwâw (2P) mwak (3P) miyiwa (3'P)
	RULES ONLY FOR THE INDICATIVE: **1.** Use the "t" as a connector for the present tense only if VS or PV begin with a vowel.	pêyâhtaki- *(carefully)* miyo- *(good)* mâyi- *(badly)* maci- *(bad/evil)* sôhki- *(hard)* pisci- *(accidently)* mwayî- *(before)* matwê- *(heard in the distance)*	miyâhta *(smell it)* nisitohta *(understand it)* kiskêyihta *(know it)* atoskâta *(work at it)* masinaha *(write it)* postiska *(put it on)* kêcikoska *(take it off)* kisîpêkina *(wash it)* kîsisa *(cook it)* itôta *(do it)* mêtawâkâta *(disrespect it)*	
CONJUNCT: **ê-** (subordinate) **kâ-** (relative clause) **ta-** (infinitive)	**2.** Change the last "a" of the VS to "ê" for 1, 2, 1P, 21, 2P for all tenses of the Indicative mood.		yôhtêna *(open it)* kipaha *(close it)* ohpina *(lift it)* yahkiwêpina *(push it)* nâkatawêyihta *(take care of it)*	**CONJUNCT:** mân (1) man (2) hk (3) miyit (3', 3'P) mâhk (1P) mahk (21) mêk (2P) ahkik (3P)

VTI-1 Future conditional forms follow the same rules (except for 3P) as with the VAIs: Drop "**ê-**" from the Conjunct mood forms, keep most of the endings, and add "**i/o**":

1	_____mâni	**1P**	_____mâhki
2	_____mani	**21**	_____mahki
		2P	_____mêko
3	_____hki	**3P**	_____hkwâwi
3'	_____miyici	**3'P**	_____miyici

EXERCISES

EXERCISE 1. In the following sentences, put the first verb into the Delayed Imperative, keeping the same subject, and the second verb into the Future Conditional form. The first is done for you.

EXAMPLE: <u>nâta</u> kimasinahikana <u>ê-kîsi-mîcisoyan</u>
          TRANSFORM: nâta**mohkan** kimasinahikana kîsi-mîciso**yani**.
          TRANSLATE: *Get your books when/if you finish eating.*

CONTINUE:

1. <u>atoskâta</u> kinêhiyawêwin <u>ê-mwayî-kîwêyan</u>.

   TRANSFORM: _____

   TRANSLATE: _____

2. <u>yôhtênamok</u> wâsênamâna <u>ê-kisitêk</u>.

   TRANSFORM: _____

   TRANSLATE: _____

3. <u>kipaha</u> iskwahtêm <u>ê-tahkâyâk</u>.

   TRANSFORM: _____

   TRANSLATE: _____

4. <u>otinêtân</u> kimaskisin <u>ê-mwayî-sipwêhtêyahk</u>.

   TRANSFORM: _____

   TRANSLATE: _____

5. <u>masinaha</u> kiwîhowin <u>ê-wî-nitawi-atoskêyêk</u>.

   TRANSFORM: _____

   TRANSLATE: _____

6. <u>postiska</u> kiskotâkay <u>ê-tahkâyâk</u>.

   TRANSFORM: _____

   TRANSLATE: _____

7. <u>kêcikoskêtân</u> kitastotininawa <u>ê-pîhtokwêyahk</u> ayamihâwikamikohk.

   TRANSFORM: _____

   TRANSLATE: _____

EXERCISE 2. In the following, identify the verb forms, then make sure of the tense agreement and transform any verb you see to make tense agreement possible. The first is done for you: a Delayed Imperative verb needs the accompanying verb in the future Conditional form.

1. <u>pêtâhkan</u> kimaskisina ispîhk <u>kimiskên</u>. (*Bring your shoes when you find them.*)
   pêtâhkan (Delayed Imperative) kimaskisina ispîhk <u>miskamani</u> (Future Conditional).

2. ati-kîwêhkahk ispîhk ê-pôni-atoskêyahk. (*Let's go home when we stop working.*)

   _____

3. nika-ayamihtân êwako nêhiyawêwin kikîsi-masinahên. (*I will read that Cree if you finish writing it.*)

   _____

4. wêpinamohkêk êwakoni masinahikana ispîhk ê-pôni-pîkopitamêk.
   (*Throw away those books when you finish tearing them up.*)

   _____

5. kocispitamohkahk anima mîciwin ê-pêtât. (*Let's taste that food if he brings it.*)

   _____

6. postiska astotin ê-tahkâyâk. (*Put on a hat if it is cold.*)

   _____

7. kipahamohkan iskwâhtêm tahkâyâw. (*Close the door if it is cold.*)

   _____

8. natohtamohkahk anima nêhiyawêwin ispîhk ana iskwêw ê-kocihtât.
   (*Let's listen to that Cree when that woman tries it.*)

   _____

9. otinamohkêk anima wiyâs ê-manisahk. (*Take that meat if he/she cuts it up.*)

   _____

10. nika-kanawâpahtên anima masinahikêwin pôni-ayamihtâw.
    (*I will look at that writing if he stops reading it.*)

    _____

EXERCISE 3. Fill in the following charts, then make the necessary changes in the sentences below:

IMPERATIVES – VTI-1

Imperatives	Negative Imperatives	Delayed Imperatives
2 verb stem	**2** _____	**2** _____ mohkan
2P _____	**2P** êkâwiya _____ mok	**2P** _____
21 _____ êtân	**21** _____	**21** _____

VTI-1

Indicative	Conjunct	Future Conditional
1	**1** ê- _____ mân	**1**
2 ki _____ n	**2**	**2** _____ mani
3	**3** ê- _____ hk	**3**
3' _____ miyiw	**3'** ê- _____ miyit	**3'**
1P	**1P**	**1P** _____ mâhki
21 ki _____ naw	**21**	**21**
2P	**2P** ê- _____ mêk	**2P**
3P _____ mwak	**3P**	**3P** _____ hkwâwi
3'P	**3'P**	**3'P** _____ miyici

The first verb is in the Imperative; place it into the Delayed Imperative. The second verb is in the Conjunct; change it to the Future Conditional.

1. nâta kimaskisina ê-nôhtê-atoskâtaman nêhiyawêwin.
   (Fetch your shoes when/if you want to work at your Cree.)

   _____

2. otinamok kimasinahikaniwâwa ê-pôni-masinahamêk âcimowina
   (Take your books when/if you stop writing stories.)

   _____

3. kêcikoskêtân astotina ê-yôhtênamahk iskwâhtêm. *(Let's take off the hats when/if we open the door.)*

   _____

4. postiska kiskotâkay ê-nâtaman mihta. *(Put on your jacket when/if you go fetch firewood.)*

   _____

5. nitawi-kanawâpahtamok cikâstêpayihcikana ê-kîsi-kisîpêkinamêk oyâkana.
   (Go to the movies when/if you finish washing the dishes.)

   _____

EXERCISE 4. Fill in the charts, then make the necessary changes in the sentences below:

VTI-1

Imperatives	Negative Imperatives	Delayed Imperatives
2 _____	2 _____	2 _____
2P _____	2P _____	2P _____
21 _____	21 _____	21 _____

VII

Indicative: verb ends in consonant before a long vowel	Conjunct:	Future Conditional:
Indicative: verb ends in consonant before a short vowel	Conjunct:	Future Conditional:

The first verb is a VTI-1 in the Imperative, put into the Delayed Imperative; the second verb is a VII in the Conjunct, put into the Future Conditional:

1. atoskâta kinêhiyawêwin ê-tipiskâk. (*Work on your Cree when/if it is night.*)

   _____

2. kêcikoskamok kimaskisiniwâwa ê-kimiwahk. (*Take off your shoes when/if it's raining.*)

   _____

3. nâtêtân wâsênikana ê-pôni-mispok. (*Let's fetch the windows when/if it stops snowing.*)

   _____

Change the tenses in the first verb to agree to the English translation, and place the second verb into the future conditional:

4. niwî-kanawâpahtênân cikâstêpayihcikana ê-nîso-kîsikâk.
   (*We will watch movies when/if it is Tuesday.*)

   _____

5. kika-nâtên cî kimasinahikana ê-kîsi-mîcisoyan.
   (*Are you going to fetch your books when/if you finish eating?*)

   _____

6. wî-natonam omaskisina wayawîtimihk ê-kîkisêpâk.
   (*He will look for his shoes outside when/if it is morning.*)

   _____

7. ta-kîsisamiyiwa otôtêma wiyâs ê-otâkwani-mîcisoyit.
   (*His/her friend is going to cook meat when/if he/she eats supper.*)

   _____

7.2 DIALOGUE EIGHT

A: tânisi ôma mâka mîna
ê-itahkamikisiyan?

B: ê-kakwê-kitohcikêyân ôma.
nicîhkêyihtên ta-kitohcikêyân.*
kiya mâka, kicîhkêyihtên cî
ta-kitohcikêyan?

A: âha, mâka namôya nikaskihtân.
nicîhkêyihtên mâka ta-nikamoyân.

B: nîsta mîna…mâka namôya
osâm nimiyohtâkosin.

A: mahti…kiya kitohcikê êkwa niya
nika-nikamon.

B: ahâw, ahpô êtikwê
kika-miyohtâkosinaw.

A: *What are you
doing as usual?*

B: *I am trying to play an instrument.
I like to play music.
How about you, do you like
to play music?*

A: *Yes, but I can't do it.
But I like to sing.*

B: *Me too…but I don't
sound so good.*

A: *Let's see…you play an instrument
and I will sing.*

B: *Okay, perhaps
we'll sound good.*

VOCABULARY

mâka mîna – *as usual*
cîhkêyihta – *like it* (VTI-1)
nikamo – *sing* (VAI)
mahti – *let's see/please*
ahpô êtikwê – *perhaps*

kitohcikê – *make music with an instrument* (VAI)
kaskihtâ – *be able/succeed* (VTI-2)
osâm – *because/excessively*
miyohtâkosi – *sound good* (VAI)

NOTES

*"ta-kitohcikêyân" is an infinitive form of an Animate Intransitive verb (VAI). Infinitive forms in Cree differ from those in English: the English infinitive forms are not marked for tense or for person and are preceded by "*to*". In Cree, however, the person (or actor of the verb) is marked using the conjunct mood endings of the verbs, no matter the type of verb. The "**ta-**" replaces the "**ê-**", the regular Conjunct mood marker. **ta-** is usually used as a future definite marker for Indicative mood verbs in the 3rd person (3, 3', 3P and 3'P) but used with the Conjunct mood endings for all persons it becomes an infinitive marker for events that happen in the past, present, and future.

Thus far, we have seen the Conjunct mood endings used in four ways:

a) as a regular Conjunct mood using the "**ê-**", where the verbs are similar to the "*-ing*" verb forms in English;

b) as a relative clause, Conjunct mood, using the "**kâ-**";

c) as a Future Conditional form without a foregoing clause marker but have most of the conjugated verbs in the conjunct ending followed by an "**i**" for 1, 2, 3, 4', 1P, 21, and an "**o**" for the 2P (the second person plural) and "**twâwi**" for the 3P form for VAI and "**hkwâwi**" for VTI-1;

d) as an infinitive form, use the "**ta-**" infinitive marker.

7.3 DIALOGUE NINE

A: tânisi ôma ê-itahkamikisiyan?
B: ê-natonamân ôma niskîsikohkâna.*
A: tânita mâka kâ-kî-nakataman?
B: ôta ôma cîki wâsaskotênikanihk.
A: ahpô êtikwê nitêm mâka mîna
   ê-kwâhcipahtwât.
B: hay, macastim! mahti wîcihin.**
A: ahâw. kika-wîcihitin***…hay!
   kiskahtikohk ôma kikikiskên
   kiskîsikohkâna.
B: iyaw! êwakoni kâ-natonamân.

A: *What are you doing?*
B: *I am looking for my glasses.*
A: *Where did you leave them?*
B: *Here, near the lamp.*
A: *Perhaps my dog, as usual,*
   ran (far) off with it.
B: *Boy! Bad dog! Please help me.*
A: *Okay. I will help you…Hey!*
   You have your glasses on
   on your forehead.
B: *Oops! Those are the ones that I'm looking for.*

VOCABULARY

natona – *look for it* (VTI-1)
tânita – *whereabouts*
ahpô êtikwê – *perhaps*
nitêm – *my dog*
macastim – *bad/evil dog*
wîcih – *help s.o.* (VTA)
kikiska – *wear* (VTI-1)

miskîsikohkâna – *eyeglasses* (pl)
nakata – *leave it* (VTI-1)
wâsaskotênikan – *lamp* (NI)
kwâhcipahtwâ – *run far off with it* (VTI-2)
mahti – *please*
miskahtik – *forehead* (NI)
êwakoni – *those are the ones*

NOTES

The inflections for marking possessions in Cree basically follow the same conjugation patterns as those of verbs. In the above marked niskîsikohkâna,* we have the inflected form of glasses owned by the speaker to say "*my glasses*". The inflected form for "*your glasses*" appears in the second last line of the above dialogue. The vocabulary lists the uninflected forms of "*glasses*" and "*forehead*" but the inflected form of "*my dog*".

The dialogue includes a couple of inverse forms of the Transitive Animate Verb "wîcih – *help someone*" in wîcihin** and kika-wîcihitin.*** This VTA-Inverse is known as the "you and me set". The structure has only eight units as shown in the chart below using "wîcih" (underlined) as an example:

IMPERATIVE	INDICATIVE – "YOU" AS SUBJECT	INDICATIVE – "YOU" AS OBJECT
<u>wîcih</u>in – *help me*	ki<u>wîcih</u>in – *you* (sg) *help me.*	ki<u>wîcih</u>itin – *I help you* (sg).
<u>wîcih</u>inân – *help us*	ki<u>wîcih</u>inân – *you help us.*	ki<u>wîcih</u>itinân – *We help you.*
	ki<u>wîcih</u>inâwâw – *you* (pl) *help me.*	ki<u>wîcih</u>itinâwâw – *I help you* (pl).

Add -**in** and -**inân** to the VTA stem for the speaker asking the listener for something as in the above Imperative. In the Indicative, with the "*you*" as subject, place the verb stem between the person indicator **ki-** and the endings -**in**, -**inân** and -**inâwâw**. For "*you*" as the object, the VTA verb stem falls between the person indicator **ki-** and the endings -**itin** and -**itinân**.

7.4 COLOURS AND CLOTHING

The animacy of the noun dictates the use of the right colour term. Colour terms in Cree are verbs. For animate nouns we would use VAI forms of the colour terms; for inanimate nouns we would use the VII forms. Below is a chart that shows the various forms of colours depending on the animacy and number of the noun whose colour is defined.

COLOUR ROOTS AND ENDINGS

ROOTS: Attach each of these →	USE THESE ENDINGS WITH 1, 2, 3, 3P, 3', and 3'P	

....

mihk _____ (red)	wâw(a) nipapakiwayân(a)	– My shirt(s) is (are) red.
	wâyiw(a) opapakiwayân(a)	– His/her shirt(s) is (are) red.
	osiw(ak) nitasikan(ak)	– My sock(s) is (are) red.
	osiyiwa otasikana	– His/her sock(s) is (are) red.
	onâkwan(wa) nipapakiwayân(a)	– My shirt(s) looks red.
	onâkwaniyiw(a) opapakiwayân(a)	– His/her shirt(s) looks red.
	onâkosiw(ak) nitasikan(ak)	– My sock(s) looks red.
	onâkosiyiwa otasikana	– His/her sock(s) looks red.

sîpihk
(blue)

askihtak
(green)

....

osâw _____ (orange)	âw(a) nipapakiwayân(a)	– My shirt(s) is (are) orange.
	âyiw(a) opapakiwayân(a)	– His/her shirt(s) is (are) orange.
	isiw(ak) nitasikan(ak)	– My sock(s) is (are) orange.
	isiyiwa otasikana	– His/her sock(s) is (are) orange.
	inâkwan(wa) nipapakiwayân(a)	– My shirt(s) looks orange.
	inâkwaniyiw(a) opapakiwayân(a)	– His/her shirt(s) looks orange.
	inâkosiw(ak) nitasikan(ak)	– My sock(s) looks orange.
	inâkosiyiwa otasikana	– His/her sock(s) looks orange.

kaskitê-osâw
(brown)

wâposâw
(yellow)

wâpisk
(white)

....

kaskitê _____ (black)	wâw(a) nipapakiwayân(a)	– My shirt(s) is (are) black.
	wâyiw(a) opapakiwayân(a)	– His/her shirt(s) is (are) black.
	siw(ak) nitasikan(ak)	– My sock(s) is (are) black.
	siyiwa otasikana	– His/her sock(s) is (are) black.
	winâkwan(wa) nipapakiwayân(a)	– My shirt(s) looks black.
	winâkwaniyiw(a) opapakiwayân(a)	– His/her shirt(s) looks black.
	winâkosiw(ak) nitasikan(ak)	– My sock(s) looks black.
	winâkosiyiwa otasikana	– His/her sock(s) looks black.

nîpâmâyât _____ (purple)	an(a) nipapakiwayân(a)	– My shirt(s) is (are) purple.
	aniyiw(a) opapakiwayân(a)	– His/her shirt(s) is (are) purple.
	isiw(ak) nitasikan(ak)	– My sock(s) is (are) purple.
	isiyiwa otasikana	– His/her sock(s) is (are) purple.
	inâkwan(wa) nipapakiwayân(a)	– My shirt(s) looks purple.
	inâkwaniyiw(a) opapakiwayân(a)	– His/her shirt(s) looks purple.
	inâkosiw(ak) nitasikan(ak)	– My sock(s) looks purple.
	inâkosiyiwa otasikana	– His/her sock(s) looks purple.

QUESTIONS WITH COLOURS:

tânisi kâ-itasinâs	têk(i)	têyik(i)
	ot(cik)	oyit

e.g., Let's use the root "mihk – *red*" to illustrate how this works. Below the root "**mihk-**" is attached to the units in the middle and right-hand column:

When the object is in simple third person (attach units from middle column):

mihkwâw – *it is red* (use for singular inanimate noun); **mihk**wâwa (for plural nouns)
mihkosiw – *it is red* (use for singular animate noun); **mihk**osiwak (for plural nouns)
mihkonâkwan – *it looks red* (use for singular inanimate noun); **mihk**onâkwanwa (plural)
mihkonâkosiw – *it looks red* (use for singular animate noun); **mihk**onâkosiwak (plural)

Use when talking about someone else's possession (attach units from right-hand column):

mihkwâyiw – *it is red* (use for singular inanimate noun); **mihk**wâyiwa (for plural nouns)
mihkosiyiwa – *it is red* (use for singular or plural animate noun; noun ends in 'a')
mihkonâkwaniyiw – *it looks red* (use for singular inanimate noun); **mihk**onâkwaniyiwa (pl)
mihkonâkosiyiwa – *it looks red* (use for singular or plural animate noun; noun ends in 'a')

EXERCISES

EXERCISE 1.

Complete the following charts, keeping in mind the animacy of the noun and the way to make possessives out of the nouns. Use the first two as guides.

- Use "ni" for *my* unless the noun begins with "mi", in which case replace the "mi" with "ni".

- Use "ki" for *your* unless the noun begins with "mi", in which case replace the "mi" with "ki".

- Use "o" for *his/her* unless the noun begins with "mi", in which case replace the "mi" with "o". Add an "a" at the end of a noun that is animate (obviation).

- Use "t" to connect the person indicators to the noun if the noun begins with a vowel.

NOUN: papakiwayân – *shirt* (NI). COLOUR-ROOT: mihk – *red*

Noun owned by 1st person	Noun owned by 2nd person	Noun owned by 3rd person
mihkwâw **ni**papakiwayân. *My shirt is red.*	**mihk**wâw **ki**papakiwayân. *Your shirt is red.*	**mihk**wâyiw **o**papakiwayân. *His/her shirt is red.*
mihkwâwa **ni**papakiwayâna. *My shirts are red.*	**mihk**wâwa **ki**papakiwayâna. *Your shirts are red.*	**mihk**wâyiwa **o**papakiwayâna. *His/her shirts are red.*
mihkonâkwan **ni**papakiwayân. *My shirt looks red.*	**mihk**onâkwan **ki**papakiwayân. *Your shirt looks red.*	**mihk**onâkwaniyiw **o**papakiwayân. *His/her shirt looks red.*
mihkonâkwanwa **ni**papakiwayâna. *My shirts look red.*	**mihk**onâkwanwa **ki**papakiwayâna. *Your shirts look red.*	**mihk**onâkwaniyiwa **o**papakiwayâna. *His/her shirts look red.*

NOUN: mitâs – *pair of pants* (NA). COLOUR-ROOT: sîpihk – *blue*

Noun owned by 1st person	Noun owned by 2nd person	Noun owned by 3rd person
sîpihkosiw **ni**tâs. *My pair of pants is blue.*	**sîpihk**osiw **ki**tâs. *Your pair of pants is blue.*	**sîpihk**osiyiwa **o**tâsa. *His/her pair of pants is blue.*
sîpihkosiwak **ni**tâsak. *My pairs of pants are blue.*	**sîpihk**osiwak **ki**tâsak. *Your pairs of pants are blue.*	**sîpihk**osiyiwa **o**tâsa. *His/her pairs of pants are blue.*
sîpihkonâkosiw **ni**tâs. *My pair of pants looks blue.*	**sîpihk**onâkosiw **ki**tâs. *Your pair of pants looks blue.*	**sîpihk**onâkosiyiwa **o**tâsa. *His/her pair of pants looks blue.*
sîpihkonâkosiwak **ni**tâsak. *My pairs of pants look blue.*	**sîpihk**onâkosiwak **ki**tâsak. *Your pairs of pants look blue.*	**sîpihk**onâkosiyiwa **o**tâsa. *His/her pairs of pants look blue.*

NOUN: miskotâkay – *jacket* (NI). **COLOUR-ROOT:** askihtak – *green*

Noun owned by 1st person	Noun owned by 2nd person	Noun owned by 3rd person

NOUN: astotin – *hat* (NI). **COLOUR-ROOT:** osâw – *orange*

Noun owned by 1st person	Noun owned by 2nd person	Noun owned by 3rd person

NOUN: tâpiskâkan – *scarf* (NA). **COLOUR-ROOT:** wâposâw – *yellow*

Noun owned by 1st person	Noun owned by 2nd person	Noun owned by 3rd person

NOUN: asikan – *sock* (NA). **COLOUR-ROOT:** wâpisk – *white*

Noun owned by 1st person	Noun owned by 2nd person	Noun owned by 3rd person

NOUN: maskisin – *shoe* (NI). **COLOUR-ROOT:** kaskitê – *black*

Noun owned by 1st person	Noun owned by 2nd person	Noun owned by 3rd person

NOUN: astis – *glove* (NA). **COLOUR-ROOT:** nîpâmâyât – *purple*

Noun owned by 1st person	Noun owned by 2nd person	Noun owned by 3rd person

EXERCISE 2. Answer the following questions:

1. tânisi kâ-itasinâstêk kiskotâkay?

   _____

2. tânisi kâ-itasinâstêki kimaskisina?

   _____

3. tânisi kâ-itasinâsot kitâs?

   _____

4. tânisi kâ-itasinâsocik kitasikanak?

   _____

5. tânisi kâ-itasinâstêyik otastotin *Jamie*?

   _____

6. tânisi kâ-itasinâstêyiki omasinahikana *James*?

   _____

7. tânisi kâ-itasinâsoyit otâpiskâkana *Conny*?

   _____

8. tânisi kâ-itasinâsoyit otastisa *Cindy*?

   _____

EXERCISE 3.

DO: Play "I spy with my little eye" using classroom objects. Have students in pairs while others guess what they see.

A.   niwâpahtên kîkway:
             (*I see something*)

                           ê-mihkwâk
                           ê-sîpihkwâk
                           ê-askihtakwâk
                           ê-osâwâk
                           ê-wâposâwâk
                           ê-wâpiskâk
                           ê-kaskitêwâk
                           ê-nîpâmâyâtahk

B.   niwâpamâw awiyak, ahpô kîkway:
             (*I see someone or something*)

                           ê-mihkosit
                           ê-sîpihkosit
                           ê-askihtakosit
                           ê-osâwisit
                           ê-wâposâwisit
                           ê-wâpiskisit
                           ê-kaskitêsit
                           ê-nîpâmâyâtisit

C.   awîna kâ-kikiskahk (colours from A above in Obviative form):
             (*Who wears*)

                           papakiwayân
                           miskotâkay
                           astotin
                           maskisin
                           iskwêwasâkay

D.   awîna kâ-kikiskawât (colours from B in Obviative form):
             (*Who wears*)

                           mitâsa
                           tâpiskâkana
                           astisa
                           asikana

EXERCISE 4.

Fill in the following colour terms with the nouns: (*Review colours with clothing*)

NOUN: miskotâkay – *coat/jacket* (NI). **COLOUR-ROOT:** mihk – *red*

Owned by 1st person	Owned by 2nd person	Owned by 3rd person
My coat is red.	*Your coat is red.*	*Her/his coat is red.* mihkwâyiw oskotâkay.
My coats are red. mihkwâwa niskotâkaya	*Your coats are red.*	*Her/his coats are red.*
My coat looks red.	*Your coat looks red.*	*Her/his coat looks red.*
My coats look red.	*Your coats look red.* mihkonâkwanwa kiskotâkaya.	*Her/his coats look red.*

NOUN: astis – *mitt/glove* (NA). **COLOUR-ROOT:** kaskitê – *black*

Owned by 1st person	Owned by 2nd person	Owned by 3rd person
My mitt is black. kaskitêsiw nitastis.	*Your mitt is black.*	*Her/his mitt is black.*
My mitts are black.	*Your mitts are black.* kaskitêsiwak kitastisak.	*Her/his mitts are black.*
My mitt looks black.	*Your mitt looks black.*	*Her/his mitt looks black.* kaskitêwinâkosiyiwa otastisa
My mitts look black.	*Your mitts look black.*	*Her/his mitts look black.*

7.5 CHAPTER SEVEN REVIEW – VTI-1

Place verb stems in the blanks; verb stems come from the second person singular (2) form of the imperative.

IMPERATIVES		NEGATIVE IMPERATIVES		DELAYED IMPERATIVES	
2 _____		**2** êkâwiya _____		**2** _____ mohkan	
2P _____ mok		**2P** êkâwiya _____ mok		**2P** _____ mohkêk	
1 _____ êtân*		**21** êkâwiya _____ êtân		**21** _____ mohkahk	

*The final "**a**" in the verb stem form changes to "**ê**" for the 1st and 2nd person forms of the indicative.

INDICATIVE	CONJUNCT	FUTURE CONDITIONAL
1 ni_____n	**1** ê-_____mân	**1.** _____mâni
2 ki_____n	**2** ê-_____man	**2** _____mani
3 _____m	**3** ê-_____hk	**3** _____hki
3' _____miyiw	**3'** ê-_____miyit	**3'** _____miyici
1P ni_____nân	**1P** ê-_____mâhk	**1P** _____mâhki
21 ki_____naw	**21** ê-_____mahk	**21** _____mahki
2P ki_____nâwâw	**2P** ê-_____mêk	**2P** _____mêko
3P _____mwak	**3P** ê-_____hkik	**3P** _____hkwâwi
3'P _____miyiwa	**3'P** ê-_____miyit	**3'P** _____miyici

RULE:

Verb stems of VTI-1 end in "**a**"; change the "**a**" to "**ê**" for the 1st and 2nd person forms of the indicative.

STANDARD VERB STRUCTURE

Person indicator or conjunct marker	Tense marker	Preverb	Verb stem	Verb ending

CHAPTER EIGHT

• • • • • • • • • • • • • • • •

TRANSITIVE ANIMATE VERBS

8. TRANSITIVE ANIMATE VERBS (VTA)

Transitive Animate Verbs (VTAs) require an animate object. Recall the VTIs which need inanimate objects in their sentence structures; without the object expressed, we would have incomplete utterances. The same applies for the VTAs. Let's compare the imperatives of both transitive verbs.

In English we can ask people to bring things over to us without a change in the verb. In Cree, we would need to know the animacy of the object that we are asking for to use the correct verb. Here are some examples:

> **VTI-2** pêtâ kimaskisin. – *Bring your shoe.*

> **VTA** pêsiw asâm. – *Bring the snowshoe.*

Notice there is a similarity to the two verbs, they start the same but end differently. Let's use verbs that are even more similar: the verb "*take*" as a VTI-1 "otina" and as a VTA "otin".

> **VTI-1** otina kimaskisin. – *Take your shoe.*

> **VTA** otin asâm. – *Take the snowshoe.*

Knowing the animacy of nouns helps in choosing the right word in all utterances. Now let's see what happens when we make plurals out of the nouns in question.

> **VTI-2** pêtâ kimaskisina. – *Bring your shoes.*

> **VTA** pêsiw**ik** asâm**ak**. – *Bring the snowshoes.*

> **VTI-1** otina kimaskisina. – *Take your shoes.*

> **VTA** otin**ik** asâm**ak**. – *Take the snowshoes.*

NOTE: There is no change to the verb form for the VTIs when the noun in question is plural. The same is not the case for the VTAs. If the object is plural then the verb also has to be in the plural, as highlighted in the above examples. This is known as number agreement, something that needs to be kept in mind when working with VTAs. If the object is plural, then the verb must show number agreement as shown in brackets below:

VTA

IMPERATIVE		NEGATIVE IMP.		DELAYED IMP.	
2	_____(ik)	**2** êkâwiya	_____(ik)	**2**	_____âhkan(ik)
2P	_____ihk(ok)	**2P** êkâwiya	_____ihk(ok)	**2P**	_____âhkêk(ok)
21	_____âtân(ik)	**21** êkâwiya	_____âtân(ik)	**21**	_____âhkahk(ik)

EXERCISES WITH VTA AND VTI IMPERATIVES

EXERCISE 1. Translate the following imperatives, paying attention to number agreement:

IMPERATIVES:

VTI-1 – otina – TAKE IT

1. Take (2) your book.

_____

2. Take (2) your books.

_____

3. Take (2P) your shoe.

_____

4. Take (2P) our shoes.

_____

5. Let's (21) take the jacket.

_____

6. Let's (21) take the jackets.

_____

VTA – otin – TAKE IT

1. Take (2) your mitt.

_____

2. Take (2) your mitts.

_____

3. Take (2P) your scarf.

_____

4. Take (2P) your scarves.

_____

5. Let's (21) take the sock.

_____

6. Let's (21) take the socks.

_____

NEGATIVE IMPERATIVES:

VTI-1 – kanawâpahta – LOOK AT IT

1. Don't look at (2) the book.

_____

2. Don't look at (2) the books.

_____

3. Don't look at (2P) the shoe.

_____

4. Don't look at (2p) the shoes.

_____

5. Let's (21) not look at the jacket.

_____

6. Let's (21) not look at the jackets.

_____

VTA – kanawâpam – LOOK AT IT

1. Don't look at (2) the mitt.

_____

2. Don't look at (2) the mitts.

_____

3. Don't look at (2P) the scarf.

_____

4. Don't look at (2P) the scarves.

_____

5. Let's (21) not look at the sock.

_____

6. Let's (21) not look at the socks.

_____

DELAYED IMPERATIVES:

VTI-1 – natona – LOOK FOR IT

1. Look for (2) your book later.

   _____

2. Look for (2) your books later.

   _____

3. Look for (2P) your shoe later.

   _____

4. Look for (2p) your shoes later.

   _____

5. Let's (21) look for the jacket later.

   _____

6. Let's (21) look for the jackets later.

   _____

VTA – natonaw – LOOK FOR IT

1. Look for (2) your mitt later.

   _____

2. Look for (2) your mitts later.

   _____

3. Look for (2P) your scarf later.

   _____

4. Look for (2P) your scarves later.

   _____

5. Let's (21) look for the sock later.

   _____

6. Let's (21) look for the socks later.

   _____

WORDS for the foregoing exercise:

mwêstas – *later*
masinahikan – *book* (NI)
maskisin – *shoe* (NI)
miskotâkay – *jacket* (NI)

êkâwiya – *don't* (use in negative imperatives)
astis – *mitt* (NA)
tâpiskâkan – *scarf* (NI)
asikan – *sock* (NI)

EXERCISE 2. Make imperatives given the following words:

mîci – *eat it* (VTI-3)
pêsiw – *bring it* (VTA)
ôsi – *boat* (NI)

môw – *eat it* (VTA)
kinosêw – *fish* (NA)
apoy – *paddle* (NA)

pêtâ – *bring it* (VTI-2)
wiyâs – *meat* (NI)

1. _____

2. _____

3. _____

4. _____

5. _____

6. _____

7. _____

8. _____

Unlike the previous verbs we have covered, the VTAs will depend on the number of the object that is spoken about. If, for example, I want to say "*I see a dog*", I would say "niwâpamâw atim." If I want to say "*I see dogs*" then the verb will have to agree in number with the plural object "*dogs*", as "niwâpamâw**ak** atim**wak**." This number agreement is highlighted in the charts on the next page by brackets.

8.1 CONJUGATION PATTERNS

Like the VAIs and the VTIs, the VTAs also have Imperatives, Negative Imperatives and Delayed Imperatives. The VTAs, however, must show number agreement if the object is plural, as shown in the forms below in brackets.

IMPERATIVE		NEGATIVE IMP.		DELAYED IMP.	
2	_____ (ik)	**2**	êkâwiya _____ (ik)	**2**	_____ âhkan(ik)
2P	_____ ihk(ok)	**2P**	êkâwiyav _____ ihk(ok)	**2P**	_____ âhkêk(ok)
21	_____ âtân(ik)	**21**	êkâwiya _____ âtân(ik)	**21**	_____ âhkahk(ik)

Like the VAIs and the VTIs, the VTAs in the Indicative and Conjunct forms can have nine possible agents/subjects carrying out the action, identified in the conjugation pattern by the following numeric system:

NO.	SUBJECT/AGENT	INDICATIVE MOOD		CONJUNCT	
1	1st person singular 'I'	ni	_____ âw(ak)	ê-	_____ ak(ik)
2	2nd person singular 'you'	ki	_____ âw(ak)	ê-	_____ at(cik)
3	3rd person singular 's/he/it'		_____ êw	ê-	_____ ât
3'	3rd person obviative 'her friend'		_____ êyiwa	ê-	_____ âyit
1P	1st person plural 'we' (excl.)	ni	_____ ânân(ak)	ê-	_____ âyâhk(ik)
21	1st person plural 'we' (incl.)	ki	_____ ânaw(ak)	ê-	_____ âyahk(ik)
2P	2nd person plural 'you'	ki	_____ âwâw(ak)	ê-	_____ âyêk(ok)
3P	3rd person plural 'they'		_____ êwak	ê-	_____ âcik
3'P	3rd person obviative plural 'their friend'		_____ êyiwa	ê-	_____ âyit

As with other verbs, all tense indicators, preverbs, and verb stems can be placed in the blank spaces in the above paradigms. VTAs follow the standard verb structure:

Indicative person indicators: "ni" and "ki" Conjunct markers: ê- or kâ- or ta-	Tense Indicators: kî- _past_ wî- _(going to)_ ka-(ta-) _(will)_ ka-kî- _(can/could)_	Preverb	Verb stems	Verb endings

TENSES

VTAs also use the following tenses that are used in other verbs:

The present (tense indicator: none):   niwâpamâw – _I see (him/her)._
The past (tense indicator: **kî**-):   nikî-wâpamâw – _I saw (him/her)._
The future intentional (tense: **wî**-):   niwî-wâpamâw – _I am going to see (him/her)._
The future definite (tense: **ka**-):   nika-wâpamâw – _I will see (him/her)._
The future definite tense for 1st and 2nd person forms is "**ka**-", and "**ta**-" for third person forms.

The future definite tenses are never used in the conjunct forms of verbs.

Another way of understanding the paradigm of verbs is to see the nature of the utterance as in who speaks, who is spoken to, and who is spoken about:

1st person subject: the speaker	2nd person subject: the one/ones spoken to	3rd person subject: the one/ones talked about
1 "ni_____âw(ak)" The speaker talking about himself/herself: "I".	**2** "ki_____âw(ak)" The addressee, i.e., the one spoken to: "you".	**3** "_____êw" The topic, i.e., the one spoken about: "she/he/it".
1P "ni_____ânân(ak)" The speaker talking about self and others but excludes the one spoken to: "We (excl.)".	**2P** "ki_____âwâw(ak)" Two or more persons spoken to: "You (plural)".	**3P** "_____êwak" Two or more persons spoken about: "they".
21 "ki_____ânaw(ak)" The speaker talking about self and others and includes the one spoken to: "We (incl.)"		**3'** "_____êyiwa" The friend, relative or pet of a 3rd person: "His/her _____"
		3'P "_____êyiwa" The friends, relatives or pets of 3rd persons: "Their_____"

Here, then, are all the paradigms for transitive animate verbs (verb stems, etc., go in the blanks):

IMPERATIVE
2	_____(ik)
2P	_____ihk(ok)
21	_____âtân(ik)

NEGATIVE IMP.
2	êkâwiya _____(ik)
2P	êkâwiya_____ihk(ok)
21	êkâwiya _____âtân(ik)

DELAYED IMP.
2	_____âhkan(ik)
2P	_____âhkêk(ok)
21	_____âhkahk(ik)

INDICATIVE MOOD
1	ni_____âw(ak)
2	ki_____âw(ak)
3	_____êw
3'	_____êyiwa
1P	ni_____ânân(ak)
21	ki_____ânaw(ak)
2P	ki_____âwâw(ak)
3P	_____êwak
3'P	_____êyiwa

CONJUNCT MOOD
1	ê-_____ak(ik)
2	ê-_____at(cik)
3	ê-_____ât
3'	ê-_____âyit
1P	ê-_____âyâhk(ik)
21	ê-_____âyahk(ik)
2P	ê-_____âyêk(ok)
3P	ê-_____âcik
3'P	ê-_____âyit

REMEMBER that the standard verb-phrase structure applies to all verbs:

Indicative person indicators: "ni" and "ki" Conjunct markers: ê- or kâ- or ta-	Tense Indicators: kî- *past* wî- (*going to*) ka-(ta-) (*will*) ka-kî- (*can/could*)	Preverbs	Verb stems	Verb endings

8.2 OBVIATION

REVIEW: The bold letters indicate the plural form of the verb used when the object in the sentence is plural; NUMBER AGREEMENT is necessary for VTAs. That is to say, if the object is plural, then the verb must also be in the plural; if the object is singular, then the verb must be in the singular.

Yet another peculiarity about VTAs is the process of obviation. All objects of VTAs undergo obviation in the third person indicators (3, 3', 3P, 3'P). Consider the following:

1.   nimôwâw kinosêw.   nimôwâw**ak** kinosêw**ak**.
        I eat fish.   *I eat fish.* (plural)

2.   kimôwâw kinosêw.   kimôwâw**ak** kinosêw**ak**.
        You eat fish.   *You eat fish.* (plural)

3.   môwêw kinosêwa.
        He eats fish.

Notice that the object of the sentence "kinosêw – *fish*" remains in its original form in both 1 and 2 but undergoes a change with the insertion of the "a" at the end of the noun in 3. This process is known as obviation; it serves to identify which is the object of the sentence. Had we left 3 without the noun "kinosêw" being obviated, we would have a situation which would leave that noun as the subject with the question of what that fish is eating left unresolved. Let's consider the case of the mystery eater:

4.   môwêw kinosêw kisîmisa.

5.   môwêw kinosêwa kisîmis.

Who eats whom?

The answer to that question depends on which of the two nouns has undergone obviation: in 4 "kisîmis – *your younger sibling*" has been obviated, so this is the object of the sentence, the one being eaten; "kinosêw – *the fish*" is the subject, the one doing the eating. So what we have in 4 is a rather cryptic situation:

4A.   *The fish eats your younger sibling.*

The situation in 5, where "kinosêw" is obviated, is the reverse of 4:

5A.   *Your younger sibling eats fish.*

In the preceding examples, we've seen a situation common to all VTAs: the process of obviation that is required in all third persons of the VTAs. For most transitive animate verbs, the objects of first and second persons need no obviation unless there are two objects: a direct object and an indirect object.

Consider the following using the VTA "asam – *feed him*":

6. nitasamâw kisîmis.
   I feed your younger brother.

7. nitasamâw kisîmis kinosêwa.
   I feed your younger brother fish.
   I feed fish to your younger brother.

In 6, we have only one object, "kisîmis", so we have no problem there; in 7, however, we have two objects, "kisîmis" and "kinosêw". One of these needs to be obviated, and depending on which is obviated, that is the one that is about to be eaten. Luckily for "kisîmis", it is the "kinosêw" which is about to be eaten. We could have had this situation where "kisîmis" is the one being obviated:

8. nitasamâw kisîmisa kinosêw.
   I feed your younger brother to the fish.

The chart below shows the forms for obviation and proximate:

NOUNS: proximate	NOUNS: obviate	VERBS: 3rd person proximate (VTA and VTI-1)	VERBS: 3rd person obviate (VTA and VTI-1)
1. Animate: Singular (VTA)	o_____a	_____êw	_____êyiwa
2. Animate: Plural (VTA)	o_____a	_____êwak	_____êyiwa
3. Inanimate: Singular (VTI-1)	o_____	_____m	_____miyiw
4. Inanimate: Plural (VTI-1)	o_____a	_____m	_____miyiwa

A peculiarity about animate nouns which undergo obviation is that they seem to lose their original animacy and number classifications. There is no way to tell if the animate noun is singular or plural unless you include a number before the noun. Also, as the example below illustrates, the animate noun which has undergone obviation seems to lose its animacy:

9. môwêw nîso kinosêwa kisîmis
   Your younger sibling eats two fish.

"*Fish*" is an animate noun so, according to the rules for making plurals out of animate nouns, we would expect the Cree word to end in a "**k**" like all animate plurals. However, although we are talking about two fish in the foregoing example, as the object of a transitive animate verb with a third person subject, it must be marked for obviation and not number.

Connect any of these units from left to right to make ten sentences: VTAs

PERSON INDICATORS	TENSE	PREVERB	VERB STEM VTA	ENDINGS
Indicative: ni (1, 1P) ki (2, 21, 2P)	kî- past wî- future intent ka- (ta-) future definite ka-kî- modal Present tense has no tense indicator.	kakwê- *(try)* nitawi- *(go and/to)* nôhtê- *(want)* nihtâ- *(can do well)* mâci- *(begin)* pêyako- *(alone)* pôni- *(stop)* ati- *(start)* pê- *(come)* pêci- *(come)* sâpo- *(through)* papâsi- *(hurriedly)* nisihkâci- *(slowly)* pêyâhtaki- *(carefully)* miyo- *(good)* mâyi- *(badly)* maci- *(bad/evil)* sôhki- *(hard)* pisci- *(accidently)* mwayî- *(before)* matwê- *(heard of in the distance)*	otin *(take it)* nâs *(fetch it)* sâmin *(touch it)* mîskon *(feel it)* pêhtaw *(hear it)* natohtaw *(listen to it)* nitawêyim *(want it)* natonaw *(search for it)* miskaw *(find it)* wâpam *(see it)* kanawâpam *(look at it)* kocispis *(taste it)* paswâs *(sniff it)* miyâm *(smell it)* nisitohtaw *(understand it)* kiskêyim *(know it)* nisitawêyim *(know it)* atoskâs *(work for someone)* masinahamaw *(write to someone)* postiskaw *(put it on)* kêcikoskaw *(take it off)* kisîpêkin *(wash it)* kîsis *(cook it)* itôtaw *(do it)* mêtawâkâs *(disrespect it)* yôhtên *(open it)* kipah *(close it)* ohpin *(lift it)* yahkiwêpin *(push it)* nâkatawêyim *(take care of it)*	**Indicative:** âw(ak) (1, 2) êw (3) êyiwa (3', 3'P) ânân(ak) (1P) ânaw(ak) (21) âwâw(ak) (2P) êwak (3P)
Conjunct : ê- (subordinate) kâ- (relative clause) ta- (infinitive)	**RULES only for the Indicative:** 1. Use the "t" as a connector for the present tense only if VS or PV begin with a vowel. **Rules for VTAs only:** **a) Number agreement:** if object is plural then the 1st and 2nd persons have to be plural. **b) Obviation:** objects of 3rd person verbs need to be marked for obviation.			**Conjunct:** ak(ik) (1) at(cik) (2) ât (3) âyit (3', 3'P) âyâhk(ik) (1P) âyahk(ik) (21) âyêk(ok) (2P) âcik (3P)

/	/	/	/	/
ni	kî-	nôhtê-	wâpam	âw(ak)

nikî-nôhtê-wâpamâw(ak)/ – *I wanted to see him/her(them).*

8.3 REVIEW – VTA

Place verb stems in the blanks; verb stems come from the second person singular (2) form of the imperative.

IMPERATIVES

2	_____(ik)
2P	_____ihk(ok)
21	_____âtân(ik)

NEGATIVE IMPERATIVES

2	êkâwiya _____(ik)
2P	êkâwiya_____ihk(ok)
21	êkâwiya_____âtân(ik)

DELAYED IMPERATIVES

2	_____âhkan(ik)
2P	_____âhkêk(ok)
21	_____âhkahk(ik)

INDICATIVE	CONJUNCT	FUTURE CONDITIONAL
1 ni_____âw(ak)	**1** ê-_____ak(ik)	**1** _____aki
2 ki_____âw(ak)	**2** ê-_____at(cik)	**2** _____aci
3 _____êw	**3** ê-_____ât	**3** _____âci
3' _____êyiwa	**3'** ê-_____âyit	**3'** _____âyici
1P ni_____ânân(ak)	**1P** ê-_____âyâhk(ik)	**1P** _____âyâhki
21 ki_____ânaw(ak)	**21** ê-_____âyahk(ik)	**21** _____âyahki
2P ki_____âwâw(ak)	**2P** ê-_____âyêk(ok)	**2P** _____âyêko
3P _____êwak	**3P** ê-_____âcik	**3P** _____âtwâwi
3'P _____êyiwa	**3'P** ê-_____âyit	**3'P** _____âyici

RULES:

a) Number agreement is needed for verbs in the 1st and 2nd persons (as marked by the brackets above): if the object is plural, then the verb also has to be plural.

b) Obviation: objects of 3rd person verbs are marked for obviation by adding an "**a**" to the noun that serves as the object of the sentence.

STANDARD VERB STRUCTURE

Person indicator or conjunct marker	Tense marker	Preverb	Verb stem	Verb ending

EXERCISES

EXERCISE 1. Conjugate the following:

1. Put the VTA "natohtaw – *listen to him*" into the 21 of the imperative.

2. Put the VTI-1 "natohta – *listen to it*" into the 21 of the imperative.

3. Put the VTA "natonaw – *look for him*" into the 1P of the Ind. Md. with plural object.

4. Put the VTI-1 "natona – *look for it*" into the 1P of the Ind. Md. with plural object.

5. Put the VTA "wîcih – *help him*" into the 3 of the Conj. Md. with PV "nitawi – *go and.*"

6. Put the VTA "nisitohtaw – *understand someone*" into the 1 of the Ind. Md.

7. Put the VTI-1 "nisitohta – *understand it*" into the 1 of the Ind. Md.

8. Put the VTA "môw – *eat it*" into the 2, past tense with plural object of the Ind. Md.

9. Put the VTA "kêcikoskaw – *take it off*" into the 3P future intentional of the Conj. Md.

10. Put the VTI-1 "kêcikoska – *take it off*" into the 21 future definite of the Ind. Md.

11. Put the VTA "postiskaw – *put it on*" into the 1P of the Ind. Md. with PV "nôhtê – *want to*" and plural object.

12. Put VTI-1 "postiska – *put it on*" into the 3` with PV "kakwê – *try to*" in the Ind. Md.

13. Put the VTI-1 "atoskâta – *work at it*" into the 2P of the Delayed Imperative.

14. Put the VTA "atoskâs – *work for someone*" into the 2P of the Delayed Imperative.

EXERCISE 2. Translate Cree to English:

môw – *eat it* (*VTA*)
natonaw – *look for someone* (*VTA*)
wîcih – *help someone* (*VTA*)

atoskâta – *work at it* (*VTI-1*)
kêcikoska – *take it off* (*VTI-1*)

1. kî-môwêyiwa kinosêwa.

_____

2. âsay cî kî-nitawi-atoskâtam nêhiyawêwin?

_____

3. sêmâk wîcihik kistêsak.

_____

4. mâka mîna cî ê-natonawacik kitastisak?

_____

5. kakwê-kêcikoskamohkan kimaskisina mwêstas.

_____

EXERCISE 3. Translate English to Cree:

natohtaw – *listen to someone* (*VTA*)
kêcikoskaw – *take it off* (*VTA*)
postiskaw – *put it on* (*VTA*)

nisitohta – *understand it* (*VTI-1*)
postiska – *put it on* (*VTI-1*)
namôya – *no/a negator*

1. *As usual I didn't listen to my older brother.*

_____

2. *Did you understand that Cree?*

_____

3. *He tried to take off his mitts.*

_____

4. *He didn't want to put on his shoes.*

_____

5. *Don't put on your mitts later, put them on now.*

_____

EXERCISE 4. Translate the following keeping in mind obviation and number agreement:

miy – *give it to someone* (VTA)
wîcih – *help someone* (VTA)
wîcêw – *accompany someone* (VTA)
wîsâm – *invite someone* (VTA)

masinahamaw – *write to someone* (VTA)
asam – *feed someone* (VTA)
môw – *eat it* (VTA)

1. *I gave that book to your older sister.*

   _____

2. *Did you give your shoes to your cousins (paternal uncle's sons)?*

   _____

3. *He invited your father to the store.*

   _____

4. *Let's help your younger brother tonight.*

   _____

5. *They fed the boys ducks.*

   _____

6. *Are you (pl) going to write to your mother?*

   _____

7. *I fed my friend bannock.*

   _____

8. *We (incl.) ate fish last night.*

   _____

9. *We (excl.) accompanied the girls to the university this morning.*

   _____

10. *Give them your books when you (pl) see them.*

   _____

EXERCISE 5. Conjugate the following:

1. Put the VTA "wîcih – *help her/him*" into the 3rd person singular of the Ind. Md.

    _____

2. Put the VTA "wîcêw – *accompany her/him*" into the 3' of the Ind. Md.

    _____

3. Put the VTA "wîsâm – *invite her/him*" into the 3P of the Ind. Md.

    _____

4. Put the VTA "kanawâpam – *look at her/him*" into the 3'P of the Ind. Md.

    _____

5. Put the VTA "kiyokaw – *visit her/him*" into the 2, past tense (with plural object) of the:

    a) Ind. Md. _____

    b) Conj. Md. _____

6. Put the VTA "wâpam – *see him/her*" into the 3 future intentional tense with preverb "nitawi – *go and*" in the:

    a) Ind. Md. _____

    b) Conj. Md. _____

7. Put the VTA "postiskaw – *put it on*" into the 3P in the past tense of:

    a) Ind. Md. _____

    b) Conj. Md. _____

8. Put the VTA "miskaw – *find him*" into the 3'P in the:

    a) Ind. Md. (future definite tense): _____

    b) Conj. Md. (future intentional tense): _____

9. Put the VTA "natohtaw – *listen to him*" into the 3' with preverb "nôhtê- – *want to*" in:

    a) Ind. Md. (past tense): _____

    b) Conj. Md. (past tense): _____

10. Put the VTA "natonaw – *look for him*" into the 3 of the:

   a) Ind. Md. (future definite tense): _____

   b) Conj. Md. (future intentional tense): _____

11. Put the VTA "wanih – *lose him*" into the 3P of the:

   a) Ind. Md. (future definite) _____

   b) Conj. Md. (future conditional) _____

12. Put the VTA "ayâw – *have/to be*" into the 3'P into the future definite tense, of the Ind Md.

   _____

13. Put VTA "kêcikoskaw – *take it off*" into the 1, past tense with preverb "kakwê- – *try to*" and plural object into the:

   a) Ind. Md. _____

   b) Conj. Md. _____

EXERCISE 6. Translate:

1. kî-môwêyiwa kinosêwa otôtêma.

2. âsay cî kî-nitawi-wâpamêw okiskinwahamâkêwa kistês?

3. wîsâmâhkanik kîtisânak.

4. mâka mîna cî ê-kî-wanihacik kitastisak tipiskohk?

5. kakwê-nitawi-kiyokawâhkan kikâwiy nîpihki.

6. âsay mîna nikî-natonawânânak awâsisak.

7. nikî-pisci-postiskawâwak ê-pîtosinâkosicik asikanak.

8. mâka mîna cî êkâ ê-nôhtê-natohtawâyêkok kimosôminawak?

9. namôya nikî-miskawâwak aniki atimwak nêtê sâkahikanihk.

10. kikî-wîcihâw cî kitôtêm ta-atoskâtahk nêhiyawêwin?

EXERCISE 7. Translate:

1. *John saw Mary eating.*

2. *The old man looked at the children playing.*

3. *The cat ate the fish that he had found.*

4. *The girl threw away her mittens when spring came.*

5. *The boys threw away their books when they finished school.*

6. *The women brought the bannock.*

7. *The man took his parents to town to see the doctor.*

8. *The young man followed the young ladies to the lake.*

9. *The child listened to his parents.*

10. *He helped her to write to her parents.*

8.4 INVERSE FORMS

There are various classes of **inverse forms** in Cree. This text will only look at what I like to call "the you and me" set and the regular inverse form where the person indicators, which used to identify the subject of the verb, become the object with a third person subject.

A. THE 'YOU AND ME' SET

This set has the second person as the subject and the first person as object or vice versa. They can be in the imperative, delayed imperative, indicative and conjunct as shown in the following charts:

IMPERATIVE		DELAYED IMPERATIVE	
2	_____in	**2**	_____ihkan
1P	_____inân	**1P**	_____ihkâhk

INDICATIVE 'YOU' AS SUBJECT		CONJUNCT 'YOU' AS SUBJECT	
2	ki_____in	**2**	ê-_____iyan
1P	ki_____inân	**1P**	ê-_____iyâhk
2P	ki_____inâwâw	**2P**	ê-_____iyêk

INDICATIVE 'I' AS SUBJECT		CONJUNCT 'I' AS SUBJECT	
2	ki_____itin	**2**	ê-_____itân
1P	ki_____itinân	**1P**	ê-_____itâhk
2P	ki_____itinâwâw	**2P**	ê-_____itakok

Let's now apply these charts along with translations using the VTA "asam – *feed someone*":

IMPERATIVE

2 asamin
Feed me.

1P asaminân
Feed us.

INDICATIVE 'YOU' AS SUBJECT

2 kit**asam**in
You (singular) *feed me.*

1P kit**asam**inân
You feed us.

2P kit**asam**inâwâw
You (plural) *feed me.*

DELAYED IMPERATIVE

2 asamihkan
Feed me later.

1P asamihkahk
Feed us later.

CONJUNCT 'YOU' AS SUBJECT

2 ê-asamiyan
You (singular) *feed me.*

1P ê-asamiyâhk
You feed us.

2P ê-asamiyêk
You (plural) *feed me.*

INDICATIVE	CONJUNCT

INDICATIVE
'I' AS SUBJECT
2 kit**asam**itin
I feed you (singular).

1P kit**asam**itinân
We feed you.

2P kit**asam**itinâwâw
I feed you (plural).

CONJUNCT
'I' AS SUBJECT
2 ê-**asam**itân
I feed you (singular).

1P ê-**asam**itâhk
We feed you.

2P ê-**asam**itakok
I feed you (plural).

B. THE REGULAR INVERSE

The regular inverse has a 3rd person subject, and the object is identified by the person indicator (if any) in the following charts:

INDICATIVE

1 ni_____ik(wak)

2 ki_____ik(wak)

3 _____ikow

3' _____ikoyiwa

1P ni_____ikonân(ak)

21 ki_____ikonaw(ak)

2P ki_____ikowâw(ak)

3P _____ikowak

3'P _____ikoyiwa

CONJUNCT

1 ê-_____it(cik)

2 ê-_____isk(ik)

3 ê-_____ikot

3' ê-_____ikoyit

1P ê-_____ikoyâhk(ik)

21 ê-_____ikoyahk(ik)

2P ê-_____ikoyêk(ok)

3P ê-_____ikocik

3'P ê-_____ikoyit

Now let's try some translations using the foregoing chart along with the following words:

INDICATIVE
1 ni_____ik

CONJUNCT
1 ê-_____it

VTA 'wâpam – *see someone*'

He sees me.	_____	_____
He saw me.	_____	_____
He will see me.	_____	_____
He's going to see me.	_____	_____

2 ki_____ik   **2** ê-_____isk

VTA 'wîsam – invite'

He invites you.   _____   _____
He invited you.   _____   _____
He will invite you.   _____   _____
He's going to invite you. _____   _____

3 _____ikow   **3** ê-_____ikot

VTA 'wîcih – help someone'

He helps him.   _____   _____
He helped him.   _____   _____
He will help him.   _____   _____
He's going to help him.   _____   _____

1P ni_____ikonân   **1P** ê-_____ikoyâhk

VTA 'wîcêw – accompany someone'

He accompanies us.   _____   _____
He accompanied us.   _____   _____
He will accompany us.   _____   _____
He's going to accompany us. _____   _____

2P ki_____ikowâw   **2P** ê-_____ikoyêk

VTA 'kanawâpam – look at someone'

He looks at you.   _____   _____
He looked at you.   _____   _____
He will look at you.   _____   _____
He's going to look at you. _____   _____

3P_____ikowak   **3P** ê-_____ikocik

VTA 'natohtaw – listen to someone'

They listen to him.   _____   _____
They listened to him.   _____   _____
They will listen to him.   _____   _____
They are going to listen to him. _____   _____

8.5 VTA-FORMS: REFLEXIVES, DIRECT FORMS AND INVERSE FORMS

SET ONE – Reflexive "iso" forms:

REFLEXIVES

IMPERATIVE		NEGATIVE IMPERATIVE		DELAYED IMPERATIVE	
2	_____iso	**2** êkâwiya _____iso		**2** _____isohkan	
2P	_____isok	**2P** êkâwiya _____isok		**2P** _____isohkêk	
21	_____isotân	**21** êkâwiya _____isotân		**21** _____isohkahk	

EXERCISE 1.

A. Translate the following using the VTA root "asam – _feed someone_":

1. _Feed yourself._ _____

2. _Feed yourselves._ _____

3. _Let's feed ourselves._ _____

B. Translate the following using the VTA root "kanawâpam – _look at someone_":

1. _Don't look at yourself._ _____

2. _Don't look at yourselves._ _____

3. _Let's not look at ourselves._ _____

C. Translate the following using the VTA root "pâhpih – _laugh at someone_":

1. _Laugh at yourself later._ _____

2. _Laugh at yourselves later._ _____

3. _Let's laugh at ourselves later._ _____

D. Translate the following using the above verb roots:

1. _Don't feed yourself._ _____

2. _Don't feed yourselves now, feed yourselves later._ _____

3. _Let's not laugh at ourselves._ _____

4. _Don't laugh at yourselves._ _____

5. _Let's not feed ourselves later._ _____

6. _Look at yourself later._ _____

INDICATIVE FORMS

VTA-DIRECT 3rd person as object	VTA-INVERSE 3rd person as subject	VTA-REFLEXIVE-1 Subject is also object
1 ni_____âw(ak)	**1** ni_____ik(wak)	**1** ni_____ison
2 ki_____âw(ak)	**2** ki_____ik(wak)	**2** ki_____ison
3 _____êw	**3** _____ikow	**3** _____isow
3' _____êyiwa	**3'** _____ikoyiwa	**3'** _____isoyiwa

wâpam – *see him/her*
asam – *feed him/her*
pâhpih – *laugh at him/her*
môh – *make him/her cry*

EXERCISE 2.

A. Translate the following using the above verb stems:

1. niwâpamâw môswa. _____

2. niwâpamik okiskinwahamâkêw. _____

3. niwâpamison. _____

4. kiwâpamâw môswa. _____

5. kiwâpamik okiskinwahamâkêw. _____

6. kiwâpamison. _____

7. wâpamêw nâpêwa. _____

8. wâpamikow okiskinwahamâkêwa. _____

9. wâpamisow nistês nipîhk. _____

10. otôtêma wâpamêyiwa môswa. _____

11. ostêsa wâpamikoyiwa okiskinwahamâkêwa. _____

12. omisa wâpamisoyiwa wâpamonihk. _____

B. Put the above sentences in the past tense.
C. Put the sentences in A in the future definite tense.
D. Put the above in the future intentional tense and use the preverb "nôhtê- – *want to.*"
E. Replace the verb stems in C with "asam – *feed someone.*"

VTA-DIRECT 3rd person as object	VTA-INVERSE 3rd person as subject	VTA-REFLEXIVE-1 Subject is also object
1 ê-_____ak(ik)	**1** ê-_____it(cik)	**1** ê-_____isoyân
2 ê-_____at(cik)	**2** ê-_____isk(ik)	**2** ê-_____isoyan
3 ê-_____ât	**3** ê-_____ikot	**3** ê-_____isot
3' ê-_____âyit	**3'** ê-_____ikoyit	**3'** ê-_____isoyit

EXERCISE 3.

A. Translate the following using the above verb stems:

1. ê-wâpamak môswa. _____

2. ê-wâpamit okiskinwahamâkêw. _____

3. ê-wâpamisoyân. _____

4. ê-wâpamat môswa. _____

5. ê-wâpamisk okiskinwahamâkêw. _____

6. ê-wâpamisoyan. _____

7. ê-wâpamât nâpêwa. _____

8. ê-wâpamikot okiskinwahamâkêwa. _____

9. ê-wâpamisot nistês nipîhk. _____

10. otôtêma ê-wâpamâyit môswa. _____

11. ostêsa ê-wâpamikoyit okiskinwahamâkêwa. _____

12. omisa ê-wâpamisoyit wâpamonihk. _____

B. Put the above sentences in the past tense.
C. Put the sentences in A in past tense with preverb "kakwê- – *try to.*"
D. Put the above in the future intentional tense and use the preverb "nôhtê- – *want to.*"
E. Replace the verb stems in C with "môh – *make someone cry.*"

SET TWO – Reflexive "oso" forms:

RELEXIVES

IMPERATIVE		NEGATIVE IMPERATIVE		DELAYED IMPERATIVE	
2	_____oso	**2** êkâwiya	_____oso	**2**	_____osohkan
2P	_____osok	**2P** êkâwiya	_____osok	**2P**	_____osohkêk
21	_____osotân	**21** êkâwiya	_____osotân	**21**	_____osohkahk

EXERCISE 4.

A. Translate the following using the VTA root "sîkah – *comb someone's hair*":

1. *Comb your hair yourself.* _____

2. *Comb your hair yourselves.* _____

3. *Let's comb our hair ourselves.* _____

B. Translate the following using the VTA root "pakamah – *hit someone*":

1. *Don't hit yourself.* _____

2. *Don't hit yourselves.* _____

3. *Let's not hit ourselves.* _____

C. Translate the following using the VTA root "wîsakah – *hurt someone by hitting*":

1. *Hurt yourself later.* _____

2. *Hurt yourselves later.* _____

3. *Let's hurt ourselves later.* _____

D. Translate the following using the above verb stems:

1. *Don't hurt yourself.* _____

2. *Don't comb your hair yourselves now, comb your hair yourselves later.*

_____

3. *Let's not comb our hair ourselves.* _____

4. *Don't hurt yourselves.* _____

5. *Let's not hurt ourselves later.* _____

6. *Hit yourself later.* _____

VTA-DIRECT 3rd person as object	VTA-INVERSE 3rd person as subject	VTA-REFLEXIVE-2 Subject is also object
1 ni_____âw(ak)	**1** ni_____ok(wak)	**1** ni_____oson
2 ki_____âw(ak)	**2** ki_____ok(wak)	**2** ki_____oson
3 _____êw	**3** _____okow	**3** _____osow
3' _____êyiwa	**3'** _____okoyiwa	**3'** _____osoyiwa
pakamahw – *hit him/her* sîkahw – *comb his/her hair* wîsakahw – *hurt him/her by hitting*	pakamah sîkah wîsakah	pakamah sîkah wîsakah

EXERCISE 5.

A. Translate the following using the above verb stems:

1. nipakamahwâw môswa. _____

2. nipakamahok okiskinwahamâkêw. _____

3. nipakamahoson. _____

4. kipakamahwâw môswa. _____

5. kipakamahok okiskinwahamâkêw._____

6. kipakamahoson._____

7. pakamahwêw nâpêwa. _____

8. pakamahokow okiskinwahamâkêwa. _____

9. pakamahosow nistês ostikwânihk. _____

10. otôtêma pakamahwêyiwa môswa. _____

11. ostêsa pakamahokoyiwa okiskinwahamâkêwa. _____

12. omisa pakamahosoyiwa ospitonihk. _____

B. Put the above sentences in the past tense.
C. Put the sentences in A in the future definite tense.
D. Put the above in the future intentional tense and use the preverb "nôhtê- – *want to.*"
E. Replace the verb stems in C with "sîkahw – *comb someone's hair.*"

VTA-DIRECT 3rd person as object	VTA-INVERSE 3rd person as subject	VTA-REFLEXIVE-1 Subject is also object
1 ê-_____ak(ik)	**1** ê-_____ot(cik)	**1** ê-_____osoyân
2 ê-_____at(cik)	**2** ê-_____osk(ik)	**2** ê-_____osoyan
3 ê-_____ât	**3** ê-_____okot	**3** ê-_____osot
3' ê-_____âyit	**3'** ê-_____okoyit	**3'** ê-_____osoyit

EXERCISE 6.

A. Translate the following using the above verb stems:

1. ê-pakamahwak môswa. _____

2. ê-pakamahot okiskinwahamâkêw. _____

3. ê-pakamahosoyân. _____

4. ê-pakamahwat môswa. _____

5. ê-pakamahosk okiskinwahamâkêw. _____

6. ê-pakamahosoyan. _____

7. ê-pakamahwât nâpêwa. _____

8. ê-pakamahokot okiskinwahamâkêwa. _____

9. ê-pakahmahosot nistês ostikwânihk. _____

10. otôtêma ê-pakamahwâyit môswa. _____

11. ostêsa ê-pakamahokoyit okiskinwahamâkêwa. _____

12. omisa ê-pakamahosoyit ospitonihk. _____

B. Put the above sentences in the past tense.
C. Put the sentences in A in the past tense with preverb "pisci- – *accidentally*."
D. Put the above in the future intentional tense and use the preverb "nôhtê- – *want to*."
E. Replace the verb stems in C with "wîsakahw – *hurt someone by hitting.*"

SET THREE – Reflexive "âso" forms:

REFLEXIVES

IMPERATIVE		NEGATIVE IMPERATIVE		DELAYED IMPERATIVE	
2 _____âso		**2** êkâwiya _____âso		**2** _____âsohkan	
2P _____âsok		**2P** êkâwiya _____âsok		**2P** _____âsohkêk	
21 _____âsotân		**21** êkâwiya _____âsotân		**21** _____âsohkahk	

NOTE: The stem's final **aw** must be deleted before adding these endings.

EXERCISE 7.

A. Translate the following using the VTA root "atâwêstamaw – *buy it for someone*":

  1. *Buy it for yourself.* _____

  2. *Buy it for yourselves.* _____

  3. *Let's buy it for ourselves.* _____

B. Translate the following using the VTA root "nâtamaw – *fetch it for someone*":

  1. *Don't fetch it for yourself.* _____

  2. *Don't fetch it for yourselves.* _____

  3. *Let's not fetch it for ourselves.* _____

C. Translate the following using the VTA root "kiskinwahamaw – *teach someone*":

  1. *Teach yourself later.* _____

  2. *Teach yourselves later.* _____

  3. *Let's teach ourselves later.* _____

D. Translate the following using the above verb stems:

  1. *Don't teach yourself.* _____

  2. *Don't teach yourselves now, teach yourselves later.* _____

  3. *Let's teach ourselves.* _____

  4. *Don't buy it for yourselves.* _____

  5. *Let's not teach ourselves later.* _____

  6. *Fetch it for yourself later.* _____

INDICATIVE FORMS

VTA-DIRECT 3rd person as object	VTA-INVERSE 3rd person as subject	VTA-REFLEXIVE-3 Subject is also object
1 ni_____âw(ak)	**1** ni_____âk(wak)	**1** ni_____âson
2 ki_____âw(ak)	**2** ki_____âk(wak)	**2** ki_____âson
3 _____êw	**3** _____âkow	**3** _____âsow
3′ _____êyiwa	**3′** _____âkoyiwa	**3′** _____âsoyiwa

atâwêstamaw - *buy it for him/her* pêtamaw - *bring it for him/her* nâtamaw - *fetch it for him/her* kiskinwahamaw - *teach him/her*	**DROP the last 'aw' from the verb stem when going to the inverse and reflexive forms.**

EXERCISE 8.

A. Translate the following using the above verb stems:

1. ninâtamawâw môswa. _____

2. ninâtamâk okiskinwahamâkêw. _____

3. ninâtamâson. _____

4. kinâtamawâw môswa. _____

5. kinâtamâk okiskinwahamâkêw. _____

6. kinâtamâson. _____

7. nâtamawêw nâpêwa. _____

8. nâtamâkow okiskinwahamâkêwa. _____

9. nâtamâsow nistês miskotâkay. _____

10. otôtêma nâtamawêyiwa môswa. _____

11. ostêsa nâtamâkoyiwa okiskinwahamâkêwa. _____

12. omisa nâtamâsoyiwa maskisina. _____

B. Put the above sentences in the past tense.

C. Put the sentences in A in the future definite tense.

D. Put the above in the future intentional tense and use the preverb "nôhtê- – *want to.*"

E. Replace the verb stems in C with "atâwêstamaw – *buy it for someone.*"

CONJUNCT FORMS

VTA-DIRECT 3rd person as object	VTA-INVERSE 3rd person as subject	VTA-REFLEXIVE-1 Subject is also object
1 ê-_____ak(ik)	**1** ê-_____it(cik)	**1** ê-_____âsoyân
2 ê-_____at(cik)	**2** ê-_____âsk(ik)	**2** ê-_____âsoyan
3 ê-_____ât	**3** ê-_____âkot	**3** ê-_____âsot
3' ê-_____âyit	**3'** ê-_____âkoyit	**3'** ê-_____âsoyit

EXERCISE 9.

A. Translate the following using the above verb stems:

1. ê-nâtamawak môswa. _____

2. ê-nâtamawit okiskinwahamâkêw. _____

3. ê-nâtamâsoyân. _____

4. ê-nâtamawat môswa. _____

5. ê-nâtamâsk okiskinwahamâkêw. _____

6. ê-nâtamâsoyan. _____

7. ê-nâtamawât nâpêwa. _____

8. ê-nâtamâkot okiskinwahamâkêwa. _____

9. ê-nâtamâsot nistês miskotâkay. _____

10. otôtêma ê-nâtamawâyit môswa. _____

11. ostêsa ê-nâtamâkoyit okiskinwahamâkêwa. _____

12. omisa ê-nâtamâsoyit maskisina. _____

B. Put the above sentences in the past tense.
C. Put the sentences in A in the past tense with preverb "nitawi- – *go and.*"
D. Put the above in the future intentional tense and use the preverb "nôhtê- – *want to.*"
E. Replace the verb stems in C with "atâwêstamaw – *buy it for someone.*"

VTA-INVERSE

The 'you and me' set:

VERBS IN REFLEXIVE FORM

SET ONE – Reflexive "iso" forms:

IMPERATIVE (commands)	NEGATIVE IMPERATIVE (commands not to do)	DELAYED IMPERATIVE (commands to do later)
2-1 _____in	**2-1** êkâwiya _____in	**2-1** _____ihkan
2(P)-1P _____inân	**2(P)-1P** êkâwiya_____inân	**2(P)-1P** _____ihkâhk
2P-1 _____ik	**2P-1** êkâwiya _____ik	**2P-1** _____ihkêk

INDICATIVE: verbs in the reflexive "iso" forms have these for the 'you and me' direct and inverse:

Direct – *"you"* as subject and *"me"* as object	Inverse – *"I"* as subject and *"you"* as object
2-1 ki_____in	**1-2** ki_____itin
2(P)-1P ki_____inân	**1P-2(P)** ki_____itinân
2P-1 ki_____inâwâw	**1-2P** ki_____itinâwâw

CONJUNCT: verbs in the reflexive form "iso" follow these forms:

Direct – *"I"* as subject and *"you"* as object	Inverse – *"You"* as subject *"I"* as object
2-1 ê_____iyan	**1-2** ê_____itân
2(P)-1P ê_____iyâhk	**1P-2(P)** ê_____itâhk
2P-1 ê_____iyêk	**1-2P** ê_____itakok

Make sentences from the above forms using the following verb stems:

wâpam – *see someone*
asam – *feed someone*
pâhpih – *laugh at someone*
môh – *make someone cry*

VERBS IN REFLEXIVE FORM

SET TWO – Reflexive "oso" forms:

IMPERATIVE (commands)	NEGATIVE IMPERATIVE (commands not to do)	DELAYED IMPERATIVE (commands to do later)
2-1 _____on	**2-1** êkâwiya _____on	**2-1** _____ohkan
2(P)-1P _____onân	**2(P)-1P** êkâwiya _____onân	**2(P)-1P** _____ohkâhk
2P-1 _____ok	**2P-1** êkâwiya _____ok	**2P-1** _____ohkêk

INDICATIVE: verbs in the reflexive "oso" forms have these for the 'you and me' direct and inverse:

Direct – *"you"* as subject and *"me"* as object	Inverse – *"I"* as subject and *"you"* as object
2-1 ki_____on	**1-2** ki_____otin
2(P)-1P ki_____onân	**1P-2(P)** ki_____otinân
2P-1 ki_____onâwâw	**1-2P** ki_____otinâwâw

CONJUNCT: verbs in reflexive "oso" form follow these forms:

Direct – *"I"* as subject and *"you"* as object	Inverse – *"You"* as subject *"I"* as object
2-1 ê-_____oyan	**1-2** ê-_____otân
2(P)-1P ê-_____oyâhk	**1P-2(P)** ê-_____otâhk
2P-1 ê-_____oyêk	**1-2P** ê-_____otakok

Make sentences with the above forms using the following verb stems:

pakamahw – *hit someone*
sîkahw – *comb someone's hair*
wîsakahw – *hurt someone by hitting*

VERBS IN REFLEXIVE FORM

SET THREE – Reflexive "âso" forms:

IMPERATIVE (commands)	NEGATIVE IMPERATIVE (commands not to do)	DELAYED IMPERATIVE (commands to do later)
2-1 _____in	**2-1** êkâwiya_____in	**2-1** _____ihkan
2(P)-1P _____inân	**2(P)-1P** êkâwiya _____inân	**2(P)-1P** _____ihkâhk
2P-1 _____ik	**2P-1** êkâwiya _____ik	**2P-1** _____ihkêk

INDICATIVE: verbs in the reflexive "âso" forms have these for the 'you and me' direct and inverse:

Direct – *"you"* as subject and *"me"* as object	Inverse – *"I"* as subject and *"you"* as object
2-1 ki_____in	**1-2** ki_____âtin
2(P)-1P ki_____inân	**1P-2(P)** ki_____âtinân
2P-1 ki_____inâwâw	**1-2P** ki_____âtinâwâw

*Note: For Inverse, drop the final "aw" of the verb stem before adding the Inverse endings.

CONJUNCT: verbs in the reflexive "âso" form follow these forms:

Direct – *"I"* as subject and *"you"* as object	Inverse – *"You"* as subject *"I"* as object
2-1 ê-_____iyan	**1-2** ê-_____âtân
2(P)-1P ê-_____iyâhk	**1P-2(P)** ê-_____âtâhk
2P-1 ê-_____iyêk	**1-2P** ê-_____âtakok

*Note: for Inverse, drop the final "aw" of the verb stem before adding the Inverse endings.

Make sentences using the above forms with the following verb stems:

atâwêstamaw – *buy it for someone*
pêtamaw – *bring it for someone*
nâtamaw – *fetch it for someone*
kiskinwahamaw – *teach it to someone*

kîsi-oyastâk ôhi nanâtohk itahkamikisiwina: Finish the following charts. Use what is here to figure out what needs to be done in the blank forms.

A. VTA -iso FORMS: IMPERATIVES: use "wâpam – *see someone*":

IMPERATIVE	NEGATIVE IMPERATIVE	DELAYED IMPERATIVE
2 ___wâpam**iso**___	**2** _____	**2** _____
2P _____	**2P** ___êkâwiya wâpam**isok**___	**2P** _____
21 _____	**21** _____	**21** ___wâpam**isohkahk**___

INDICATIVE FORMS: VTA – wâpam "*see someone*" in the past tense:

VTA-DIRECT 3rd person as object	VTA-INVERSE 3rd person as subject	VTA-REFLEXIVE-1 Subject is also object
1 nikî-**wâpam**âw(ak)	**1** _____	**1** nikî-**wâpam**ison
2 _____	**2** kikî-**wâpam**ik(wak)	**2** _____
3 _____	**3** kî-**wâpam**ikow	**3** _____
3' kî-**wâpam**êyiwa	**3'** _____	**3'** kî-**wâpam**isoyiwa

wâpam – *see him/her*
asam – *feed him/her*
pâhpih – *laugh at him/her*
môh – *make him/her cry*

WORDS: okiskinwahamâkêw – *teacher;* okiskinwahamâkan – *student;* môswa – *moose;* nipiy – *water;* wâpam – *see someone.*

TRANSLATE:

1. niwâpamison. _____

2. nikî-wâpamâw môswa. _____

3. niwâpamik môswa. _____

4. wâpamisow môswa nipîhk. _____

5. wî-wâpamêw okiskinwahamâkana. _____

6. ta-wâpamikow okiskinwahamâkêwa. _____

B. VTA -OSO FORMS: IMPERATIVES: use "sîkah – *comb someone's hair*."

IMPERATIVE	NEGATIVE IMPERATIVE	DELAYED IMPERATIVE
2 _____	2 ___êkâwiya sîkah**oso**___	2 _____
2P _____	2P _____	2P ___sîkah**osohkêk**___
21 ___sîkah**osotân**___	21 _____	21 _____

INDICATIVE FORMS: VTA sîkah "*comb someone's hair*" in the future definite tense:

VTA-DIRECT 3rd person as object	VTA-INVERSE 3rd person as subject	VTA-REFLEXIVE-2 Subject is also object
1 _____	1 nika-**sîkah**ok(wak)	1 _____
2 kika-**sîkahw**âw(ak)	2 _____	2 kika-**sîkah**oson
3 **ta-sîkahw**êw	3 **ta-sîkah**okow	3 _____
3' _____	3' _____	3' ta-**sîkah**osoyiwa
pakamahw – *hit him/her* sîkahw – *comb his/her hair* wîsakahw – *hurt him/her by hitting*	pakamah sîkah wîsakah	pakamah sîkah wîsakah

WORDS: nitiskwêm – *my woman (wife)*; nitânis – *my daughter*; osîmisa – *her/his younger sibling.*

TRANSLATE:

1. nika-sîkahoson. _____

2. niwî-sîkahwâw nitânis. _____

3. nisîkahok nitiskwêm. _____

4. ta-sîkahosow nitânis. _____

5. kî-sîkahwêw osîmisa. _____

6. wî-sîkahokow otiskwêma. _____

C. VTA -âso FORMS: IMPERATIVES: use "nâtamaw – *fetch something for someone*" in the following forms (drop the "aw" from the end for the forms):

IMPERATIVE	NEGATIVE IMPERATIVE	DELAYED IMPERATIVE
2 _____	**2** _____	**2** ___ nâtam**âsohkan** _____
2P ___nâtam**âsok**_____	**2P** _____	**2P** _____
21 _____	**21** ___ êkâwiya nâtam**âsotân**_	**21** _____

INDICATIVE FORMS: VTA nâtamaw "*fetch/get something for someone*" in future intention:

VTA-DIRECT 3rd person as object	VTA-INVERSE 3rd person as subject	VTA-REFLEXIVE-3 Subject is also object
1 niwî-**nâtamaw**âw(ak)	**1** _____	**1** niwî-**nâtam**âson
2 _____	**2** kiwî-**nâtam**âk(wak)	**2** _____
3 wî-**nâtamaw**êw	**3** _____	**3** wî-**nâtam**âsow
3' _____	**3'** wî-**nâtam**âkoyiwa	**3'** _____
atâwêstamaw – *buy it for him/her* pêtamaw – *bring it for him/her* nâtamaw – *fetch it for him/her* kiskinwahamaw – *teach him/her*	**DROP the last 'aw' from the verb stem when going to the inverse and reflexive forms.**	

WORDS: maskisin – *shoe;* nohkom – *my grandmother;* nistês – *my older brother.*

TRANSLATE:

1. niwî-nâtamâson nimaskisina. _____

2. nikî-nâtamawâw omaskisina nohkom. _____

3. nika-nâtamâk nimaskisina nitânis. _____

4. ta-nâtamâsow omaskisina nistês. _____

5. wî-nâtamawêw omaskisiniyiwa ostêsa. _____

6. nâtamâkow omaskisina okiskinwahamâkêwa. _____

SUBORDINATE CLAUSES

Choose the correct subordinate clause in each of the follow sentences:

1. *I'm going to drink coffee before (if) going to work.*
   niwî-minihkwân pihkahtêwâpoy

   _____ ê-mwayî-nitawi-atoskêyân.
   _____ ta-mwayî-nitawi-atoskêyân.
   _____ ta-kî-mwayî-nitawi-atoskêyân.
   _____ mwayî-nitawi-atoskêyâni.
   _____ kâ-mwayî-nitawi-atoskêyân.

2. *My mother called me to go and eat.*
   nikî-natomik nikâwiy

   _____ ta-nitawi-mîcisoyân.
   _____ ê-nitawi-mîcisoyân.
   _____ nitawi-mîcisoyâni.
   _____ kâ-nitawi-mîcisoyân.
   _____ ta-kî-nitawi-mîcisoyân.

3. *I fed my dog fish because she was hungry.*
   nikî-asamâw nitêm kinosêwa ayisk

   _____ kâ-nôhtêhkatêt.
   _____ ta-kî-nôhtêhkatêt.
   _____ nôhtêhkatêci.
   _____ ta-nôhtêhkatêt.
   _____ ê-nôhtêhkatêt.

4. *I usually help my older brother when he goes to work.*
   niwîcihâw mâna nistês ispîhk

   _____ ta-kî-nitawi-atoskêt.
   _____ kâ-nitawi-atoskêt.
   _____ ê-nitawi-atoskêt.
   _____ ta-nitawi-atoskêt.
   _____ nitawi-atoskêci.

5. *If you want to see your older sister you should come here tomorrow.*
   kîspin kinôhtê-wâpamâw kimis

   _____ ê-pê-itohtêyan ôta wâpahki.
   _____ ta-pê-itohtêyan ôta wâpahki.
   _____ ta-kî-pê-itohtêyan ôta wâpahki.
   _____ pê-itohtêyani ôta wâpahki.
   _____ kâ-pê-itohtêyan ôta wâpahki.

Choose the correct grammatical forms from each line to fit with the English version of the following story [Note: where only one form is given, it is correct and must be included]:

kayâs, ispîhk   ê-kî-awâsisîwiyân,   mihcêtwâw mâna nikî-kostên ta-kî-nitawiminêyân.
kayâs, tânispîhk kâ-kî-awâsisîwiyân,   nikî-kospîn ta-nitawiminêyân.
A long time ago when I was a child, there were a lot of times I went into the forest to go berry-picking.

mihcêtwâw mâna niwî-wanisinin   ayisk êkî ê-nâkatawêyihtamân nimêskanâm.
mihcêtwâw   nikî-wanisinin   êkâ kâ-nâkatawêyihtamân
A lot of times I got lost because I did not pay attention to my path.

êkosi mâni-mâka, nikî-ati-wanohtân!   kêtahtawê kâ-mâtâhwak maskwa!
              kâ-kî-ati-wanôhtêyân!   kâ-mâtâhwit niskwa!
That's the way it was, I eventually got lost! All of a sudden I saw bear tracks!

"piko ta-pêyâhtakisiyân,"   kititêyihtên. namoya nikî-ninitawêyihtên ta-nakiskawit
   "ta-kî-pêyâhtakisiyân,"   nititêyihtên. namôya   ninitawêyihtên   ta-nakiskawak
"I will have to be careful," I thought. I did not want to meet up with

maskwa. kisihkâc nikî-ati-pa-pimohtân.   kêtahtawê kâ-pêhtawak awiyak sakâhk.
        nisihkâc ê-kî-ati-pa-pimohtêyân.   kâ-pêhtawit
a bear. Slowly I began walking. All of a sudden I hear someone in the bush.

nikîmôtâpin sakâsihk ohci, kâ-wâpamak maskwa ê-matwê-môminêt. kêsiskaw êkota
nikîmôtapin   ochi, kâ-wâpamit   kâ-matwê-môminêt.
I peek from a small bush, (from there) I see a bear, it was eating berries. Quickly from

ohci tapasîw! pihtaw ôma nikî-wanisinin, mâka kiyâm! kinwêsk nipimiyâmon! iyaw!
   nitapasîn! pîhtaw ôta niwî-wanisinin   kâ-pimiyâmoyân!
there I fled! Unfortunately I was lost, but no matter! I fled for a long time! Holy!

kêtahtawê kâ-takopahtâyân   kikapêsiwinihk
        ê-takopahtâyan   nikapêsiwinihk.
All of a sudden I arrived (running) at my camp.

DO: Go through the following story, isolating verb stems, and thus creating a word list.

pêyakwâw ê-nîpihk nohtâwîpan kî-atoskêhikow atâwêwikimâwa ta-kîskatahâhtikwêt. êkosi tahto-kîsikâw nikî-pôsinân ê-nitawi-nikohtêyâhk natimihk. nohtâwiy kî-kîskatahâhtikwêw êkwa niyanân nîtisânak – nistês, nisîmis êkwa niya – nikî-âwacimihtânân, nohcimihk ohci isko nâsipêtimihk. kwayask nikî-mâh-mâkwahikon anihi mihta!

kinwêsk nikî-pimahkamikisinân êkotê, kapê-kîsik ê-nikohtêyâhk, êkotê mina mâna ê-kî-âpihtâ-kîsikani-mîcisoyâhk. mêtoni mihcêt mihta nikî-ati-oyastânân wâsakâm sîpîhk ispîhk nohtâwiy kâ-ati-mihtotihkêt, kwayask kî-ispâw anima mihtot!

nîstâw nikî-pê-wîcihikonân ispîhk kâ-kîsihtâyâhk anima mihtot, ê-pê-tahkopitahk otôtihk, mâmihk ta-isipitahk, ê-sakahpitahk anima mihtot. nititikonân nohtâwiy ta-pôsiyâhk ôsihk mâka mâka-mîna namôya ninatohtên, ê-akâwâtamân ta-pôsiyân tahkohc mihtotihk.

êkosi nikitimâkinâkonân nohtâwiy, nikî-pakitinikonân tahkohc mihtotihk ta-pôsiyâhk. êkos îsi nikî-ati-misakânân âmaciwêspimowinihk. kwayask nikî-cîhkêyihtên.

One summer my late father was hired to cut firewood by the store manager. Every day we would get on the canoe to go cut firewood up-river. My father would cut down the trees and my siblings and I – my older brother, my younger brother and I – would haul the firewood down, from deep in the forest to the shoreline. Those logs sure gave me a tough time.

We were busy there for a long time, chopping firewood all day, we would eat our lunch over there too. Eventually we had lots of firewood all along the shore of the river when my father started to make a raft, that raft was piled high with firewood!

My brother-in-law came to help when we had finished the raft, he came to tie the raft to his boat to pull that raft down river. My father told us to get in the boat but as usual I wouldn't listen, wanting to get on top of the raft instead.

My father took pity on us and he let us ride on top of the raft. In that fashion we arrived by boat at Stanley Mission. I was so happy.

WORD LIST
Find the root words in the above story and list them here with grammatical category.

_____

_____

_____

_____

_____

_____

_____

_____

_____

8.6 TRANSITIVE VERB PAIRS: VTA AND VTI-1 *(Unless marked otherwise)*

ENGLISH: *"it" refers to any noun.*	TRANSITIVE ANIMATE	TRANSITIVE INANIMATE
Taste it.	kocispis*	kocispita
Like the taste of it.	wîhkipw-**	wîhkista
Eat it.	môw	mîci (VTI-3)
See it.	wâpam	wâpahta
Look at it.	kanawâpam	kanawâpahta
Hear it.	pêhtaw	pêhta
Listen to it.	natohtaw	natohta
Understand it.	nisitohtaw	nisitohta
Recognize it.	nisitawêyim	nisitawêyihta
Know it.	kiskêyim	kiskêyihta
Fetch it.	nâs*	nâta
Choose it.	nawasôn	nawasôna
Take it (buy it).	otin	otina
Bring it.	pêsiw	pêtâ (VTI-2)
Try it.	kocih	kocihtâ (VTI-2)
Feel it.	mîskon	mîskona
Touch it.	sâmin	sâmina
Smell it.	miyâm	miyâhta
Have it.	ayâw	ayâ (VTI-2)
Look for it.	naton	natona
Find it.	miskaw	miska
Fry it.	sâsâpiskisw-**	sâsâpiskisa
Boil it.	pakâsim	pakahtâ (VTI-2)
Put it in the oven.	pîhtâpiskahw-**	pîhtâpiskaha
Cook it.	kîsisw-**	kîsisa

*Transitive animate verb stems ending in "s" have that changed to a "t" in the conjugation. The change occurs in the 2l of the Imperative and all the forms of the Indicative mood and Conjunct mood.

**The ending of the root here is simply to indicate that we need a "w" before putting in the verb endings in the conjugation.

Some VTA verbs do not have a VTI counterpart. These include:

Feed him – asam   *Visit him* – kiyokaw   *Invite him* – wîsâm

Invite him/Call him over – natom   *Help him* – wîcih   *Accompany him* – wîcêw

A. FOODS: INANIMATES

The following foods are inanimate. We would use the VTI class 3 verb "mîci – *eat it*" if we are talking about eating these. The VTI class 3 verbs (which end in a short "**i**") follow the VAI conjugation pattern, as does the VTI class 2 (which end in a long "**â**"). For the liquids we would use the VAI verb "minihkwê – *drink*".

MEATS:

wiyâs – *meat*
kohkôsiwiyâs – *pork/ham*
kohkôsopwâm – *ham*
atihkowiyâs – *caribou meat*
mitêh – *heart*
mitêyaniy – *tongue*
pimîhkân – *pemmican*
paskwâwi-mostosowiyâs – *buffalo meat*
amiskowiyâs – *beaver meat*

mostosowiyâs – *beef*
kohkôsiwiyin – *bacon*
môsowiyâs – *moose meat*
sikopicikaniwiyâs – *ground meat*
wîniy – *bone marrow*
micakisîsa – *sausages*
kâhkêwak – *dried meat*
pâhkahâhkwâniwiyâs – *chicken meat*
mâyatihkowiyâs – *mutton*

BERRIES AND OTHER FOODS:

mînis – *berry*
wîsakimina – *cranberries*
nîpiminâna – *cranberries*
mitêhimina – *strawberries*
otisîhkân – *turnip*
nîpiya – *lettuce/salad*
kiscikâna – *potatoes*
wiyitihp – *brain*
pimiy – *oil/lard/grease*
tohtôsâpoy – *milk*
iskwêsisâpoy – *beer*
nihtiy – *tea*
pihkahtêwâpoy – *coffee*
kisâstêwâpoy – *Kool-Aid*
mîcimâpoy – *soup*
sîwinôs/sîwâs – *candy*
âmôsîsipâskwat – *honey*
pêskomina – *pepper*
askîwisîwihtâkan – *pepper*
sîwinikan – *sugar*
mîciwin – *food*
wîhkês – *muskrat-root*
paskwâwîhkaskwa – *sage*

iyinimina – *blueberries*
maskêkomina – *cranberries*
takwahiminâna – *chokecherries*
misâskwatômina – *Saskatoon berries*
kâ-mihkwaskwâki – *beets*
napatâkwa – *potatoes*
askipwâwa – *potatoes*
tohtôsâpôwipimiy – *butter*
manahikan – *cream*
wâwi – *egg*
iskotêwâpoy – *liquor*
maskihkîwâpoy – *herb tea*
sîwâpoy – *pop*
sôminâpoy – *wine*
osâwâpoy – *orange juice*
âmômêyi – *honey*
sîsipâskwat – *maple sugar*
wîsakat – *pepper*
sîwihtâkan – *salt*
wîhtikowimîciwin – *popcorn*
ohpihkasikan – *yeast*
wîhkaskwa – *sweet-grass*
maskihkiy – *medicine*

B. FOODS: ANIMATES

The following foods are animate. We would use the VTA "**môw**" with these foods.

amisk – *beaver*
anikwacâs(k) – *gopher/squirrel*
anômin – *oatmeal*
apisimôsos – *deer*
apistacihkos – *antelope*
atihk – *caribou*
atihkamêk – *whitefish*
ayôskanak – *raspberries*
iyinikinosêw – *jackfish*
kihc-ôkiniy – *tomato*
kinosêw – *fish*
mahtâmin – *corn*
manôminak – *rice*
maskimocisak – *beans*
maskosîmina – *wild rice*
maskwa – *bear*
mâyatihk – *sheep*
miniy – *Mariah fish*
misihêw – *turkey*
miskwamiy – *ice*
môswa – *moose*
mwâkwa – *loon*
namêkos – *trout*
namêpin – *sucker*
namêw – *sturgeon*
namêscêkos – *dried fillets*
niska – *goose*

okâw – *pickerel*
okiniyak – *wild rosehips*
osâwâs – *an orange*
oskâtâsk – *carrot*
otônapiy – *tullabee*
pâhkahâhkwân – *chicken*
pahkwêsikan – *bannock*
pakân – *nut*
paskwâwi-mostos – *buffalo*
paspaskiw – *birch grouse*
picikwâs – *apple*
pihêw – *partridge/grouse*
pihkasikan – *toast*
pîswêhkasikanisak – *buns*
sâpôminak – *gooseberries*
sîsîp – *duck*
sîwihkasikan – *cake*
sîwihkasikanak – *baked goods*
sîwinikan – *sugar*
wâkâs – *banana*
wâpinôminak – *rice*
wâpos – *rabbit*
wâwa – *eggs*
wâwi – *an egg*
wâwâskêsiw – *elk*
wîhcêkaskosîs – *onion*
wîhkihkasikan – *cake*
yîwahikanak – *ground meat/fish*

C. KITCHEN VOCABULARY

môhkomân – *knife* (NI)
cîstahâsêpon – *fork* (NI)
êmihkwân – *spoon* (NA)
oyâkan – *plate* (NI)
minihkwâcikan – *cup* (NI)
askihk – *pail* (NA)
sîsîpaskihk – *kettle* (NA)
sâsâpiskisikan – *frying-pan* (NA)

sâsêskihkwân – *frying-pan* (NA)
kocawâkanis – *match* (NI)
akocikan – *cupboard* (NI)
kotawânâpisk – *stove* (NI or NA)
kêsiskawihkasikan – *microwave* (NI)
sêkowêpinâpisk – *oven* (NI)
âhkwacikan – *freezer* (NI)
tahkascikan – *fridge* (NI)

D. ANIMATE INTRANSITIVE VERBS
(used with meals, etc.)

mîciso – *eat*
minihkwê – *drink*
kîspo – *be full*
nôhtêhkatê – *be hungry*
nôhtêyâpâkwê – *be thirsty*
wîhkohkê – *make a feast*
asahkê – *feed people*
mîcisosi – *eat a little*
kitânawê – *eat everything*
minihkwêsi – *drink a little*

kîsitêpo – *cook*
paminawaso – *cook*
kîkisêpâ-mîciso – *eat breakfast*
âpihtâ-kîsikani-mîciso – *eat lunch*
otâkwani-mîciso – *eat supper*
nawacî – *roast*
apwê – *roast over a fire*
apwânâskohkê – *make fish-roast stick*
mawimosi – *pray over food*
nîminikê – *serve out food*

E. HOLIDAYS

ocêhtowi-kîsikâw – *New Year's Day*
mitêhi-kîsikâw – *Valentine's Day*
kihci-niyânano-kîsikâw – *Good Friday*
âpisisiniwi-kîsikâw – *Easter Sunday*
kihci-okimâskwêwi-kîsikâw – *Victoria Day*
okâwîmâwi-kîsikâw – *Mother's Day*
ohtâwîmâwi-kîsikâw – *Father's Day*
mêtawêwi-kîsikâw – *Dominion Day (July 1)*
tipahamâtowi-kîsikâw – *Treaty Day*

kihci-asotamâkêwini-kîsikâw – *Treaty Day*
sôniyâskâw – *Treaty Day* (Lac La Ronge area)
otatoskêwi-kîsikâw – *Labour Day*
nanâskomowi-kîsikâw – *Thanksgiving Day*
cîpayi-kîsikâw – *Halloween (Day)*
cîpayi-tipiskâw – *Halloween (Night)*
onôtinitowi-kîsikâw – *Remembrance Day*
manitowi-kîsikâw – *Christmas Day*
makosî-kîsikâw – *Christmas Day* (Lac La Ronge area)

EXERCISES

EXERCISE 1. On the following pages, read the text, then answer the questions.

pêyakwâw êsa[1] *Shaking-Spear* pimohtêw mêskanâhk. wâpamêw[2] mostoswa.
"tânisi," itwêw[3] awa nâpêw.
"môw, môw,"[4] itwêw awa pêyak mostos. koskohtawêw[5] ôhi mostoswa *Shaking-Spear*!
"hay! awas! namôya ninôhtê-mîcison," itwêw awa *Shaking-Spear*.

QUESTIONS:

1. tânitê awa *Shaking-Spear* kâ-pimohtêt?[6] _____

2. awîniwa[7] kâ-wâpamât? _____

3. tânisi kâ-itât[8] ôhi mostoswa? _____

4. tânisi kâ-itikot[9] ôhi mostoswa? _____

5. tânisi kâ-isi-naskwêwasihât?[10] _____

....

1 These two foregoing words are the standard way of beginning a story in Cree. It translates to *"Once, as it happens..."*
2 This is the Transitive Animate Verb (VTA), which translates as *"He sees* (someone or something Animate)." The object, that person or something Animate being seen by a third person subject of a VTA, always ends with an "a" and cannot be distinguished if it is Singular or Plural unless a number precedes it. That is why the next word for "cows," which you know is Animate, ends in an "a" looking like a pluralized Inanimate noun. This process is known as obviation and occurs after all VTAs with third person subjects.
3 Animate Intransitive Verb (VAI) *"say."*
4 This is the VTA for *"eat* (something Animate)."
5 This is the VTA meaning *"He is surprised by what the person says."* Note the obviation on the noun for cows and the Demonstrative pronoun preceding it. The Demonstrative pronoun is one normally used for Inanimate nouns but occurs here because of the Obviation of the object "cows."
6 This verb is in a Relative Clause. That is why "kâ-" is used and the "t" at the end is the third person ending when verbs are in this form. Answer using the Indicative Mood.
7 "Who" in the Obviate form is used because of the VTA *"see* (someone or something Animate)" in the third person which follows it. *"awiyiwa* or *awinihi"* can be used interchangeably with *"awîniwa"* in 2.
8 VTA for *"he says to him/her."*
9 VTA-Inverse for *"Someone says something to her/him."*
10 VTA *"answer him"* with Preverb "isi-", meaning *"way/manner."*

âsay mîna[1] pimohtêw mêskanâhk *Shaking-Spear*. wâpamêw mâyacihkosa.

"tânisi," kâ-itât êsa ôhi mâyacihkosa.

"pâ, pâ,"[2] kâ-itikot pêyak mâyacihkosa. wahwâ![3] koskohtawêw!

"hay, awas! namôya niya kipâpâ!" kâ-itât êsa.

ati-sipwêhtêw. kwayask[4] kisiwâsiw![5]

QUESTIONS:

1. âsay mîna cî pimohtêw mêskanâhk *Shaking-Spear*? _____

2. awîniwa êkwa kâ-wâpamât? _____

3. tânisi kâ-itikot ôhi mâyacihkosa? _____

4. tânisi kâ-isi-naskwêwasihât? _____

5. ati-kisiwâsiw cî awa nâpêw? _____

----

1 The two words together mean "*Once again.*"
2 Together, sounds like pâpâ, slang for "*Father.*"
3 An exclamation similar to "*My gracious!*" in English.
4 "*Very.*"
5 VAI "*be angry.*"

âsay mîna pimohtêw mêskanâhk *Shaking-Spear*. ispatinâhk wâpamêw mistikwa. mâtow êsa awa mistik.
"tânêhki kâ-mâtoyan,"[1] isi-kakwêcimêw[2] ôhi mistikwa.
"ayisk tahto-kîsikâw[3] awa pêyak atim ê-sikisit,"[4] kâ-isi-mâtot awa mistik. kitimâkihtawêw[5] ôhi mistikwa.
"haw, cêskwa kika-wîcihitin,"[6] itwêw êsa awa nâpêw. ati-masinahikêw.

QUESTIONS:

1. tânitê kâ-wâpamât mistikwa awa nâpêw? _____

2. tânisi kâ-itât ôhi mistikwa? _____

3. tânêhki awa mistik kâ-mâtot? _____

4. kitimâkihtawêw cî ôhi mistikwa? _____

5. tânisi kâ-ati-itahkamikisit? _____

---

1   *"Cry"* in the second person singular form of a Relative Clause.
2   VTA *"he/she asks him."*
3   *"Every day."*
4   VTA-Inverse *"he/she urinates on me."*
5   VTA *"he hears pitiable sounds and feels for him."*
6   VTA-Inverse *"I will help you."*

ati-sipwêhtêw *Shaking-Spear*. cîhkêyihtam[1] ayisk ê-wîcihât[2] mistikwa.
mwêscasîs[3] êsa pê-takohtêw[4] awa atim. wahwâ! koskwâpisin![5] ayamihtâw[6] anima kâ-kî-masinahahk[7]
Shaking-Spear:
"*Out of Order*" ê-itastêyik.[8]
êkwâni namôya kaskihtâw[9] ta-sikit.[10] ati-sipwêhtêw. kisiwâsiw!
kwayask cîhkêyihtam awa mistik.

QUESTIONS:

1. tânêhki awa *Shaking-Spear* kâ-cîhkêyihtahk? _____

2. tânispîhk kâ-pê-takohtêt awa atim? _____

3. tânisi kâ-itastêyik anima kâ-koskwâpisihk? _____

4. kaskihtâw cî ta-sikit mistikohk? _____

5. cîhkêyihtam cî awa mistik? _____

....

1 Transitive Inanimate Verb class 1 *"be happy"* in the third person.
2 VTA *"help him/her"* in the third person Conjunct Mood.
3 *"A little while later."*
4 VAI *"arrive by foot"* with Preverb *"pê-."*
5 VAI *"be surprised by a sight."*
6 VTI class 2 *"read it."*
7 VTI class 1 *"write it"* in a Relative Clause using third person subject.
8 VII class 2 *"be set in such a way"* in the Conjunct Mood using third person obviative inanimate subject.
9 VTI class 2 *"be successful at something."*
10 VAI *"pee"* in the Infinitive form using third person subject.

EXERCISE 2. Identify the grammar points, then answer the questions about the story:

pêyakwâw êsa *Shaking-Spear* kî-<u>pa</u>-pimohtêw sisonê sâkahikani<u>hk</u>. kî-<u>wâpamêw</u> maskwa.
kâsôpayihow <u>ta</u>-kakwê-paspît! namôya wâpam<u>iko</u>w maskwa.
"wâpam<u>ici</u> maskwa nika-kakwê-môw<u>ik</u>," êkosi <u>itêyihta</u>m.
nisihkâc ati-tapasîw. pêht<u>âko</u>w maskwa! wahwâ kwayask sôhkêpahtâw.
iskwahtawîpâhtâw ispatinâhk. nawaswâ<u>tiko</u>w maskwa! wîsta maskwa iskwahtawîpâhtâw.
"tânisi mâka <u>ta-kî</u>-isi-paspîyân," itêyihtam. ati-nîhtaciwêpâhtâw. wîsta maskwa
kakwê-nîhtaciwêpâhtâw. namôya kaskihtâw! osâm apisâsiniyiwa nistam anihi oskâta.
mêtoni ati-tihtipipayiw ana maskwa!

GRAMMAR POINTS

Future Conditional of VTA-Inverse: _____

Reduplication: _____

Locative: _____   VTA: _____

VTI: _____   VTA-Inverse: _____

Modal: _____   Infinitive: _____

WORD LIST

kâsôpayiho – *hide quickly* (VAI)
itêyihta – *think* (VTI-1)
sôhkêpâhtâ – *run fast* (VAI)
nîhtaciwêpahtâ – *run downhill* (VAI)
apisâsin – *it is small* (VII)
osâm – *because*
kwayask – *right/extremely*
pêhtâkow – *he is heard by him* (VTA-Inverse-Irregular form)
nawaswâs – *chase* (VTA – last **s** changes in conjugation to **t**)

paspî – *be saved* (VAI)
tapasî – *escape/run away* (VAI)
iskwahtawîpâhtâ – *run uphill* (VAI)
kaskihtâ – *succeed* (VTI-2)
tihtipipayi – *roll* (VAI)
nistam – *first/in front*
nisihkâc – *slowly*

QUESTIONS

1.   tânitê awa *Shaking-Spear* kâ-pimohtêt? _____

2.   awîniwa kâ-wâpamât *Shaking-Spear*? _____

3.   tânêhki awa kâ-kâsôpayihot? _____

4.   tânitê kâ-iskwahtawîpâhtât? _____

5.   tânisi kâ-ispayihikot maskwa? _____

EXERCISE 3. INTERMEDIATE LEVEL PICTURE-TEXT QUESTION AND ANSWER

Using the following vocabulary, read the story on the following five pages and answer the questions.

VOCABULARY

VERBS:

âcimo – *tell a story* (VAI)
napakiska – *flatten it* (VTI-1)
kâtâ – *hide it* (VTI-2)
âcimostaw – *tell him/her a story* (VTA)
mispon – *it is snowing* (VII)
wayawîpahtâ – *run outside* (VAI)
otina – *take it* (VTI-1)
sôhkiyowêw – *there is a strong wind* (VII)
nanôyacih – *tease him/her* (VTA)
itâpi – *look (somewhere)* (VAI)
mwêstasisini – *be late* (VAI)
kiyâski – *tell a lie* (VAI)
kwêyâtisi – *be (get) ready* (VAI)
pâhpih – *laugh at him/her* (VTA)
itahkamikisi – *be busy/do* (VAI)
nititik – *she/he says to me* (VTA-Inv)
nitâpwêhtâk – *he/she belives me* (VTA-Inv)

kîkisêpâ-mîciso – *eat breakfast* (VAI)
itwê – *say* (VAI)
kisowi-kanawâpam – *look at in anger* (VTA)
pâhpi – *laugh* (VAI)
wayawîpahtâ – *run it outside* (VTI-2)
nâcipahtâ – *run for it* (VTI-2)
isi – *say to him/her* (VTA)
wêpâstan – *it blows about* (VII)
wîhtamaw – *tell him/her* (VTA)
tâpwêhtaw – *believe him/her* (VTA)
masinaha – *write it* (VTI-1)
astêw – *it is there* (VII)
pâhpihkwê – *smile* (VAI)
ispayihiko – *it happens to one* (VAI)
itasinâstêw – *it is coloured thus* (VII)

NOUNS and other items to be used in conjunction with the above:

nikiskinwahamâkosihk – *at/to my class*
nitêm – *my dog*
âcimowin – *a story*
wâpiskastis – *a white mitt*
maskisin – *shoe*
têhtapiwin – *chair*
wayawîtimihk – *outside*
mâka mîna – *as usual*
asici – *also*
sêhkêpayîs – *car*
nistam – *first*

nitokiskinwahamâkêm – *my teacher*
tahto-kîsikâw – *every day*
astis – *mitt/glove*
kaskitêwastis – *a black mitt*
miskotâkay – *coat/jacket*
nipêwin – *bed*
kwayask – *right/very*
macastim – *bad dog*
napakaskisin – *flat shoe*
mêskanaw – *road*
pakahkam – *perhaps*

kâ-pôni-kîkisêpâ-mîcisoyân nikî-ati-kwêyâtisin. nikî-natonên niskotâkay kâ-kaskitêwâk.
nikî-miskên êwako. nikî-natonawâwak nitastisak kâ-kaskitêsicik. nikî-miskawâwak
nikaskitêwastisak. nikî-natonên nimaskisina. tâniwêhâ êtikwê nimaskisina.

Q1. tânisi kâ-itahkamikisit ispîhk kâ-pôni-mîcisot awa?

_____

Q2. natonam cî oskotâkay?

_____

Q3. tânisi kâ-itasinâstêyik oskotâkay?

_____

Q4. natonawêw cî owâpiskastisa?

_____

Q5. miskam cî omaskisina?

_____

ninatonên nimaskisina sîpâ têhtapiwinihk. namôya êkota nimiskên. ninatonên nimaskisina sîpâ nipêwinihk. namôya mîna êkota nimiskên. nikanawâpamâw nitêm. pâhpihkwêw nitêm. "tânita mâka mîna kâ-kâtâyan nimaskisina," nititâw. namôya nânitaw itwêw.

Q6. tânita nistam kâ-natonahk omaskisina?

_____

Q7. miskam cî omaskisina sîpâ têhtapiwinihk?

_____

Q8. tânita mîna kâ-natonahk omaskisina awa?

_____

Q9. miskam cî omaskisina sîpâ nipêwinihk?

_____

Q10. tânisi otêma kâ-itahkamikisiyit?

_____

wayawîtimihk nititâpin. wahwâ! ati-yîkwaskwan. wî-mispon pakahkam. niwâpahtên
nimaskisina wayawîtimihk ê-astêki. nikanawâpamâw nitêm. kwayask misi-pâhpiw!
"macastim!" nititâw. mâka mîna êsa ê-wayawîpahtwât nimaskisina.

Q11. tânitê awa kâ-itâpit?

Q12. tânisi kâ-isiwêpahk?

Q13. wî-mispon cî?

Q14. kîkwây asici kâ-wâpahtahk wayawîtimihk?

Q15. tânisi kâ-itât otêma?

niwayawîpahtân ê-nâcipahtâyân nimaskisina. mâci-mispon! wahwâ! ati-sôhkiyowêw mîna.
aspin kâ-wêpâstahki nimaskisina mêskanâhk isi. kwayask matwê-pâhpiw nitêm ispîhk
sêhkêpayîs kâ-napakiskahk nimaskisina. nisihkâc nitotinên ninapakaskisina.
nikisowi-kanawâpamâw nitêm.

Q16. tânêhki awa kâ-wayawîpahtât?

_____

Q17. tânisi kâ-ati-isiwêpahk?

_____

Q18. tânitê kâ-isi-wêpâstahki maskisina?

_____

Q19. tânêhki anihi otêma kâ-sôhki-pâhpiyit?

_____

Q20. tânisi kâ-itôtawât otêma?

_____

tâpwê mâni-mâka nimwêstasisinin nikiskinwahamâkosihk. nikakwê-wîhtamawâw
nikiskinwahamâkêm tânisi awa nitêm kâ-isi-nanôyacihit mâka namôya nitâpwêhtâk.
nititik ta-masinahamwak tânisi mâna kâ-itahkamikisiyân tahto-kîsikâw.
ôma âcimowin kâ-masinahamân, namôya nikiyâskin.

Q21. mwêstasisiniw cî awa?

_____

Q22. kakwê-wîhtamawêw cî okiskinwahamâkêma kâ-ispayihikot?

_____

Q23. tâpwêhtâk cî?

_____

Q24. tânisi kâ-itikot okiskinwahamâkêma?

_____

Q25. kêko âcimowin kâ-masinahahk?

_____

8.7 CHAPTER EIGHT REVIEW – VTA

Place verb stems in the blanks; verb stems come from the second person singular (2) form of the imperative.

IMPERATIVES		NEGATIVE IMPERATIVES		DELAYED IMPERATIVES	
2	_____(ik)*	**2** êkâwiya_____(ik)		**2** _____âhkan(ik)	
2P	_____ihk(ok)	**2P** êkâwiya _____ihk(ok)		**2P** _____âhkêk(ok)	
21	_____âtân(ik)	**21** êkâwiya_____âtân(ik)		**21** _____âhkahk(ik)	

*the brackets indicate number agreement for 1st and 2nd person forms needed if the object of the verb is plural.

VTA-DIRECT

INDICATIVE		CONJUNCT		FUTURE CONDITIONAL	
1 ni_____âw(ak)		**1** ê-_____ak(ik)		**1** _____aki	
2 ki_____âw(ak)		**2** ê-_____at(cik)		**2** _____aci	
3 _____êw		**3** ê-_____ât		**3** _____âci	
3' _____êyiwa		**3'** ê-_____âyit		**3'** _____âyici	
1P ni_____ânân(ak)		**1P** ê-_____âyâhk(ik)		**1P** _____âyâhki	
21 ki_____ânaw(ak)		**21** ê-_____âyahk(ik)		**21** _____âyahki	
2P ki_____âwâw(ak)		**2P** ê-_____âyêk(ok)		**2P** _____âyêko	
3P _____êwak		**3P** ê-_____âcik		**3P** _____âtwâwi	
3'P _____êyiwa		**3'P** ê-_____âyit		**3'P** _____âyici	

VTA-INVERSE

INDICATIVE		CONJUNCT		FUTURE CONDITIONAL	
1 ni_____ik(wak)		**1** ê-_____it(cik)		**1** _____ici	
2 ki_____ik(wak)		**2** ê-_____isk(ik)		**2** _____iski	
3 _____ikow		**3** ê-_____ikot		**3** _____ikoci	
3' _____ikoyiwa		**3'** ê-_____ikoyit		**3'** _____ikoyici	
1P ni_____ikonân(ak)		**1P** ê-_____ikoyâhk(ik)		**1P** _____ikoyâhki	
21 ki_____ikonaw(ak)		**21** ê-_____ikoyahk(ik)		**21** _____ikoyahki	
2P ki_____ikowâw(ak)		**2P** ê-_____ikoyêk(ok)		**2P** _____ikoyêko	
3P _____ikowak		**3P** ê-_____ikocik		**3P** _____ikotwâwi	
3'P _____koyiwa		**3'P** ê-_____ikoyit		**3'P** _____ikoyici	

RULE:
Number agreement is needed for the 1st and 2nd person forms; obviation markers are needed for objects of 3rd person verbs forms.

STANDARD VERB STRUCTURE

Person indicator or conjunct marker	Tense marker	Preverb	Verb stem	Verb ending

VERB CHARTS

VAI, VTI (CLASS 2 AND CLASS 3)

IMPERATIVE MOOD

2 _____

2P _____ k

21 _____ tân

DELAYED IMPERATIVE

2 _____ hkan

2P _____ hkêk

21 _____ hkahk

INDICATIVE MOOD

1 ni _____ n   **1P** ni _____ nân

2 ki _____ n   **21** ki _____ naw

3 _____ w   **2P** ki _____ nâwâw

3' _____ yiwa   **3P** _____ wak

  3'P _____ yiwa

CONJUNCT MOOD

1 ê- _____ yân   **1P** ê- _____ yâhk

2 ê- _____ yan   **21** ê- _____ yahk

3 ê- _____ t   **2P** ê- _____ yêk

3' ê- _____ yit   **3P** ê- _____ cik

3'P ê- _____ yit

RULE: change **ê** to **â** for the Indicative Mood in the following persons: **1, 2, 1P, 21, 2P** (the first and second persons) if verb stem ends in ê.

VTI-1

IMPERATIVE MOOD

2 _____ a

2P _____ amok

21 _____ êtân

DELAYED IMPERATIVE

2 _____ mohkan

2P _____ mohkêk

21 _____ mohkahk

RULE: all verb stems of VTI-1 verbs end in "**a**"; change the "**a**" to "**ê**" for 21 of the Imperative Mood and the first and second persons of the Indicative Mood. This change is reflected in these charts.

INDICATIVE MOOD

1 ni _____ n   **1P** ni _____ nân

2 ki _____ n   **21** ki _____ naw

3 _____ m   **2P** ki _____ nâwâw

3' _____ miyiw   **3P** _____ mwak

  3'P _____ miyiwa

CONJUNCT MOOD

1 ê- _____ mân   **1P** ê- _____ mâhk

2 ê- _____ man   **21** ê- _____ mahk

3 ê- _____ hk   **2P** ê- _____ mêk

3' ê- _____ miyit   **3P** ê- _____ hkik

3'P ê- _____ miyit

VTA-DIRECT

IMPERATIVE MOOD

2 _____ (ik)

2P _____ ihk(ok)

21 _____ âtân(ik)

DELAYED IMPERATIVE

2 _____ âhkan(ik)

2P _____ âhkêk(ok)

21 _____ âhkahk(ik)

INDICATIVE MOOD

1 ni _____ âw(ak)   **1P** ni _____ ânân(ak)

2 ki _____ âw(ak)   **21** ki _____ ânaw(ak)

3 _____ êw   **2P** ki _____ âwâw(ak)

3' _____ êyiwa   **3P** _____ êwak

  3'P _____ êyiwa

CONJUNCT MOOD

1 ê- _____ ak(ik)   **1P** ê- _____ âyâhk(ik)

2 ê- _____ at(cik)   **21** ê- _____ âyahk(ik)

3 ê- _____ ât   **2P** ê- _____ âyêk(ok)

3' ê- _____ âyit   **3P** ê- _____ âcik

3'P ê- _____ âyit

CONJUGATION PATTERNS (VAI, VTI-1, VTA)

IMPERATIVE

NEGATIVE IMPERATIVE
- use *êkâwiya* in front of the regular Imperative
DELAYED IMPERATIVE

VAI		VTI-1		VTA		VAI		VTI-1		VTA	
2	___	**2**	___	**2**	___	**2**	___hkan	**2**	___mohkan	**2**	___âhkan
2P	___k	**2P**	___mok	**2P**	___ihk	**2P**	___hkêk	**2P**	___mohkêk	**2P**	___âhkêk
21	___tân	**21**	___êtân	**21**	___âtân	**21**	___hkahk	**21**	___mohkahk	**21**	___âhkahk

NOTE THE SIMILARITIES AND DIFFERENCES IN THESE PARADIGMS:

The VAI endings can also be used for VTI-2 and VTI-3. All classes of verbs use the same person indicators and all use the various conjunct markers previously mentioned; only the **ê** is used here as an example. The person indicators and conjunct markers are NEVER used together:

Ind. Person	Subj. Mark	VAI Endings:		VTI-1 endings		VTA endings	
		Ind.	Conj.	Ind.	Conj.	Ind.	Conj.
1	ni / ê-	-n	-yân	-n	-mân	-âw(ak)	-ak(ik)
2	ki / ê-	-n	-yan	-n	-man	-âw(ak)	-at(cik)
3	ê	-w	-t	-m	-hk	-êw	-ât
3'	ê-	-yiwa	-yit	-miyiw	-miyit	-êyiwa	-âyit
1P	ni / ê	-nân	-yâhk	-nân	-mâhk	-ânân(ak)	-âyâhk(ik)
21	ki / ê-	-naw	-yahk	-naw	-mahk	-ânaw(ak)	-âyahk(ik)
2P	ki / ê	-nâwâw -	yêk	-nâwâw	-mêk	-âwâw(ak)	-âyêk(ok)
3P	ê-	-wak	-cik	-mwak	-hkik	-êwak	-âcik
3'P	ê-	-yiwa	-yit	-miyiwa	-miyit	-êyiwa	-âyit

TENSE INDICATORS: all of these are used no matter what the verb is:

PAST: something has already happened; use: kî-
FUTURE INTENTIONAL: something is going to happen; use: wî-
FUTURE DEFINITE: something will happen; For 1, 2, 1P, 21, and 2P use: ka-; For 3, 3', 3P, and 3'P use: ta-
MODAL: for "can/could/would/should" use: ka-kî-

RULES:

FOR VAI: change ê to â if verb stem ends in ê for 1, 2, 1P, 21, 2P of the Indicative Mood;
FOR VTI-1: change a to ê for 1, 2, 1P, 21, 2P of the Indicative Mood;
FOR VTA: number agreement needed for 1, 2, 1P, 21, 2P
    OBJECT of 3, 3', 3P, 3'P is marked by an "-a" known as Obviation
FOR ALL: if verb stem or preverb begins with a vowel: connect the person indicator to the rest of the verb-structure by a "t." This rule applies only in the present tense.

THE STANDARD VERB STRUCTURE IS AS FOLLOWS:

Person indicator	Tense indicator	Preverb-	Verb stem	Ending

VOCABULARY LIST

The following abbreviations are for the grammatical items here:

1st – first person, speaker
2nd – second person, addressee/person spoken to
3rd – third person, person spoken about

an – animate
in – inanimate

NA – animate noun
NI – inanimate noun

pl / P – plural
PR – pronoun
PV – preverb
sg – singular

VAI – animate intransitive verb
VII – inanimate intransitive verb
VTA – transitive animate verb
VTI-1 – transitive inanimate verb, class 1
VTI-2 – transitive inanimate verb, class 2
VTI-3 – transitive inanimate verb, class 3

A

acâhk – *star* (NA)
acâhkos – *star* (NA)
ahcahk – *spirit* (NA)
ahcâpiy – *a bow* (NA)
ahpô êtikwê – *maybe*
akask – *an arrow* (NA)
akâwâs – *desire s.o.* (VTA)
akâwâta – *desire s.t.* (VTI-1)
akihcikê – *count* (VAI)
akik – *mucus* (NA)
akim – *count someone* (VTA)
akimâw – *it is counted* (VTA-3rd sg)
akocikan – *a shelf, a cupboard* (NI)
akohp – *a blanket* (NA)
amisk – *beaver* (NA)
amiskowiyâs – *beaver meat* (NI)
ana – *that* (PR-an)
anihi – *those* (PR-in)
aniki – *those* (PR-an)
anikwacâsk – *gopher/squirrel* (NA)
anima – *that* (PR-in)
anita – *there*
anohc – *today/at the present time*
anohc kâ-askîwik – *this year*
anohc kâ-ispayik – *this week*
api – *sit* (VAI)
apisâsin – *it is small* (VII)

apisimôsos – *deer* (NA)
apisis – *a little bit*
apisîs – *a little bit*
apistacihkos – *antelope* (NA)
apoy – *a paddle* (NA)
apwânâskohkê – *make fish-roast stick* (VAI)
apwê – *roast over a fire* (VAI)
asahkê – *feed people* (VAI)
asam – *feed someone* (VTA)
asawâpi – *look about* (VAI)
asâm – *a snowshoe* (NA)
asicâyihk – *beside/against*
asicâyihtak – *wall* (NI)
asikan – *a sock* (NA)
asiniy – *stone* (NA)
askihk – *pail* (NA)
askihtakosiw – *it is green* (VAI)
askihtakwâw – *it is green* (VII)
askipwâwa – *potatoes* (NI)
askiy – *land* (NI)
askîwin – *year* (NI)
askîwi-sîwihtâkan – *pepper* (NI)
astêw – *it is there*
astêwa – *they are there*
astis – *a mitt/glove* (NA)
astotin – *a hat* (NI)
atâmihk – *beneath/under*
atâmipihk – *underwater*

atâwêstamaw – *buy it for him/her* (VTA)
atâwêwikamik – *a store* (NI)
atâwêwikimâw – *store manager* (NA)
ati- – *begin* (PV)
atihk – *caribou* (NA)
atihkamêk – *white-fish* (NA)
atihkowiyâs – *caribou meat* (NI)
atim – *a dog* (NA)
atoskaw – *work for s.o.* (VTA)
atoskâta – *work at it* (VTI-1)
atoskê – *work* (VAI)
atoskêh – *make s.o. work* (VTA)
awa – *this* (PR-an)
awas – *go away*
awasi-tipiskohk – *night before last night*
awasi-wâpahki – *day after tomorrow*
awasitâkosîhk – *day before yesterday*
awâsis – *a child* (NA)
awâsis-nâkatawêyimâwasowin – *a daycare* (NI)
awâsisihkân – *a doll* (NA)
awâsisîwi – *be a child* (VAI)
awiyak – *someone* (PR-an)
awîna – *who*
awîna êtikwê – *I wonder who*
awîniki – *who* (pl)
ayamâkanis – *a telephone* (NI)
ayamihâ – *pray* (VAI
ayamihcikê – *read* (VAI)
ayamihêwi-kîsikâw – *Sunday/It is Sunday* (VII)
ayamihêwikimâw – *a priest* (NA)
ayamihtamaw – *read it for s.o.* (VTA)
ayamihtâ – *read it* (VTI-2)
ayâw – *she/he is there* (VAI 3rd sg)
ayâwak – *they are there* (VAI 3rd pl)
ayênânêw – *8*
ayênânê(wo)mitanaw – *80*
ayênânêwosâp – *18*
ayîki-pîsim – *the Frog Moon; April*
ayîkis – *a frog* (NA)
ayôskanak – *raspberries* (NA)
aywêpi – *rest* (VAI)
âcimo – *tell a story* (VAI)
âcimostaw – *tell him/her a story* (VTA)
âcimowin – *a story* (NI)
âha – *yes*
âhcanis – *a ring* (NA)

âhkik – *seal* (NA)
âhkosîwikamik – *a hospital* (NI)
âhkwacikan – *freezer* (NI)
âhkwatin – *it freezes* (VII)
âkayâsimo – *speak English*
âmaciwêspimowinihk – *at Stanley Mission, SK*
âmow-mêyi – *honey* (NI)
âmow-sîsipâskwat – *honey* (NI)
âniskotâpân – *great-great-grandparent
    / great-great-grandchild*
ânômin – *oatmeal* (NA)
âpihtaw – *a half*
âpihtawanohk – *halfway*
âpihtâ-kîsikani-mîciso – *eat lunch* (VAI)
âpihtâ-kîsikâw – *it is noon* (VII)
âpisisinowi-kîsikâw – *Easter Sunday*
âskaw – *sometimes*
âstam – *come here*
âstamitê – *over this way*
âtotêw – *s/he tells a story about s.o.* (VTA)
âwacimihtê – *haul firewood* (VAI)
âyîtâwâyihk – *on either side*

c

cahkâyâsin – *it is chilly* (VII)
capasis – *below*
capasîs – *lower down*
cêskwa – *wait*
cihcipayapisikanis – *a bicycle* (NI)
cihcipayîsi-sôniskwâtahikê – *go
    roller-blading* (VAI)
cikâscêpayihcikanis – *television* (NI)
cikâstêpayihcikan – *a movie* (NI)
cipahikanis – *minutes*
cî – *a polarity question indicator*
cîhkêyihta – *like it* (VTI-1)
cîhkêyim – *like someone* (VTA)
cîki – *near*
cîpayi-kîsikâw – *Halloween* (Day)
cîpayi-tipiskâw – *Halloween* (Night)
cîstahâsêpon – *fork* (NI)
cîwêw – *it is calm, peaceful* (VII)
cîwêyâw – *it is very calm* (VII)

E

ê-akimiht – *it is counted*
êkâwiya – *don't*
êkosi – *that's it*
êkosi itôta – *do it that way*
êkosi pitamâ – *that's it for now*
êkota – *there*
êkotê – *over there*
êkwa – *now/and*
êmihkwân – *spoon* (NA)
êsa – *evidently*
êtikwê – *maybe/about*
êwako – *that one*
êyikohk – *until*

H

hâw – *okay*
hâw mâka – *okay then*

I

ici – *at that time*
ihkopîwi-pîsim – *the Frost Moon; November*
isi – *toward / manner in which something is done*
isi-wêpan – *it happens* (VII)
isipita – *pull it toward* (VTI-1)
isiyihkâsow – *she/he is named* (VAI)
isko – *as far as/up to*
iskonikan – *reserve* (NI)
iskotêwâpoy – *liquor* (NI)
iskwâhtawîpahtâ – *run up(hill/stairs)* (VAI)
iskwâhtêm – *a door* (NI)
iskwêsis – *girl* (NA)
iskwêsisâpoy – *beer* (NI)
iskwêw – *woman* (NA)
iskwêwasakay – *a woman's skin* (NA)
iskwêwasâkay – *a woman's dress/coat* (NI)
iskwêyânihk – *at the last place*
ispatinaw – *hill* (NI)
ispayihiko – *s.t. happens to s.o.* (VAI)
ispayiki – *if/when it comes about*
ispayin – *it comes about* (VII)
ispâw – *it is high* (VII)
ispimihk – *up/upstairs*
ispimihtak – *ceiling* (NI)
ispîhk – *when*
itahkamikisi – *do* (VAI)

K

itahtopiponê – *be of a certain age* (VAI)
itapi – *sit it that way* (VAI)
itâpi – *look that way* (VAI)
itêyihta – *think that* (VTI-1)
itohtah – *take s.o. some place* (VTA)
itohtatâ – *take it somewhere* (VTI-2)
itôta – *do it* (VTI-1)
itôtaw – *do it to s.o.* (VTA)
itwah – *point to s.o.* (VTA)
itwaha – *point to it* (VTI-1)
itwê – *say* (VAI)
iyini-kinosêw – *jack-fish* (NA)
iyinimina – *blueberries* (NI)
îkatêna – *take it away* (VTI-1)

K

ka-pêhitin – *I will wait for you*
kah – *oh*
kahkiyaw – *all*
kakwâtaki- – *very* (PV)
kakwê- – *try to* (PV)
kakwêcihkêmowin – *question* (NI)
kanawâpahta – *look at it* (VTI-1)
kanawâpam – *look at it* (VTA)
kapâ – *get out (of a vehicle)* (VAI)
kapê-kîsik – *all day*
kapê-tipisk – *all night*
kapêsiwikamik – *a hotel* (NI)
kapêsiwin – *camp* (NI)
kaskatin – *ice freezes* (VII)
kaskêyihta – *be lonesome* (VTI-1)
kaskêyim – *be lonesome for s.o.* (VTA)
kaskih – *be successful with s.o.* (VTA)
kaskiho – *succeed* (VAI)
kaskihtâ – *be able/succeed* (VTI-2)
kaskikwâso – *sew* (VAI)
kaskitê-osâwâw – *it is brown* (VII)
kaskitê-osâwisiw – *it is brown* (VAI)
kaskitêsiw – *it is black* (VAI)
kaskitêwastis – *a black mitt* (NA)
kaskitêwâw – *it is black* (VII)
kawisimo – *lay down (to sleep)* (VAI)
kayâhtê – *originally*
kâ-mihkwaskwâki – *beets* (NI)
kâ-tipiskaman – *you have a birthday*
kâhkêwak – *dried meat* (NI)

kâkîsimo – *pray (traditional)* (VAI)
kâkwa – *porcupine* (NA)
kâmwâtan – *it is quiet* (VII)
kâsîhikan – *a chalk brush* (NI)
kâsîhkwâkan – *towel* (NI)
kâsîhkwê – *wash face* (VAI)
kâsîpitêhow – *brush teeth* (VAI)
kâsîyâkanê – *dry dishes* (VAI)
kâskipâso – *shave* (VAI)
kâsô – *hide* (VAI)
kâsôpayiho – *hide quickly* (VAI)
kâtâ – *hide it* (VTI-2)
kâya – *don't*
kêcikoska – *take it off* (VTI-1)
kêcikoskaw – *take it off* (VTA)
kêkâ-mitâtaht – *9*
kêkâ-mitâtahtomitanaw – *90*
kêkâ-mitâtahtosâp – *19*
kêkâ-nistomitanaw – *29*
kêkâ-nîsitanaw – *19*
kêkâc – *almost*
kêsiskaw – *in a hurry*
kêsiskawihkasikan – *micro-wave* (NI)
kêtayiwinisê – *undress* (VAI)
kihc-ôkiniy – *tomato* (NA)
kihci-asotamâkêwini-kîsikâw – *Treaty Day*
kihci-kiskinwahamâtowikamik – *university*
kihci-niyânano-kîsikâw – *Good Friday*
kihci-okimâskwêwi-kîsikâw – *Victoria Day*
kihciniskêhk – *to the right*
kihiw – *an eagle* (NA)
kikâwiy – *your mother*
kikosis – *your son*
kimis – *your older sister*
kimiwan – *It rains* (VII)
kimiwan – *rain* (NI)
kimiwanasâkay – *raincoat* (NI)
kimiwasin – *It is drizzling* (VII)
kimosôm – *your grandfather*
kinanâskomitin – *I thank you*
kinêpik – *snake* (NA)
kinosêw – *a fish* (NA)
kinosiw – *s/he is long* (VAI)
kinwêsk – *for a long time*
kipah – *close it* (VTA)
kipaha – *close it* (VTI-1)

kipahotowikamik – *jail* (NI)
kisâstêw – *it is hot* (VII)
kisâstêwâpoy – *kool-aid* (NI)
kiscikâna – *potatoes* (NI)
kisê-pîsim – *the Great Moon, January*
kisik – *and also*
kisinâw – *it is very cold* (VII)
kisipanohk – *at the end*
kisitêw – *it is hot* (VII)
kisiwâk – *nearby*
kisiwâsi – *be angry* (VAI)
kisiwi-kanawâpam – *look at s.o. in anger* (VTA)
kisîmis – *your younger sibling*
kisîpêkin – *wash it* (VTA)
kisîpêkina – *wash it* (VTI-1)
kisîpêkinastê – *bathe/shower* (VAI)
kisîpêkinikê – *wash clothes* (VAI)
kisîpêkiyâkanê – *wash dishes* (VAI)
kiskêyihta – *know it* (VTI-1)
kiskêyim – *know it* (VTA)
kiskinwahamaw – *teach him/her* (VTA)
kiskinwahamâkê – *teach* (VAI)
kiskinwahamâtowikamik – *a school* (NI)
kistâpitêho – *brush teeth* (VAI)
kistês – *your older brother*
kistikân – *a garden/farm* (NI)
kitawâsimis – *your child*
kitânawê – *eat everything* (VAI)
kitânis – *your daughter*
kitimâkihtaw – *hear a sad tale from s.o.* (VTA)
kitimâkinaw – *have pity on s.o.* (VTA)
kitisiyihkâson – *you are named* (VAI-2nd sg)
kititahtopiponân – *you are of that age* (VAI-2nd sg)
kitohcikê – *play music* (VAI)
kitohcîn – *you are from* (VAI-2nd sg)
kitowêhkwâmi – *snore* (VAI)
kitôtêm – *your friend*
kiwîcêwâkan – *your companion* (NA)
kiwîhowin – *your name* (NI)
kiya – *you* (PR)
kiya mâka – *how about you*
kiyawâw – *you (pl)* (PR)
kiyâm – *no matter*
kiyânaw – *us/we (includes the one spoken to)* (PR)
kiyâski – *tell a lie* (VAI)
kiyokaw – *visit s.o.* (VTA)

kiyokê – *visit (VAI)*
kiyôtê – *to visit (far away) (VAI)*
kîhkêhtak – *a corner (NI)*
kîkisêp – *this past morning (VII)*
kîkisêpâ-mîciso – *eat breakfast (VAI)*
kîkisêpâki – *in the morning*
kîkisêpâw – *it is morning (VII)*
kîkisêpâyâw – *it is morning (VII)*
kîkway – *something*
kîkwây – *what?*
kîkwây asici – *what else?*
kîkwâya – *what (pl)*
kîmôtâpi – *sneak a peek (VAI)*
kîsapwêw – *it is warm (VII)*
kîsapwêyâw – *it is warmish (VII)*
kîsihtâ – *finish it (VTA-2)*
kîsik – *the sky (NI)*
kîsikâw – *it is day (VII)*
kîsis – *cook it (VTA)*
kîsisa – *cook it (VTI-1)*
kîsitêpo – *cook (VAI)*
kîsitêw – *it is cooked (VII)*
kîskatahâhtikwê – *cut down trees (VAI)*
kîskipita – *tear it off (VTI-1)*
kîskis – *cut it (VTA)*
kîskisa – *cut it (VTI-1)*
kîsta – *you too (PR)*
kîstawâw – *you (pl) too (PR)*
kîstânaw – *we too (includes the one spoken to) (PR)*
kîwê – *go home (VAI)*
kîwêpayi – *drive home (VAI)*
kîwêtinohk – *north*
kocawâkanis – *match (NI)*
kocih – *try s.o. (VTA)*
kocihowin – *exam (NI)*
kocihtâ – *try it (VTI-2)*
kocispis – *taste it (VTA)*
kocispita – *taste it (VTI-1)*
kohkom – *your grandmother*
kohkôs – *a pig (NA)*
kohkôsiwiyâs – *pork/ham (NI)*
kohkôsiwiyin – *bacon (NA)*
kohkôsopwâm – *ham (NI)*
kohtâwiy – *your father*
kospi – *go inland (VAI)*
kosta – *be scared of it (VTI-1)*

kostaw – *be scared of s.o. (VTA)*
kotak – *another*
kotak askîwiki – *next year*
kotak ispayiki – *next week*
kotawânâpisk – *stove (NI)*
kotawê – *make a camp-fire (VAI)*
kôna – *snow (NA)*
kwayask – *very much*
kwâhcipahtwâ – *run off with it (VTI-2)*
kwâskohti – *jump (VAI)*
kwâskwêpicikê – *go fishing (VAI)*
kwâskwêtahikê – *play golf (VAI)*
kwêyâtisi – *get ready (VAI)*

M

macastim – *bad/evil dog*
maci- – *evil (PV)*
maci-kîsikâw – *it is a bad day (VII)*
mahtâmin – *corn (NA)*
mahti – *please/let's see*
makosî-kîsikâw – *Christmas Day (TH area)*
manahikan – *cream (NI)*
manahisôniyâwân – *a mine (NI)*
manipis – *tear it off (VTA)*
manipita – *tear it off (VTI-1)*
manis – *cut it (VTA)*
manisa – *cut it (VTI-1)*
manitowi-kîsikâw – *Christmas Day*
manôminak – *rice (NA, pl)*
masinaha – *write it (VTI-1)*
masinahamaw – *write to someone (VTA)*
masinahikan – *a book (NI)*
masinahikanâhcikos – *a pencil (NA)*
masinahikanâpiskos – *a small chalkboard (NI)*
masinahikanêkin – *paper (NI)*
masinahikê – *write (VAI)*
masinahikêsîs – *secretary (NA)*
masinahikêwâpisk – *a chalkboard (NI)*
masinahikêwin – *writing (NI)*
masinahikêwinâhtik – *pen (NA)*
maskasiy – *fingernail (NA)*
maskatêpwê – *barbecue (VAI)*
maskêkômina – *cranberries (NI)*
maskihkiy – *medicine (NI)*
maskihkîwâpoy – *herb-tea (NI)*
maskihkîwikamik – *a drug store (NI)*

maskihkîwikamikos – *clinic* (NI)

maskihkîwiskwêw – *a nurse* (NA)

maskihkîwiyiniw – *a doctor* (NA)

maskimocisak – *beans* (NA, pl)

maskisin – *a shoe* (NI)

maskosis – *a bear cub* (NA)

maskosiy – *grass* (NI)

maskosîmina – *wild rice* (NA, pl)

maskosîs – *a small piece of grass* (NI)

maskwa – *bear* (NA)

matay – *a belly* (NI)

matwê- – *heard (of) in the distance* (PV)

matwêhkwâmi – *snore* (VAI)

mawiso – *pick/harvest berries* (VAI)

mâci- – *begin*

mâcî – *hunt* (VAI)

mâka – *but*

mâka mîna – *as usual*

mâkwah – *make it difficult for s.o.* (VTA)

mâmihk – *down river*

mâna – *usually*

mâskisin – *s/he is crippled* (VAI)

mâtâh – *come upon s.o.'s tracks* (VTA)

mâto – *cry* (VAI)

mâyatihk – *sheep* (NA)

mâyatihkowiyâs – *mutton* (NI)

mâyi- – *bad* (PV)

mêkwâc – *at this time, now*

mêskanaw – *road* (NI)

mêstakay – *a hair*

mêtawâkâs – *disrespect it* (VTA)

mêtawâkâta – *disrespect it* (VTI-1)

mêtawêwi-kîsikâw – *Dominion Day*

mêtawêwikamik – *gym*

mêtoni – *very*

micakisîsa – *sausages* (NI)

misicihcân – *a thumb* (NI)

micihciy – *a hand* (NI)

mihcêt – *a lot*

mihcêtwâw – *lots of times*

mihcikwan – *a knee* (NI)

mihkosiw – *it is red* (VAI)

mihkwâw – *it is red* (VII)

mihtawakay – *an ear* (NI)

mihti – *firewood* (NI)

mihtot – *raft* (NI)

mihtotihkê – *make a raft* (VAI)

mikisiw – *an eagle* (NA)

mikisiwi-pîsim – *the Eagle Moon, February*

mikiskâw – *it is early winter* (VII)

mikiskohk – *last early part of winter*

mikot – *a nose* (NI)

mikwayaw – *a neck* (NI)

minah – *give someone a drink* (VAI)

minihkwâcikan – *cup* (NI)

minihkwê – *drink* (VAI)

minihkwêsi – *drink a little* (VAI)

minihkwêwikamik – *bar* (NI)

minôs – *a cat* (NA)

mipwâm – *thigh* (NI)

misakâ – *arrive by boat/canoe* (VAI)

misatim – *a horse* (NA)

misâskatômina – *Saskatoon berries* (NI)

misi- – *big* (PV)

misihêw – *turkey* (NA)

misit – *a foot* (NI)

miska – *find it* (VTI-1)

miskaw – *find it* (VTA)

miskâhtik – *a forehead* (NI)

miskât – *a leg* (NI)

miskîsik – *an eye* (NI)

miskîsiko-maskihkîwiyiniw – *optometrist* (NA)

miskîsikohkâna – *eye-glasses* (NI-pl)

miskon – *liver* (NI)

miskotâkay – *coat* (NI)

miskwamiy – *ice* (NA)

mispiskwan – *back* (NA)

mispiton – *an arm* (NI)

mispon – *It snows* (VII)

mistahi – *lots*

mistatim – *horse* (NA)

mistik – *tree* (NA)

mistik – *log* (NI)

mistiko-nâpêw – *a carpenter* (NA)

mistikowat – *a box* (NI)

mistikwân – *a head* (NI)

mitâs – *a pair of pants* (NA)

mitâtaht – *10*

mitâtahtomitanaw – *100*

mitêh – *heart* (NI)

mitêhi-kîsikâw – *Valentine's Day*

mitêhimina – *strawberries* (NI)

mitêyaniy – *tongue (NI)*
mitôn – *a mouth (NI)*
miy – *give it to s.o. (VTA)*
minay – *Mariah fish (NA)*
miyâhta – *smell it VTI-1)*
miyâm – *smell it (VTA)*
miyâskam – *it goes past*
miyo- – *good (PV)*
miyo-kîsikâw – *it is a good day (VII)*
miyohtâkosi – *sound good (VAI)*
miyohtâkwan – *it sounds good (VII)*
miyoskamik – *last late spring*
miyoskamin – *it is late spring (VII)*
miywêyihta – *like it (VTI-1)*
miywêyim – *like someone (VTA)*
mîci – *eat it (VTI-3)*
mîcimâpoy – *soup (NI)*
mîciso – *eat (VAI)*
mîcisosi – *eat a little (VAI)*
mîcisowikamik – *café NI)*
mîcisowinâhtik – *table (NI)*
mîciwin – *food (NI)*
mîkis – *a bead (NA)*
mîkisîhkâcikê – *bead (VAI)*
mîkwan – *a feather (NA)*
mîna – *also*
mînis – *berry (NI)*
mîpit – *a tooth (NI)*
mîpit-maskihkîwiyiniw – *dentist*
mîskon – *feel it (VTA)*
mîskona – *feel it (VTI-1)*
mohcihk – *down/on the ground*
mohcihtak – *on the bare floor*
mostos – *a cow (NA)*
mostosowiyâs – *beef (NI)*
mow – *eat it (VTA)*
môh – *make someone cry (VTA)*
môhkomân – *knife (NI)*
môminê – *pick and eat berries (VAI)*
môniyâw – *Caucasian(NA)*
môsâhkin – *pick someone up (VTA)*
môsâhkina – *pick it up (VTI-1)*
môsowiyâs – *moose meat (NI)*
môswa – *moose (NA)*
mwâkwa – *loon (NA)*
mwêstas – *later*
mwêstasisini – *be late (VAI)*

N

nahapi – *sit down (VAI)*
nahâpi – *see clearly (VAI)*
nahihta – *listen well (VTI-1)*
nakiskaw – *meet up with s.o. (VTA)*
namahcîhk – *to the left*
namêkos – *trout (NA)*
namêpin – *sucker (NA)*
namêscêkos – *dried fillets (NA)*
namêw – *sturgeon (NA)*
namôya – *no, not (negates)*
namôya cêskwa – *not yet*
namôya katâc – *not necessary*
namôya kîhtwâm – *not again*
namôya nânitaw – *all's well*
namôya osâm – *not very*
namôya wâhyaw – *not far*
nanâskomowi-kîsikâw – *Thanksgiving Day*
nanôyacih – *tease someone (VTA)*
napakaskisin – *a flat shoe NI)*
napakiska – *flatten with foot (VTI-1)*
napatâkwa – *potatoes (NI)*
naskwêwasih – *answer s.o. (VTA)*
natimihk – *up river*
natohta – *listen to it (VTI-1)*
natohtaw – *listen to s.o. (VTA)*
natom – *invite/call s.o. (VTA)*
natona – *search for it (VTI-1)*
natonaw – *search for s.o. (VTA)*
nawacî – *roast (VAI)*
nawaswâs – *chase (VTA)*
nâcipahtâ – *run for s.t. (VTI-2)*
nâha – *that (PR-an)*
nâkatawêyihta – *take care of it (VTI-1)*
nâkatawêyim – *take care of it (VTA)*
nâpêw – *man (NA)*
nâs – *fetch/get him/her (VTA*
nâsipêtimihk – *at the shore*
nâta – *fetch it (VTI-1)*
nâtamaw – *fetch it for him/her (VTA)*
nêhi – *those (PR-in)*
nêhiyaw – *a Cree (NA)*
nêhiyawê – *speak Cree (VAI)*
nêhiyawêwin – *Cree language (NI)*
nêki – *those over there (PR-an)*
nêma – *that over there (PR-in)*
nê(wo)mitanaw – *40*

nêtê – *over there*

nêwo – *4*

nêwo-kîsikâw – *Thursday/it is Thursday* (VII)

nêwosâp – *14*

nicâhkos – *my cross cousin (female to female), sister-in-law*

niciwâm – *my cousin (male to male)*

niciwâmiskwêm – *my cousin (female to female)*

nihtâ- – *ability to* (PV)

nihtâwiki – *be born* (VAI)

nihtiy – *tea* (NI)

nikamo – *sing* (VAI)

nikamowin – *song* (NI)

nikâwiy – *my mother*

nikâwîpan – *my late mother*

nikâwîs – *my maternal aunt*

nikohtê – *make firewood* (VAI)

nikosis – *my son*

nikotwâsik – *6*

nikotwâso-kîsikâw – *Saturday/it is Saturday* (VII)

nikotwâsomitanaw – *60*

nikotwâsosâp – *16*

nimis – *my older sister*

nimosôm – *my grandfather*

ninanâskomon – *I give thanks/I am grateful*

ninîkihikwak – *my parents*

nipâ – *sleep* (VAI)

nipêwin – *a bed* (NI)

nipiy – *water* (NI)

nisihkâc – *slowly*

nisihkâci- – *slowly* (PV)

nisikos – *my aunt/mother-in-law*

nisis – *my uncle/father-n-law*

nisitohta – *understand it* (VTI-1)

nisitohtaw – *understand s.o.* (VTA)

nisîmis – *my younger sibling*

niska – *a goose* NA)

niski-pîsim – *the Goose Moon, March*

nistam – *at/in front, first*

nistês – *my older brother*

nisto – *3*

nisto-kîsikâw – *Wednesday/it is Wednesday* (VII)

nistomitanaw – *30*

nistosâp – *13*

nitawâsimis – *my child*

nitawêmâw – *my cousin (female to male/male to female)*

nitawêyihta – *want it* (VTI-1)

nitawêyim – *want it* (VTA)

nitawi- – *go and* (PV)

nitawiminê – *go berry picking* (VAI)

nitânis – *my daughter*

nitêm – *my dog*

nitihtâwâw – *my fellow parent-in-law*

nitipiskên – *I have a birthday*

nitisiyihkâson – *I am named* (VAI-1st sg)

nititahtopiponân – *I am of that age* (VAI-1st sg)

nititikonân – *he says to us* (VTA-Inv)

nitohcîn – *I am from* (VAI-1st sg)

nitomisin – *I have an older sister/s* (VAI)

nitômisin – *I am greasy/oily* (VAI)

niwîkimâkan – *my spouse*

niya – *I/me* (PR)

niyanân – *us/we (excludes the one spoken to)* (PR)

niyâ – *lead/go ahead* (IPC)

niyânan – *5*

niyânano-kîsikâw – *Friday/It is Friday* (VII)

niyânanomitanaw – *50*

niyânanosâp – *15*

nîhcâyihk – *down/downstairs*

nîhtaciwêpahtâ – *run downhill* (VAI)

nîmihito – *dance* (VAI)

nîmihitowin – *a dance* (NI)

nîminikê – *serve out food* (VAI)

nîpawi-napakihtaki-sôskwaciwê – *go snow-boarding* (VAI)

nîpawi-sôskwaciwêyâpoko – *ski* (VAI)

nîpâmâyâtan – *it is purple* (VII)

nîpâmâyâtisiw – *it is purple* (VAI)

nîpiminâna – *cranberries* (NI)

nîpin – *it is summer* (VII)

nîpinohk – *last summer*

nîpiy – *leaf* (NI)

nîpiya – *lettuce/salad* (NI)

nîsitanaw – *20*

nîsitanaw pêyakosâp – *21*

nîso – *2*

nîso-kîsikâw – *Tuesday/it is Tuesday* (VII)

nîsosâp – *12*

nîsta – *me too* (PR)

nîstanân – *us too (excludes the one spoken to)*

nîstâ – *my brother-in-law (vocative)*
nîstâw – *my cross cousin (male to male), brother-in-law*
nîtim – *my cross cousin (female to male), brother/sister-in-law*
nîtisân – *my sibling*
nohcâwîs – *my paternal uncle*
nohcimihk – *inland/in the forest*
nohkom – *my grandmother*
nohtâwiy – *my father*
nohtâwîpan – *my late father*
nôcihitowi-pîsim – *the Mating Moon, September*
nôhtê- – *want to (PV)*
nôhtêhkatê – *be hungry (VAI)*
nôhtêhkwasi – *be sleepy (VAI)*
nôhtêyâpâkwê – *be thirsty (VAI)*
nôsisim – *my grandchild*
nôtâpân – *my great grandparent/great grandchild*

O

ocêhtowi-kîsikâw – *New Year's Day*
ohci – *from*
ohcitaw piko – *have to*
ohcî – *be from (VAI)*
ohkoma – *his/her grandmother*
ohkomimâw – *a grandmother*
ohkomimâwi – *be a grandmother (VAI)*
ohpahowi-pîsim – *the Flying Up Moon, August*
ohpihkasikan – *yeast (NI)*
ohpikihâwasowinihk – *within a family*
ohpin – *lift it (VTA)*
ohpina – *lift it (VTI-1)*
ohtâwiya – *her/his father*
ohtâwîmâw – *a father*
ohtâwîmâwi – *be a father (VAI)*
ohtâwîmâwi-kîsikâw – *Father's Day*
okanawêyihcikêw – *conservation officer (NA)*
okanawêyimâwasow – *baby-sitter (NA)*
okâw – *pickerel (NA)*
okâwiya – *his/her mother*
okâwîmâw – *a mother*
okâwîmâwi-kîsikâw – *Mother's Day*
okâwîmâwi – *be a mother (VAI)*
okimâhkân – *a Chief (NA)*
okimâw – *a boss (NA)*
okiniyak – *wild rose-hips (NA)*

okisîpêkihtakinikêw – *janitor*
okiskinwahamâkan – *a student (NA)*
okiskinwahamâkêw – *a teacher (NA)*
okistikêw – *a farmer (NA)*
okitêyihcikêw – *probation officer (NA)*
okosisa – *her/his son*
okosisi – *have a son (VAI)*
okosisimâw – *a son*
omisa – *her/his older sister*
omisi – *have an older sister (VAI)*
omisi – *this way*
omisimâw – *an older sister*
omosôma – *his/her grandfather*
omosômimâw – *a grandfather*
omosômimâwi – *be a grandfather (VAI)*
onôtinitowi-kîsikâw – *Rememberance Day*
opakitahwâw – *commercial fisherman (NA)*
opimohtahiwêw – *bus driver (NA)*
opîkiskwêstamâkêw – *a lawyer (NA)*
osâm – *because/excessively*
osâwâpoy – *orange juice (NI)*
osâwâs – *orange (NA)*
osâwâw – *it is orange (VII)*
osâwisiw – *it is orange (VAI)*
osîhcikêwiyiniw – *a maintenance person (NA)*
osîmimâw – *a younger sibling*
osîmisa – *his/her younger sibling*
osîmisi – *have a younger sibling (VAI)*
oskana kâ-asastêki – *Regina*
oskâtâsk – *carrot (NA)*
ospwâkan – *a pipe (NA)*
ostêsa – *his/her older brother*
ostêsi – *have an older brother (VAI)*
ostêsimâw – *an older brother*
otah – *defeat s.o. (VTA)*
otatoskêwi-kîsikâw – *Labour Day*
otawâsimisa – *her/his child*
otawâsimisi – *have a child (VAI)*
otâhk askîwin – *last year*
otâhk ispayiw – *last week (VAI)*
otâkosiki – *this evening*
otâkosin – *evening (VII)*
otâkosîhk – *yesterday*
otâkwani-mîciso – *eat supper (VAI)*
otânisa – *her/his daughter*
otânisi – *have a daughter (VAI)*

otânisimâw – *a daughter*
otâstawêhikêw – *a firefighter* (NA)
otin – *take someone* (VTA)
otina – *take it* (VTI-1)
otisîhkân – *turnip* (NI)
otônapiy – *tullabee* (NA)
otôtêma – *her/his friend*
otôtêmiwâwa – *their friend*
owanihikêw – *a trapper* (NA)
owîkimâkana – *her/his spouse*
owîkimâkani – *have a spouse* (VAI)
oyastâ – *set in place* (VTI-2)
oyâkan – *plate* (NI)
ôcêw – *a housefly*
ôhi – *these* (PR-in)
ôki – *these* (PR-an)
ôma – *this* (PR-in)
ôsi – *boat* (NI)
ôsisimi – *have a grandchild* (VAI)
ôta – *here*
ôtê – *over here*
ôtênaw – *town* (NI)

P

pahkipêstâw – *it rains heavy/downpour* (VII)
pahkisimotâhk – *west*
pahkopê – *wade* (VAI)
pahkwêsikan – *bannock* (NA)
pakahkam – *perhaps*
pakamah – *hit him/her* (VTA)
pakâhtâ – *boil it* (VTI-2)
pakân – *nut* (NA)
pakâsim – *boil it* (VTA)
pakâsimo – *swim* (VAI)
pakitin – *allow/let s.o. go* (VTA)
pakosêyimo – *beg/hope, wish, desire* (VAI)
pakwâhtêhon – *a belt* (NI)
pakwâs – *dislike someone* (VTA)
pakwâta – *dislike it* (VTI-1)
papakiwayân – *a shirt* (NI)
papâmi-atâwê – *go shopping* (VAI)
papâmi-mânokê – *go camping* (VAI)
papâmiskâ – *paddle about* (VAI)
papâmohtê – *walk about* (VAI)
pasikô – *get up/stand up* (VAI)
paskinam – *s/he breaks s.t. off* (VTI)

paskisam – *s/he cuts it* (VTI-1)
paskowi-pîsim – *the Moulting Moon, July*
paskwâwi-mostos – *buffalo* (NA)
paskwâwi-mostoso-wiyâs – *buffalo meat* (NI)
paskwâwihkaskwa – *sage* (NI)
pasow – *s/he smells it* (VAIt)
paspaskiw – *birch grouse* (NA)
paspî – *be saved* (VAI)
paswâs – *sniff it* (VTA)
paswâta – *sniff it* (VTI-1)
pawâcakinasîsi-pîsim – *the Frost
  Exploding Moon, December*
pâcimâsîs – *a little while later*
pâhkahâhkwân – *chicken* (NA)
pâhkahâhkwâni-wiyâs – *chicken meat* (NI)
pâhpi – *laugh* (VAI)
pâhpih – *laugh at s.o.* (VTA)
pâhpihkwê – *smile* (VAI)
pâkâhtowê – *play baseball, play soccer* (VAI)
pâmwayês – *before*
pâskâwihowi-pîsim – *the Hatching Moon, June*
pâskinam – *s/he uncovers s.t.* (VTI-1)
pâskisam – *s/he shoots at it* (VTI-1)
pâsow – *s/he dries up* (VAI)
pâtimâ – *at a later time*
pê- – *come/in this direction* (PV)
pê-itohtê – *come this way* (VAI)
pêci- – *come* (PV)
pêhêw – *s/he waits for s.o.* (VTA)
pêhta – *hear it* (VTI-1)
pêhtaw – *hear someone* (VTA)
pêhtâkow – *he is heard by him* (VTA-Inv)
pêsiw – *bring someone* (VTA)
pêskomina – *pepper* (NI)
pêtamaw – *bring it for him/her* (VTA)
pêtâ – *bring it* (VTI-2)
pêyak – *1*
pêyak ispayiw – *one week*
pêyako- – *alone* (PV)
pêyako-kîsikâw – *Monday/it is Monday* (VII)
pêyakosâp – *11*
pêyakwan – *the same*
pêyakwâw – *once*
pêyâhtaki- – *carefully* (PV)
pêyâhtakisi – *be careful* (VAI)
picikwâs – *apple* (NA)

pihêw – *a grouse* (NA)
pihkasikan – *toast* (NA)
pihkahtêwâpoy – *coffee* (NI)
pihkahtêwâpôhkê – *make coffee* (VAI)
pikw îspî – *anytime*
pimahkamikisi – *be busy* (VAI)
pimiciwan – *there is a current* (VII)
pimihamo – *migrate* (VAI)
piminawaso – *cook* (VAI)
pimipahtâ – *run* (VAI)
pimipayi – *drive* (VAI)
pimisin – *s/he lays down* (VAI)
pimiy – *oil/lard/grease* (NI)
pimiyâmo – *flee along* (VAI)
pimihkân – *pemmican* (NI)
pimohtê – *walk* (VAI)
pimotêw – *s/he shoots arrows at s.o.* (VTA)
pinâskowi-pîsim – *Leaf Falling Moon, October*
pipon – *it is winter* (VII)
piponasâkay – *parka* (NI)
piponohk – *last winter*
pisci- – *accidently* (PV)
pisiw – *a lynx* (NA)
pitamâ – *for now*
piyêsîs – *a bird* (NA)
pîcicî – *dance round dance* (VAI)
pîhcâyihk – *inside*
pîhtâpiskah – *bake it* (VTA)
pîhtâpiskaha – *bake it* (VTI-1)
pîhtokamihk – *indoors*
pîhtokwê – *enter* (VAI)
pîmiciwan – *there is a cross-current* (VII)
pîmisin – *s/he lays sideways* (VAI)
pîsim – *sun/month* (NA)
pîsimohkân – *a clock* (NA)
pîsimwasinahikan – *calendar* (NI)
pîswêhkasikan – *bread* (NA)
pîswêhkasikanisak – *buns* (NA)
pîwan – *it drifts (blizzard)* (VII)
pîwâpisk – *metal* (NI)
pîwâpiskowiyiniw – *a mechanic* (NA)
postayiwinisê – *get dressed* (VAI)
postiska – *put it on* (VTI-1)
postiskaw – *put it on* (VTA)
pôni- – *stop* (PV)
pôni-âpihtâ-kîsikâki – *this afternoon*

pôni-âpihtâ-kîsikâw – *it is afternoon* (VII)
pôsi – *get in (a vehicle)* (VAI)
pôsi – *go boating/canoeing* (VAI)
pôsihin – *give me a ride* (VTA-Inv)
pwâtisimo – *danced pow-wow* (VAI)
pwâtisimowin – *a pow-wow* (NI)

s
sakahikan – *a nail* (NI)
sakahpita – *tie it to s.t.* (VTI-1)
sakâw – *a bush* (NI)
sakâw – *it is bushy* (VII)
sasîpihta – *be stubborn* (VTI-1)
saskan – *it melts(chinook)* (VII)
sâkahikan – *lake* (NI)
sâkâstênohk – *east*
sâkihêw – *s/he loves s.o.* (VTA)
sâkinêw – *s/he holds it out* (VTA)
sâkipakâwi-pîsim – *the Budding Moon, May*
sâmin – *touch it* (VTA)
sâmina – *touch it* (VT-1)
sâpo- – *through* (PV)
sâponikan – *a needle* (NI)
sâpôminak – *gooseberries* (NA)
sâsâpiskis – *fry it* (VTA)
sâsâpiskisa – *fry it* (VTI-1)
sâsâpiskisikan – *frying-pan* (NA)
sâsêskihkwân – *frying-pan* (NA)
sâwanohk – *south*
sêhkêpayîs – *a car* (NA)
sêkihêw – *s/he scares s.o.* (VTA)
sêkowêpinâpisk – *oven* (NI)
sêmâk – *right away*
sêsâwipahtâ – *jog* (VAI)
sêsâwî – *exercise* (VAI)
sêsâwohtê – *walk for exercise* (VAI)
sikâk – *a skunk* (NA)
sikopicikani-wiyâs – *ground meat* (NI)
simâkanis – *a police person* (NA)
simâkanisihkân – *a soldier* (NA)
simâkanisîwikamik – *a Police Station* (NI)
sisonê – *along*
sîkah(w) – *comb his/her hair* (VTA)
sîkaho – *comb hair* (VAI)
sîkahon – *a comb* (NI)
sîkipêstâw – *it is pouring rain*

sîkwan – *It is spring* (VII)

sîkwanohk – *last spring*

sîpâ – *under*

sîpâyihk – *under*

sîpihkosiw – *it is blue* (VAI)

sîpihkwâw – *it is blue* (VII)

sîpiy – *a river* (NI)

sîsipâskwat – *maple sugar* (NI

sîsîp – *a duck* (NA)

sîsîpaskihk – *kettle* (NA)

sîwâpoy – *soda-pop* (NI)

sîwâs – *candy* (NA)

sîwihkasikan – *cake* (NA)

sîwihkasikanak – *baked goods* (NA)

sîwihtâkan – *salt* (NI)

sîwinikan – *sugar* (NA)

sîwinôs – *candy* (NA)

sôhkânipahtâ – *run fast* (VAI)

sôhki- – *hard* (PV)

sôhkiyowêw – *it is very windy* (VII)

sôminâpoy – *wine* (NI)

sôminisak – *raisins* (NA)

sôniskwâtahikê – *skate* (VAI)

sôniskwâtahikê-mêtawê – *play hockey* (VAI)

sôniyâskâw – *Treaty Day* (Lac La Ronge area)

sôniyâw – *money* (NA)

sôskwaciwê – *slide (go sledding)* (VAI)

T

tahkascikan – *fridge* (NI)

tahkâyâw – *it is cold* (VII)

tahkohc – *on top*

tahkon – *carry someone* (VTA)

tahkona – *carry it* (VTI-1)

tahkopis – *tie s.o. up* (VTA)

tahkopita – *tie it* (VTI-1)

tahto-kîsikâw – *every day*

tahto-tipiskâw – *every night*

takohtê – *arrive walking* (VAI)

takon – *add to it* (VTA)

takona – *add to it* (VTI-1)

takopahtâ – *arrive running* (VAI)

takopayi – *arrive by vehicle* (VAI)

takosini – *arrive* (VAI)

takwahiminâna – *chokecherries* (NI)

takwâki-pîsim – *the Autumn Moon, September*

takwâkin – *it is fall* (VII)

takwâkohk – *last fall*

tapasî – *flee* (VAI)

tastawâyihk – *in between*

tâna – *which (singular animate)*

tânêhki – *why? how come?*

tânihi – *which (plural inanimate)*

tâniki – *which (plural animate)*

tânima – *which (singular inanimate)*

tânimayikohk – *how much?*

tânisi – *how / how are you?*

tânispîhk – *when*

tânita – *where abouts?*

tânitahto – *how many?*

tânitahtopiponêyan – *how old are you?*

tânitahtwâw – *how many times?*

tânitê – *where (in general)*

tânitowahk – *what kind?*

tâniwâ – *where is (singular animate)*

tâniwê – *where is (singular inanimate)*

tâniwêhâ – *where is (plural inanimate)*

tâniwêhkâk – *where are (plural animate)*

tâniyikohk – *how much?*

tâpiskâkan – *a scarf/tie* (NA)

tâpiskâkan – *a horse-collar* (NI)

tâpwê – *it is true*

tâpwê mâni-mâka – *it is so true*

tâpwê takahki – *truly great*

tâpwêhtaw – *believe s.o.* (VTA)

tâwâyihk – *in the middle*

têhamâ – *play cards* (VAI)

têhtapi – *ride/sit on top of* (VAI)

têhtapiwin – *a chair* (NI)

têpakohp – *7*

têpakohpomitanaw – *70*

têpakohposâp – *17*

têpiska – *fit it* (VTI-1)

têpiskaw – *fit it* (VTA)

têpwê – *shout* (VAI)

tihkiso – *melt* (VAI)

tihkitêw – *It melts* (VII)

tihtipipayi – *roll* (VAI)

tihtipiwêpiska – *ride (a bike)* (VTI-1)

tipahamâtowi-kîsikâw – *Treaty Day*

tipahikan – *time*

tipiska – *have a birthday* (VTI-1)

tipiskâki – *tonight* (VII)

tipiskâw – *it is night* (VII)

tipiskâwi-pîsim – *moon* (NA)

tipiskohk – *last night* (VII)

tohtôsâpoy – *milk* (NI)

tohtôsâpôwipimiy – *butter* (NI)

tômihkwê – *put on make-up* (VAI)

w

wanâh – *distract someone* (VTA)

wanih – *lose s.o.* (VTA)

waniho – *lose one's way* (VAI)

wanihtâ – *lose something* (VTI-2)

wanikiskisi – *forget* (VAI)

wanisini – *be lost* (VAI)

waniskâ – *get up* (VAI)

wanohtê – *lose one's way on path* (VAI)

wawânêyihta – *be confused* (VTI-1)

wawâninâkwan – *it is twilight* (VII)

wayawî – *go out* (VAI)

wayawîpahtâ – *run outside* (VAI)

wayawîpahtwâ – *run it outside* (VTI-2)

wayawîtimihk – *outside*

wayawîtimiskwâht – *just outside the door*

wâhkômâkan – *a relative*

wâhyaw – *far*

wâhyawês – *a bit of a ways*

wâkâs – *banana* (NA)

wâpahki – *tomorrow*

wâpahta – *see it* (VTI-1)

wâpakosîs – *mouse* (NA)

wâpam – *see it* (VTA)

wâpamon – *mirror* (NI)

wâpan – *it is dawn* (VII)

wâpikwaniy – *flower* (NI)

wâpikwanîwinâkosiw – *it is pink* (VAI)

wâpikwanîwinâkwan – *it is pink* (VII)

wâpinôminak – *rice* (NA)

wâpiskastis – *a white mitt* (NA)

wâpiskâw – *it is white* (VII)

wâpiskisiw – *it is white* (VAI)

wâpos – *rabbit* (NA)

wâposâwâw – *it is yellow* (VII)

wâposâwisiw – *it is yellow* (VAI)

wâsakâm – *along the shore/around*

wâsaskotênikan – *lamp* (NI)

wâsâw – *a bay* (NI)

wâsênikan – *a window* (NI)

wâsêpicikanis – *a light switch* (NI)

wâsêskwan – *it is clear/sunny* (VII)

wâskahikan – *a house* (NI)

wâskâhikan – *a screwdriver* (NI)

wâstêpakâw – *leaves change colour* (VII)

wâti – *cave, hole* (NI)

wâwâskêsiw – *elk* (NA)

wâwi – *an egg* (NI)

wêpaha – *sweep it away* (VTI-1)

wêpahikê – *sweep* (VAI)

wêpâstan – *it blows* (VII)

wêpin – *throw it away* (VTA)

wêpina – *throw it away* (VTI-1)

wiya – *she/he* (PR)

wiyasiwêwikamik – *court house* (NI)

wiyasiwêwiyiniw – *a band councillor*

wiyasiwêwiyiniwikamik – *a Band Office* (NI)

wiyawâw – *they/them* (PR)

wiyâs – *meat* (NI)

wiyitihp – *brain* (NI)

wîcêw – *accompany s.o.* (VTA)

wîcih – *help s.o.* (VTA)

wîhcêkaskosîs – *onion* (NI)

wîhkaskwa – *sweet-grass* (NI)

wîhkês – *muskrat-root* (NI)

wîhkihkasikan – *cake* (NA)

wîhkihp(w) – *like the taste of it* (VTA)

wîhkista – *like the taste of it* (VTI-1)

wîhkohkê – *make a feast* (VAI)

wîhtamaw – *tell s.o.* (VTA)

wîhtikowi-mîciwin – *popcorn* (NI)

wîki – *reside/inhabit/live* (VAI)

wînêyihta – *detest it* (VTI-1)

wînêyim – *detest someone* (VAT)

wîniy – *bone marrow* (NI)

wîpac – *soon/early*

wîpâci-kîsikâw – *it is a miserable day* (VII)

wîsakahw – *hurt him/her by hitting* (VTA)

wîsakat – *pepper* (NI)

wîsakîmina – *cranberries* (NI)

wîsâm – *invite s.o.* (VTA)

wîsta – *she/he too* (PR)

wîstawâw – *they too* (PR)

wîsti – *beaver lodge* (NI)

wîtisâni – *have a sibling* (VAI)

wîtisânihtowinihk – *within a family*

Y

yahki-sôskoyâpawi – *cross-country ski* (VAI)
yahkiwêpin – *push it* (VTA)
yahkiwêpina – *push it* (VTI-1)
yîkatê- – *aside* (PV)
yîkatê-api – *sit aside* (VAI)
yîkatêkâpawi – *stand aside* (VAI)
yîkowan – *it is foggy* (VII)
yîkwaskwan – *it is cloudy* (VII)
yîwahikanak – *ground meat/fish* (NA)
yôhtên – *open it* (VTA)
yôhtêna – *open it* (VTI-1)
yôtin – *it is windy* (VII)

BIBLIOGRAPHY

ahkami-nêhiyawêtân. Saskatchewan Cree Language Retention Committee. Jean L. Okimâsis and Arok Wolvengrey, eds. Vol. 1, Nos. 1, 2, 3, 4, 1997, and Vol. 2, Nos. 1, 2, 1998.

Bloomfield, Leonard. *Sacred Stories of the Sweetgrass Cree.* Saskatoon: Fifth House Publishers, 1993.

Faries, Rev. E. A. *A Dictionary of the Cree Language.* Toronto: Church of England, 1938.

Kelsey, Henry. *A Dictionary of the Hudson's Bay Indian Language.* London: HBC, 1669.

MacKenzie, Alexander. *Voyages From Montreal ... 1789-1793.* Edmonton: Hurtig, Rutland, Vt. Tuttle: 1971.

Nehithowewin. La Ronge: Curriculum Resource Unit, Lac La Ronge Indian Band, Education Branch, 1995.

O'Grady, William, and Michael Dobrovolsky. *Contemporary Linguistics Analysis,* 3rd ed. Toronto: Copp Clark, Ltd., 1996.

Okimâsis, Jean L. *Cree: Language of the Plains* (textbook). Regina: Canadian Plains Research Center, 2004.

Okimâsis, Jean L., and Solomon Ratt. *Cree: Language of the Plains* (textbook). Regina: Canadian Plains Research Center, 1999.

_____. *Cree: Language of the Plains* (workbook). Regina: Canadian Plains Research Center, 1999.

Okimâsis, Jean, and Arok Wolvengrey. *How to Spell It in Cree (The Standard Roman Orthography).* Regina: miywâsin ink, 2008.

Pyles, Thomas, and John Algeo. *The Origins and Development of the English Language.* 3rd ed. Toronto: Harcourt, Brace, and Jovanovich, 1982.

Ratt, Solomon. *How to Say It in Cree.* Saskatoon: SICC Press, 1995.

_____. *How to Say It in Cree.* La Ronge: Northern Lights School Division, No. 113, 1996.

_____. *A Handbook for Cree Language Teachers.* Regina: SIFC Press, 1994.

_____. *Teaching Cree through Actions and Pictures.* Saskatoon: SICC Press, 1997.

_____. *Input Exercises for Cree.* Saskatoon: SICC Press, 1997.

_____. *Peter Okisikâm.* Saskatoon: SICC Press, 1995.

Wolvengrey, Arok. *nêhiýawêwin: itwêwina / Cree: Words.* Regina: Canadian Plains Research Center, 2001.

NOTES